BY THE SAME AUTHOR

*Approaching Zero: Data Crime & the Computer Underworld* (with Paul Mungo) London 1992

*Approaching Zero: The Extraordinary World of Hackers, Phreakers, Virus Writers and Keyboard Criminals* (with Paul Mungo) New York 1992

*Los Piratas del Chip: La Mafia Informatica al Desnudo* (with Paul Mungo) Barcelona 1992

*Delinquance Assistée par Ordinateur: La Saga des "Hackers" Nouveaux Flibustiers "High Tech"!* (with Paul Mungo) Paris 1993

*Cheating at Cards – Plastic Fraud: Sharp Practices and Naïve Systems* Hove 1994

*Beware of Your Bank* Hove 1995

*The Guru Guide: Unlocking & Firmware Repair of Nokia GSM Mobiles* Hove 2001

# STATE SECRETS

## The Kent-Wolkoff Affair

### Bryan Clough

Hideaway Publications Ltd

First published 2005 by Hideaway Publications Ltd, 4 Erroll Road, Hove, East Sussex.

This book has been printed digitally by Lightning Source UK Ltd

British Library Cataloguing in Publication Data.

A catalogue record for this book
is available from the British Library.

Espionage – World War II – Foreign Relations

ISBN 0 9525477 3 2

Cover by Bizbro Web Design

# Copyright Notice

# Contents

# Acknowledgments

My thanks to all those who have ploughed these fields before, even though understandably most reached the wrong conclusions by having to rely on official reports and cover stories that had been designed to mislead. Before the availability of the MI5 files in the National Archives, I formed many interim opinions that would later be proved wrong. The staff at the National Archives at Kew and those at my local Library in Hove have always been very helpful, particularly Nina, Sue and Zoe.

My thanks to Patricia Craig, for sharing her views on Joan Miller. I really liked her book and it is a pity that Joan was such a fibber.

My thanks also to various experts in their fields, who have been unfailingly generous in their help. Among these, I must mention Stephen Dorril, Professor Colin Holmes, Hugh Thomas, Keith Thompson, Jeff Wallder, the late John Warburton and the Donovan family.

Grateful thanks to Genny Lawson, Peter Hopley and Mike Morley for their proof reading; and to Friederich von Petersdorff and Phil Tomaselli who pointed out several factual errors.

Finally, my thanks to Nik Bizzell-Browning of Bizbro Web Design who designed the cover and the associated website www.statesecrets.co.uk.

# Principal Characters

### Winston S. Churchill (1874-1965)

Prime Minister Neville Chamberlain brought Churchill into the British War Cabinet as First Lord of the Admiralty on 4 September 1939, after he had spent the previous nine years in the 'political wilderness'.

He replaced Chamberlain as Prime Minister on 10 May 1940.

### Hélène Louise de Munck aka Agent M/1 (1915-?)

A Belgian-born mystic, she was the second MI5 undercover agent whom Maxwell Knight assigned to cover Anna Wolkoff. She read Anna's fortune and told her what she wanted to hear. She testified at the trials of Kent and Wolkoff that Anna had handed her a Coded Letter that was intended for William Joyce.

### James McGuirk Hughes alias P.G. Taylor, etc. (1897-1983)

A private Intelligence Agent who did subcontract work for Scotland Yard. A man with several aliases, he was a member of Captain Ramsay's Right Club (as Hughes) and a senior member of Mosley's Fascist party (as Taylor). He set up Anna Wolkoff's 'attempt to communicate with William Joyce' by handing her a Coded Letter addressed to Joyce. After she had passed the Coded Letter to Hélène de Munck, this led to Wolkoff being categorised as a 'Foreign Agent'. Earl Jowitt referred to him as Mr X in his summary of Anna's trial and he falsely reported that 'he could not be found' when Anna wanted to call Hughes as a witness.

## Kurt Jahnke (1882-1945)

A legendary German spy and saboteur who operated in the United States during WWI.

During the Thirties, he ran the Jahnke Büro, a semi-private Intelligence Service in Berlin, which was the reported recipient of material leaked from the American Embassy in London.

## The Earl Jowitt (1885-1957)

A Labour politician who was the Solicitor-General in Churchill's War Cabinet, he led for the prosecution at the trials of Kent and Wolkoff.
After the war, he became the Lord Chancellor and was one of the Law Lords who dismissed William Joyce's final appeal, after Jowitt had persuaded Lord Macmillan to change his original decision.
He later wrote misleading accounts of the Kent and Wolkoff trials.

## William Joyce aka Lord Haw-Haw (1906-1946)

A member of Captain Ramsay's Right Club and a former member of Mosley's Fascist party, he fled to Germany on 26 August 1939, after being tipped off that he had been listed for internment.

As Lord Haw-Haw, he became the most notorious broadcaster of Nazi propaganda.

After the war, he was captured and executed for High Treason.

## Joseph P. Kennedy (1888-1969)

Patriarch of the famous clan, he served as Ambassador at the American Embassy in London from 1938 to 1940.
He favoured a negotiated peace with Hitler and was extremely defeatist with regard to Britain's chances of survival in 1940.
He waived Tyler Kent's diplomatic immunity, thus paving the way for his flat to be searched and his later arrest.

**Tyler Gatewood Kent (1911-1988)**

He joined the American Embassy in London in October 1939 where he worked as a code and cipher clerk.

He was introduced to Anna Wolkoff in February 1940 and they became friendly.

When Maxwell Knight searched his flat on 20 May 1940, he discovered 'masses' of American Embassy documents and he admitted showing these to Anna Wolkoff and Captain Ramsay. After a secret trial in October 1940, he was sentenced to seven years' penal servitude.

**Maxwell Knight (1900-1968)**

MI5's 'agent runner', he planted moles in Captain Ramsay's Right Club and other Right Wing and Fascist organisations.

He set up a sting that entrapped Anna Wolkoff and then produced a 'sexed-up' report of the Kent-Wolkoff Affair.

He testified at Kent's trial.

# PRINCIPAL CHARACTERS

## Guy Maynard Liddell (1892-1958)

The Director of MI5's Counter Espionage Division, he was Knight's boss. He approved Knight's 'sexed-up' report and testified at Kent's trial. His wartime Diaries are now in the National Archives.

## Marjorie Norah Mackie née Amor aka Agent M/Y (1898-1975)

Knight's principal undercover agent on the Right Club case, she succeeded in winning the confidence of Mrs. Ramsay who invited her to join the Right Club and introduced her to Anna Wolkoff.

## Joan Priscilla Miller (1918-1984)

A young MI5 secretary who, at Maxwell Knight's request, played a small part in the Kent-Wolkoff Affair.

Forty years later, she exaggerated her own part for the purposes of a book.

## Sir Oswald Ernald Mosley (1896-1980)

The leader of Britain's most important Fascist party, he was interned during the war, as were his wife, the former Diana Mitford, and over 750 of his followers.

## Captain Archibald Henry Maule Ramsay (1895-1955)

The Conservative MP for Peebles, he founded the anti-Jewish Right Club in 1939 and advocated a peace deal with Hitler.

He was interned without trial from May 1940 to September 1944.

## Franklin D. Roosevelt (1882-1945)

Elected President in 1932, 1936, 1940 and 1944. He brought America into war with Germany as quickly as he could consistent with electoral considerations and a vocal isolationist lobby.

He died shortly after being re-elected for a fourth term and just before the cessation of hostilities in Europe.

## Mr Justice Tucker (1888-1975)

He presided over the secret trials of Kent and Wolkoff in 1940 and, in announcing their sentences in open court, he denounced William Joyce as a traitor.

He was given the unique opportunity of making his prophecy come true when he presided over Joyce's own trial for High Treason in 1945. This was decidedly irregular.

## Anna Wolkoff (1902-1973?)

A Russian-born dress designer who had acquired British nationality in 1935.

She was a member of Captain Ramsay's Right Club and represented herself as his aide-de-camp. After being introduced to Tyler Kent in February 1940, they became friendly and he allowed her to see his collection of Embassy documents.

She was arrested on 20 May 1940 and tried in secret in October 1940. She was handed down ten years' penal servitude.

# Introduction

On 12 November 1941, the *Washington Times-Herald* published an article by Arthur Sears Henning in which he reported a question that had been asked by Richard R. Stokes, a Labour MP, in the British House of Commons. Stokes, who had formed a Parliamentary Peace Aims Group, could always be relied upon to ask potentially embarrassing questions on the conduct of the war. On this occasion, his question was whether a British subject who had sent telegrams to Mr. Roosevelt and thereby evaded censorship had been prosecuted. Herbert Morrison, the Home Secretary, had given non-committal replies.

Henning elaborated by explaining that the British subject in question was actually Prime Minister Winston Churchill and that his correspondence with Roosevelt had started before he had stepped up as Prime Minister on 10 May 1940. Among the matters that Churchill and Roosevelt were supposed to have touched upon was a more vigorous prosecution of the European war and the possibilities of America taking a more active part in support of Britain.

According to one version, the device of the Lend-Lease legislation for circumventing the United States neutrality law and the Johnson Act forbidding the extension of credit to Britain as a war debt defaulter was also discussed. If this version were correct, it flew in the face of received history, which said that Roosevelt had only conceived the Lend-Lease formula on 17 December 1940, six weeks after his re-election for an unprecedented third term. He had signed law H.R. 1776, popularly known as the Lend-Lease Act, on 11 March 1941.

Henning explained that the correspondence between Churchill and Roosevelt had passed through the American Embassy in London and that Tyler Kent, a young American employed as a clerk in the Embassy, had made copies and had shown them to Captain Archibald Ramsay, the Conservative MP for Peebles.

The leak of this correspondence soon became known and responsibility was traced to young Kent, whereupon the vengeance of the British and American governments for this breach of trust was swift and certain. After Joseph P. Kennedy, the American Ambassador had discharged Kent, he was immediately arrested, held in jail for six months and, after a secret trial, he was sentenced to seven years' penal servitude. Captain Ramsay was also placed in detention but according to Henning, the White House professed to have no knowledge on the subject.

No paper other than the *Washington Times-Herald* ran the story, although Tyler Kent, Captain Archibald Ramsay and Anna Wolkoff, a Russian-born dress designer, were all languishing in British jails. All three had been implicated in what would become popularly known as 'The Tyler Kent Affair' in the United States or 'The Kent-Wolkoff Affair' in Britain. Kent eventually saw a copy of Henning's article in May 1944 when he confirmed that it was 'essentially correct'.

Over thirty years later, when the correspondence between Churchill and Roosevelt was released into the public domain, it was discovered that both the war leaders had acted innocently and with the utmost propriety. Churchill had evidently begged for assistance but Roosevelt had regretfully turned him down, by citing the need to get Congressional approval before America could provide any help. There was not a single shred of evidence to support the claim that Roosevelt had made any pre-war commitments to Churchill, there were no discussions on how to circumvent the United States neutrality law and the Johnson Act forbidding the extension of credit nor any mention whatsoever of the Lend-Lease device.

Two American academics who reviewed the Churchill-Roosevelt correspondence acknowledged that it was 'always possible to dismiss official files as selective [but] in this case it would have taken a vast conspiracy stretching from London to

Washington and lasting for over thirty-five years, an unlikely possibility'.[1]

Now, following the release of the MI5 files on Kent, Ramsay, Wolkoff and others into the National Archives, it has at last become possible to reconstruct the full story.

On 21 August 1939, representatives of the Governments of the German Reich and the Union of Soviet Socialist Republics agreed a Treaty of Non-Aggression. It was ratified two days later and its declared aim was 'because both nations were desirous of strengthening the cause of peace between Germany and the USSR and proceeding from the fundamental provisions of the Neutrality Agreement concluded in April 1926'.

Its real aim expressed in a 'strictly secret' protocol was to carve up the Baltic States (Estonia, Latvia and Lithuania) and to determine whether it was in the interests of both parties to maintain an independent Polish state. In the event of some territorial or political rearrangement of the Polish state becoming necessary, it was agreed that the line of the rivers Narew, Vistula and San would become the boundary of their respective spheres of influence. In other words, Nazi Germany would invade Poland from the West and the Soviets from the East. They would then divide the country between them, in accordance with their strictly secret protocol.

Next, the SS took twelve prisoners out of the Buchenwald concentration camp and made them dress in Polish uniforms. They were taken to the frontier where a Polish-speaking SS Officer announced on the radio that they had come to invade Germany. The prisoners were shot and the SS men fled.

On 1 September 1939, Hitler told the Nazi Reichstag that Poland had tried to invade Germany and that the Wehrmacht was returning their fire. It was total nonsense because

---

[1] Kimball, Warren F., and Bartlett, Bruce. "Roosevelt and Prewar Commitments to Churchill: The Tyler Kent Affair." *Diplomatic History* Vol. 5, No. 4 (Fall 1981), pp. 291-312.

Generalfeldmarschall Walther von Brauchitsch had carefully planned the attack, codenamed Fall Weiss (Case White).

In anticipation of Germany's intentions, Britain and France had guaranteed Poland's independence on 30 March 1939, in the mistaken belief that this would cause Hitler to abandon his military ambitions. They were wrong and after their ultimatum had been ignored, the British and French Governments declared war on Germany on 3 September 1939.

World War II had begun but in the beginning it was a very tame affair with neither side wanting to cause too much offence to the other. Chamberlain had been correctly advised that Hitler was not universally popular in Germany and that should Britain stand up to him over the Polish issue then arrangements would be made for his removal. Britain took the bold initiative of sending wave after wave of bombers over Germany, showering the populace with leaflets. But when a popular uprising failed to materialise, the British experts debated the literary merits of their offerings. Noel Coward put it into perspective by asking 'Are we trying to bore the Germans to death?' The question was raised in Parliament 'Why not drop bombs?' A minister replied that this was not possible because they might damage private property.

The truth of the matter was that neither Chamberlain nor Hitler had ever wanted their countries to be at war with each other. Both had been misled: Hitler had been assured that Britain would fail to honour its commitment to Poland and Chamberlain believed that he would soon be able to sort out a peace deal that would allow Britain to step gracefully aside while things in Europe sorted themselves out. Chamberlain had confided to his sister that he had 'a hunch' that the war would be over before the Spring[2].

However, there were others in Britain who believed that if Hitler were allowed to get his own way yet again then he would soon become unstoppable, as each military success fuelled further ambition.

---

[2] Neville to Ida Chamberlain, 5 November 1939. Neville Chamberlain papers 18/1/1129 cited by Graham Stewart in *Burying Caesar*.

Chamberlain's military advisers had also assured him that Britain had nothing to fear from Germany. In their experience, it was always easier to defend than to attack and the French Maginot line, a string of forts along most but not all of France's borders, would ensure that there would be no prolonged trench warfare, as in WWI. There wasn't any prolonged trench warfare, so Chamberlain's military advisers were right but for the wrong reasons.

What happened was that Soviet troops entered Eastern Poland on 17 September 1939; and German troops occupied Warsaw on 1 October. Organised Polish resistance ended on 6 October 1939.


In a clever political move, Chamberlain had invited Winston Churchill to join the War Cabinet, coincident with his declaration of war. Several newspapers had been clamouring for Churchill's return to Government office and, according to Lord Hankey[3], Chamberlain had consulted him on whether or not Churchill should be in the War Cabinet. Hankey had advised that 'public opinion would expect it'. Chamberlain may have also perceived that this would muzzle the man who had been the greatest critic of appeasement. Churchill accepted the invitation and on 4 September 1939 he became the First Lord of the Admiralty, the same position that he had held at the outbreak of WWI. In the event, both men supported each other.

The following day, President Roosevelt declared American neutrality, as he was required to do under the provisions of the Neutrality Act, a piece of legislation originally introduced in 1935 after Italy had invaded Ethiopia. It was designed to prevent America from becoming embroiled in any 'foreign' wars, by placing an embargo on arms shipments to any belligerents, without making any distinction between 'aggressor' and 'victim'. It was amended in 1937 as a result of the Spanish Civil War to embrace civil wars and also to include an embargo on strategic materials. However, Roosevelt had chosen to ignore it when

---

[3] Stephen Roskill, *Hankey: Man of Secrets* (23 August 1939).

China needed aid, after being invaded by Japan later that same year.

The Neutrality Act was only one of the hurdles that Roosevelt would have to overcome, should he want to provide aid officially to any of the belligerents in the European conflict. There was also the Johnson Act of 1934, which prohibited loans except renewals or re-financings, to any Government that was in default on the payment of its obligations to the American Government. Britain was among the countries in default, a legacy of WWI. The Neutrality Act also reinforced the provisions of the Johnson Act, by making belligerency a reason for the denial of loans. In fact, the Neutrality Act was soon relaxed but in his statement to the press on 4 November 1939, Roosevelt forgot to mention that the arms embargo had been lifted.

Nevertheless, Britain was in double trouble under the Johnson Act because it was both a defaulter and a belligerent. Therefore, any business had to be 'Cash and Carry' so formidable obstacles remained because Britain had a heavy adverse trade balance with the United States and it had only a very limited war chest in terms of dollar securities and gold. France was also in the same boat.

The problems were compounded by a widely held belief that America should avoid all European commitments. Charles Lindbergh, the aviator who had thrilled the world with the first solo flight across the Atlantic Ocean, was among the prominent spokesmen who aired these views. Joseph P. Kennedy, the American Ambassador in London and the patriarch of the famous clan, was also a prominent isolationist. He was very chummy with Chamberlain and heartily approved of his appeasement policies.

Two further problems faced the future war leaders. Churchill had been out-of-step with the Conservative Party since 1931 and until being recalled by Chamberlain, he had been in a 'political wilderness'. Roosevelt was approaching the end of his second term as President and although not yet a 'lame duck President', no previous incumbent had ever been re-elected for a third term.

With elections coming up in November 1940, there was a big question mark over his future.

Hitler had become an icon during the Thirties and many in Germany and elsewhere came to believe in his magic. He had clearly valued the support of his British sympathisers, which he consolidated through a charm offensive. He had even tried to charm British Intelligence and shortly after becoming Chancellor, he had invited an exchange of information on Communist activities. The invitation dated 31 January 1933 came from the Politzei President and was routed through the German Embassy in London.

The Politzei President's invitation was passed to Lord Trenchard, the Commissioner of the Metropolitan Police. The Metropolitan Police is better known as 'Scotland Yard' but its activities are not confined to the metropolis. It also runs 'Special Branch', an important part of the British Intelligence community. Trenchard formally accepted the invitation on 24 March 1933 and the exchange of information took place in Berlin from 30 March to 9 April 1933. The event was described as 'The Liquidation of Communism, Left Wing Socialism and Pacifism in Germany'.[4]

Captain Guy Liddell and Captain Frank Foley (1884-1958) were the representatives of British Intelligence. After serving in WWI, Liddell had joined Scotland Yard in 1919 and he moved to MI5 in 1931, coincident with the transfer of responsibility for monitoring Communist activities. He became the Director of MI5's 'B' Division, where he controlled the entire spectrum of Counter Espionage. Officially, Frank Foley was the British Passport Control Officer in Berlin but the job also provided cover for an MI6 man.

Their host was Ernst 'Putzi' Hanfstaengel (1887-1975) a personal friend of Hitler who had become the Führer's Personal Liaison Officer with the Foreign Press. Although he was said to be a man with considerable influence, the visitors found him to

---

[4] KV 4/111.

be 'quite unbalanced'. Seemingly, he believed the conspiracy theories of Mrs. Nesta H. Webster, including 'the International Jewish conspiracy'. He had evidently made a careful study of Mrs. Webster's books and was under the impression that Communism was a movement controlled by the Jews.

Nevertheless, the visitors found Hanfstaengel 'extremely likeable' and he was undoubtedly well disposed towards Britain. He even proposed that Britain should establish a bureau in Berlin where its representatives could work on documents found in recent raids.

Later, they met another Nazi leader named Bürger-Neuss who seemed to have a fanatical hatred of the Jews. He produced a map that purported to show that International Jewry was being controlled from London. He also showed them a photograph of a Jew addressing a meeting of 40 or 50 people in London's Hyde Park. Liddell and Foley tried to explain that such meetings had little or no significance but Bürger-Neuss 'seemed unconvinced'.

They were then shown around Karl Liebknecht Haus, the former Communist Headquarters now renamed the Horst Wessell Haus in tribute to a Nazi who was held up as a martyr after being murdered by Communists.

The delegation was also provided with documents that the Nazis had obtained after taking over the occupation of the former Communist Headquarters. Their host for this part of their visit was Staatsanwalt Diehls, a young man aged about 30-35, who explained that it was his intention to eliminate Communism in its widest sense by the inclusion of left-wing pacifist organisations. Diehls told them that they had already arrested 'some thousands' and that the question of what to do with them was becoming 'a serious problem'. Diehls asked, 'Perhaps the British Government could set aside an island somewhere which could be jointly used as a penal settlement?'

The general question of relations with Russia was discussed and it soon became evident to the visitors that the Nazis were on the horns of a dilemma. They had become increasingly dependent upon Russo-German trade which they valued while simultaneously trying to make political capital out of the insidious effects of Soviet influence on German interests.

The visitors formed the impression that the Nazis earnestly wanted to cooperate with British Intelligence but, having had responsibility for countering Soviet influence in Britain since 1919, Liddell was not convinced that the Soviet threat was as serious as their hosts had been trying to make out, so the offer of establishing a bureau in Berlin was not taken up.

In fact, the privileged visit by the two British Intelligence men into the inner sanctum of the Nazi political police might have had the opposite effect to what their hosts had intended. Hitherto, MI5 had only run a section for countering Communist political subversion but from 1934 it also embraced the British Fascist parties and other organisations of the extreme right. It was a critically important change.

Frank Foley stayed on as the British Passport Control Officer in Berlin but he continually exceeded his official duties by advising visa applicants how they could circumvent the regulations. After Foley's flexible attitude became known, large queues of people seeking an escape route regularly formed outside his offices and he is now credited with having saved some 10,000 souls from the Nazi concentration camps or worse.

Putzi Hanfstaengel would eventually fall foul of Hitler and after believing that his life was in danger, he fled to Zurich in March 1937 and then went to London. His former colleagues tried to lure him back to Germany by telling him that it had been 'a joke' but he couldn't see the funny side.

Putzi told his English friends that he was waiting for Hitler to fall when he would be asked to return to Germany as Head of the Fourth Reich. The call never came and he was interned on the outbreak of war. Later, he was transferred to Washington and while still in captivity, he produced political assessments of events in Germany. None of these was considered 'important'.[5]

---

[5] KV 2/469.

Guy Liddell was given a rude awakening on 4 September 1939, the second day of the war. He learned from Lord Lothian, the British Ambassador in Washington, that there was a Soviet spy in the Foreign Office who had been passing secrets to his Soviet spymasters for 'a long time'. There was also another Soviet spy in the Committee of Imperial Defence, Britain's top security body.

The information would prove to be correct and although it would be easy enough to find the first spy, the second spy would be much more elusive. In all probability the man in question was Donald Maclean, the son of a prominent politician, who was eventually unmasked in 1951.

The two wartime leaders, Winston Churchill and Franklin Roosevelt, would certainly have some work to do, if they were to get their acts together. But would they have ever corresponded on such politically sensitive matters as:

• How to circumvent the Neutrality and Johnson Acts, so that the United States could help Britain by becoming its major supplier of war matériel?

• How the United States could arrange the financing of the war through a massive War Loan that would be euphemistically called 'Lend-Lease' in America and 'Lease-Lend' in Britain?

• How Britain could help to ensure Roosevelt's re-election in November 1940?

But if they had, then there would have been a lot of interest on both sides of the Atlantic in getting sight of their correspondence. Particularly when in the run-up to the Presidential Elections, Roosevelt had repeatedly assured the electorate that 'I have said this before but I shall say it again and again and again; your boys are not going to be sent into any foreign wars'[6].

On 29 December 1940 a few weeks after his re-election for a third term, Roosevelt delivered one of his famous Fireside Chats. He said 'If Great Britain goes down, the Axis powers will control

---

[6] FDR, Speech in Boston, 30 October 1940.

the continents of Europe, Asia, Africa, Australia, and the high seas and they will be in a position to bring enormous military and naval resources against this hemisphere. It is no exaggeration to say that all of us, in all the Americas, would be living at the point of a gun, a gun loaded with explosive bullets, economic as well as military'.

Roosevelt continued in this same vein with the German monitors picking up his every word, 'The American appeasers ignore the warning to be found in the fate of Austria, Czechoslovakia, Poland, Norway, Belgium, the Netherlands, Denmark and France. They tell you that the Axis powers are going to win anyway; that all of this bloodshed in the world could be saved, that the United States might just as well throw its influence into the scale of a dictated peace, and get the best out of it that we can. They call it a 'negotiated peace'. Nonsense! Is it a negotiated peace if a gang of outlaws surrounds your community and on threat of extermination makes you pay tribute to save your own skins? Such a dictated peace would be no peace at all. It would be only another armistice, leading to the most gigantic armament race and the most devastating trade wars in all history. And in these contests the Americas would offer the only real resistance to the Axis powers ...'

Shortly after Roosevelt's Fireside Chat, British Intelligence noticed the impact that it had made on the Nazi Government. It was panic stations and Peace Feelers started pouring into London from all directions, often at the rate of one a week, prompting Churchill to instruct Anthony Eden the Foreign Secretary on 20 January 1941, that 'Our attitude to all such suggestions should be absolute silence'.[7]

Evidently, Churchill was satisfied that his relationship with Roosevelt would eventually bear fruit.

---

[7] FO 371/26542.

# 1: A Miller's Tale

Tyler Gatewood Kent joined the American Foreign Service in March 1934. In those days, jobs were scarce and he was probably fortunate to get taken on as a junior clerk. He had a flair for languages and he must have hoped that his lowly job would lead to bigger things. He was a bachelor, a condition of his employment, and he was posted to the American Embassy in Moscow, which had been newly opened following a breakdown in diplomatic relations as a consequence of the Bolshevik Revolution.

Kent was transferred to the American Embassy in London in October 1939, by which time he spoke 'wonderful Russian'. Having had a Russian mistress, thoughtfully provided by the NKVD, would have helped. His transfer to London was not a promotion. In fact, his salary was reduced from $2,500 to $2,250 p.a. due to a differential between the two locations.

As a junior clerk, his job included the coding and decoding of cables and 'radios'. However, because London acted as a hub for Embassy traffic within Europe, he was able to read many messages exchanged between the White House and its various European outposts.

Kent then started collecting copies of the correspondence that he considered 'interesting'. Often, he simply helped himself to a spare copy that would otherwise have been scrapped but at other times he made an extra copy for himself. He kept his collection of Embassy documents in an unlocked suitcase in his London flat. Being a 'serviced' flat, to which the housemaid and cook had access, there was no lock on the door, just a bolt on the inside when he wanted privacy.

Evidently, Joseph Kennedy, the American Ambassador, had also been collecting copies of Embassy correspondence. These were interesting times and it is not unusual for an Ambassador to collect material from which he could later write up his memoirs. Kennedy evidently did write up his Diplomatic Memoirs although these have never been published in their entirety possibly because his two sons, Jack and Bobby, did not consider that they would have been helpful to their own political careers. Fragments have subsequently appeared in *Hostage to Fortune* (2001), edited by Amanda Smith, Kennedy's granddaughter.

Whether or not Kent was influenced by Kennedy's actions is not relevant because those who are in the wrong often look for excuses and by helping himself to copies of Embassy correspondence, Kent was clearly in the wrong. He then exacerbated the wrong by allowing Captain Ramsay and Anna Wolkoff to examine his collection. After his arrest, Kent signed a statement in which he admitted that he had obtained a collection of Embassy documents and that he had shown them to Ramsay and Wolkoff, so this was never in dispute.

However, Kent's excuse was that his collection of documents contained evidence that Churchill and Roosevelt had been conspiring to bring America into the war. This was not necessarily true, but true or false, Kent's claims could have been politically damaging had he been allowed to make them in public because in May 1940 Churchill had only just stepped up as Prime Minister and Roosevelt had less than six months remaining on his Presidential franchise.

Moreover, with the German juggernaut already smashing its way through the Netherlands, Belgium and France, the prospect of a German invasion had become a very real threat for which Britain was entirely unprepared.

The Tyler Kent Affair would become a cause célèbre in the United States and it could have had important political consequences in Britain had it not been kept closely under wraps by official censorship and other measures. By 1981, the story had pretty much run out of steam when one of the MI5 operatives who had worked on the case decided that she had a story to tell.

Her name was Joan Miller.


Joan Miller joined MI5 on 4 September 1939, the day after Britain had declared war on Germany, to undertake clerical duties. She was a very attractive 21-year-old[1] and having previously worked for Elizabeth Arden the cosmetics company she knew how to make the most of her natural assets. Her father Anthony[2] had been a Lieutenant in the 5th Gloucester Regiment in WWI so she came from the 'right background'. A product of a broken marriage, she had been to boarding school and an old school friend had suggested that she should apply for a job.

Much to her surprise, Miller found herself working in 'The Scrubs' - Wormwood Scrubs Prison in Hammersmith - where MI5 had been re-housed as a wartime emergency measure in the mistaken belief that it was bombproof. She was assigned to the Transport Section headed up by the 6th Earl of Cottenham who was otherwise known as Mark Pepys, a former racing driver who had driven for Alvis at Brooklands. He was considered a 'gentleman driver' because he always took his valet with him to the racing circuits, to make sure he was suitably attired.

One of Miller's duties in MI5 was handing out the petrol vouchers that had been introduced as part of the wartime rationing restrictions. Before long, she was talent spotted by William Younger[3], another new recruit who had recently come down from Oxford. He introduced her to his boss Maxwell Knight, MI5's 'agent runner', who had a requirement for a young secretary who was prepared to take on an unusual assignment.

Knight was a former Naval Midshipman and preparatory school teacher who had joined MI5 in 1931[4]. Within MI5 he was known as 'M'[5] (for Maxwell) but in the outside world he usually

---

[1] Joan Priscilla Miller was born in Bristol on 19 March 1918.
[2] Anthony Guy Miller was granted a Regular Army Emergency Commission on 9 December 1939 as a Lieutenant. He served in the Army Catering Corps and remained in the army after the war, finishing up as Mess Manager at the Royal Military Academy Sandhurst. He retired in 1954 with the rank of Major.
[3] William Younger (1917-1961) was the stepson of Dennis Wheatley, the writer, who was a friend of Maxwell Knight's. After the war, Younger wrote detective novels under the name of 'William Mole'. He also had some poetry published.
[4] It has often been wrongly reported that Knight joined MI5 in 1924 or 1925.
[5] Vernon Kell, the Director General of MI5, had already claimed 'K'. Knight's activities bore no resemblance to Ian Fleming's fictional 'M'.

appeared as Captain King of the War Office. He ran Section B5b whose mission was countering Political Subversion and he gathered intelligence mainly by placing and running 'moles' in extreme political organisations. The Communist Party and its sympathisers were initially his prime concern but from 1934 the British Fascist parties assumed increasing importance, after Hitler had come to power and had declared his intentions.

Knight who was a keen amateur naturalist enjoyed a second career after the war as a radio and television broadcaster. He also wrote several books that reflected his interest in all kinds of animals and insects, having previously failed to make an impact with two tame 'thrillers' published in the Thirties.


Over the years, the British Secret Service has been a fertile ground for nourishing writers of spy fiction with John Buchan, Somerset Maugham, A.E.W. Mason, Graham Greene, Compton Mackenzie, Ian Fleming and John Le Carré (David Cornwell) as stellar examples. Two of Maxwell Knight assistants: John Bingham, who was the model for John Le Carré's 'Smiley', and William Younger also tried their hands at detective fiction.

Forty years on in October 1980, the former Joan Miller (now known as Joanna Phipps) decided to continue the tradition, by writing about her 'Personal Exploits in MI5's Most Secret Station'. It was based on the facts as she knew them, suitably modified to portray herself in the starring role. She had sidestepped the restrictions imposed by the Official Secrets Acts by moving to Malta, where she was outside British jurisdiction.

Her motivation was money. Having turned sixty and having lived life to the full she was being hounded by creditors. She also had health problems, her figure had ballooned and she had taken to wearing tent-like garments. In public, she wore dark glasses that helped to hide the puffiness of her face.

Miller desperately wanted to write a bestseller and she was fully prepared to lie as much as necessary to achieve her ends. A magazine article appeared on 18 October 1981 in which she was colourfully described as 'MI5's Mistress of Espionage'[6]. It was a trailer for the book that she was said to be writing on 'an unnamed Mediterranean island'.

The Kent-Wolkoff Affair was the only case of any consequence with which Miller had claimed an involvement. Kent and his partner-in-crime Anna Wolkoff were members of Captain Ramsay's Right Club, which had never got off the ground in the way Ramsay had hoped. After the declaration of war, its few activists comprised a small group of middle-aged women who fancifully called themselves 'The Inner Circle'. Wolkoff was the most prominent among these and she claimed to be Ramsay's aide-de-camp.

The Inner Circle met mainly at the Russian Tea Rooms, a small café on Harrington Road near South Kensington Underground Station. Somewhat surprisingly, while the *hoi polloi* were limited to the subsistence amounts prescribed by their ration books, the better off could still patronise the cafés and indulge to their heart's content. Even delicacies including caviar were available and reputedly the Russian Tea Rooms served the best caviar in London.

Wolkoff's parents ran the café and even with caviar on the menu this was a very big comedown. Before the Bolshevik Revolution, her father Admiral Nicolas Wolkoff had been the Naval Attaché at the Russian Embassy in London and some time previously her mother had been a Lady-in-Waiting for the Empress. After the Revolution, the Wolkoffs had opted to stay in London but they held bitter memories having been deprived of their former privileges. Anna, the eldest of their four children, shared their bitterness.

The magazine article on Miller had evidently touched a raw nerve because Whitehall reacted by asking its American counterparts to withdraw the material on Tyler Kent that had been released into the National Archives in Washington. It was withdrawn on 6 November 1981.

---

[6] Barrie Penrose, *MI5's Mistress of Espionage*: *The Sunday Times Colour Magazine* (18 October 1981).

Weidenfeld & Nicolson, a London publisher, had offered Miller a contract and introduced her to Patricia Craig, an established writer who agreed to 'ghost' the book. It was slated for publication in May 1984 but shortly before the due date the Treasury Solicitor stepped in and persuaded Weidenfeld's not to go ahead.

Miller died in June 1984 and Jonquil Hepper, her daughter, and Patricia Craig offered the manuscript to an Irish publisher, Brandon. A deal was done but once again the Government intervened shortly before publication and, as a consequence, the book was officially banned for sale in Britain for several years[7].

Brandon published Miller's book *One Girl's War* in 1986 two years after her death. It was a jolly good read but like most books in this genre the author had relied heavily on previously published work, some of which was decidedly dubious.

Yet according to the cover, it was the book 'Whitehall Wants to Ban'. Most readers would have been at a loss to understand why but eventually everything would unfold when MI5 files for that era were released into Britain's National Archives.

Although the files had been heavily 'weeded', there was still enough relevant information to piece together one of the most controversial stories in Anglo-American relationships.


On arriving in London, Tyler Kent began to socialise amongst the American and White Russian émigré communities, which was hardly surprising given his American roots, his experience of Soviet Russia and his 'wonderful Russian'. One old émigré acknowledged that Kent knew many new Russian words that had not previously been heard in London. Another spoke of the photographs that he had brought with him. He became much sought after for social gatherings.

Then aged 28, he was considered a snappy dresser. He acquired a mistress, Irene Danischewsky, an attractive Russian-

---

[7] Steve MacDonogh, *Open Book: One Publisher's War*, 1999.

born woman after meeting her at a Russian New Year Ball on 20 January 1940[8].

At some stage, Kent also met Barbara Allen, the American-born wife of Sam Allen, a wealthy businessman. Barbara ran the American Club and she took Kent to the Russian Tea Rooms on or about the 21 February 1940 and introduced him to Anna Wolkoff[9]. Kent and Wolkoff shared the same outlook that the war was nothing more than a Jewish conspiracy and they soon hit it off. Before long he invited her to his flat and allowed her to read his collection of Embassy documents, some of which appeared to support their beliefs.

Some time during March 1940, Wolkoff introduced Kent to Captain Ramsay. Kent then invited Ramsay to peruse his cache of Embassy documents whereupon Ramsay asked Wolkoff to obtain copies of two telegrams that Churchill had sent to Roosevelt. It had been Ramsay's intention to show these to Prime Minister Chamberlain, as evidence of the conspiracy that was being conducted behind his back. In those days, when photocopiers were largely 'a thing of the future', this meant that Wolkoff had to visit a photographer, which she did.

However, Ramsay would run out of time because Churchill became Prime Minister on 10 May 1940. Both Kent and Wolkoff were arrested on 20 May 1940 and after secret trials, they were sent down for seven and ten years. Ramsay was arrested on 23 May 1940 and detained without trial until 24 September 1944.

According to Miller's version of events, she had been the undercover agent who had been instrumental in breaking up this dangerous spy ring, she had been the main prosecution witness at Wolkoff's trial and she had been at the receiving end of a death threat uttered by Wolkoff on seeing her in court.

---

[8] KV2/840 (39).
[9] Previous reports that Mrs. Betty Straker had made the introductions are wrong. Mrs. Straker introduced Kent to Wolkoff's parents and possibly to his mistress, Irene Danischewsky.

Although Miller had worked on the Kent-Wolkoff case, she greatly exaggerated her part for the purposes of her book, by claiming an earlier involvement and to have carried out tasks performed by the two undercover agents who had testified at Kent's trial: Marjorie Mackie and Hélène de Munck.

Miller must have assumed that she could get away with her deception because the agents' names had never been previously published in Britain. Evidently, she was initially unaware that they had testified under their real names, that copies of Kent's trial transcript had become available in the United States and that the 'death threat' supposedly uttered by Wolkoff in court was actually just a piece of nonsense invented by a newspaper to spice up its report on the trials. Although the sentences had been announced in open court, the trials had been held in secret so some imaginative reporting had been required.

When Miller discovered that Kent's trial transcript was telling a different story, she changed hers to suit. In her 1981 version, she claimed to have performed de Munck's role in the sting operation that MI5 had mounted against Wolkoff but later[10] she reinstated 'Helen' (de Munck).

In other respects, Miller continued to insist that she had played an important role in the Affair but the truth was that she had played no part whatsoever in the sting operation nor had she been a witness at Wolkoff's trial. Here she was on safer ground because no transcript had ever been released, although according to the Earl Jowitt 'When the Judge decided that the case against Kent should be tried separately from that against Anna Wolkoff, it became necessary to call the same evidence in both cases.'[11]

Maxwell Knight was at the heart of the Kent-Wolkoff Affair having planted Marjorie Mackie in Captain Ramsay's Right Club

---

[10] Anthony Masters' biography of Maxwell Knight *The Man Who Was M* published in 1984, shortly after Miller's death contains her original version.
[11] As Sir William Jowitt, he had been the Solicitor General and he had led for the Prosecution at the trials. Later, as the Earl Jowitt, he summarised the cases in his book, *Some Were Spies* (1954).

in August 1939. She was the Assistant Secretary of the Christian Defence Movement and having separated from her husband, she had reverted to using her maiden name of Amor. On 4 October 1939, she was given a job in Censorship to satisfy Captain Ramsay's wish to have a contact there.

Mackie was introduced to Anna Wolkoff on 6 December 1939 and quickly discovered her superstitious nature, her interest in spiritualism, clairvoyance, astrology and anything to do with the occult[12]. Wolkoff also boasted about her contacts at various Embassies and her ability to send correspondence abroad without troubling the Censor. In February 1940 at Mackie's urging, she had tried to send a letter through the Belgian Embassy but as she had never received any acknowledgment she fretted about the reliability of her Belgian contacts[13].

Knight, who was also interested in the occult, inserted Hélène de Munck, a Belgian-born mystic, into the operation on 1 February 1940 so that he could play mind games with Wolkoff and investigate the connections that she had claimed to have in Belgium.

Marjorie Mackie introduced Joan Miller to Anna Wolkoff on 9 April 1940 simply to satisfy Anna's wish to have a contact within MI5. She believed that one of the young secretaries could be educated into 'our way of thinking' and Miller, who was 22 at the time, played her part to perfection.

Although de Munck may have planted the idea in her head, this was not altogether crazy because MI5 and Censorship were then sharing the facilities of Wormwood Scrubs Prison and with Mackie ostensibly working in Censorship she could conceivably have known some of the secretaries, at least by sight.

After accepting Knight's assignment, Miller just happened to visit the Russian Tea Rooms one evening when Mackie and Wolkoff were present. Mackie just happened to spot Miller sitting by herself and so she went over and went through the

---

[12] KV 4/227 page 49.
[13] Germany had not invaded Belgium and it was neutral when Anna Wolkoff had attempted to send her letter.

motions of introducing herself. She then introduced Miller to Wolkoff. Wolkoff was suitably impressed and further meetings followed.

On one occasion when they were in the Russian Tea Rooms, Wolkoff pointed out Miller to de Munck and asked her 'what she thought about her?' She evidently placed great faith in de Munck's mystic powers even though she would later dismiss her as a 'drug fiend' [14].

In due course, Knight provided Miller with some titbits of information that she could pass on to Wolkoff to establish her credentials. Wolkoff was so pleased with Miller's contributions that she gave her some *haute couture* creation that she had admired, as a token of her appreciation.

Wolkoff also introduced Miller to a 'Mrs. Freeman', an alias adopted by Captain Ramsay's wife whose husband sometimes called himself 'Mr. Freeman' but MI5 were aware of their subterfuges.

When de Munck told Wolkoff that she was visiting her relatives in Belgium, she was asked to check out the reliability of her contacts there, and Wolkoff duly provided their names and addresses.

Wolkoff expressed herself pleased with the contributions made by de Munck and, as a reward, she was promised an introduction to Captain Ramsay although this never happened. Neither de Munck nor Miller was invited to join the Right Club, despite Miller's claim to have been enrolled. The three women saturated Wolkoff with their attention and continually encouraged her to carry out subversive activities.

Knight put a fourth agent on the case on 16 April 1940, just one week after Joan Miller. Anna evidently already knew Knight's fourth agent, identified only as 'Special Source', and they had dinner together at the Russian Tea Rooms. She told him that she had been obtaining 'a great deal of information through Tyler Kent' and claimed that he had given her confidential

---

[14] Miller also claimed that 'Helen' had an addiction.

information regarding 'the North Sea battles', arising out of the Norwegian campaign.

On 18 May 1940, Knight briefed Herschel Johnson, the Counsel at the American Embassy, about MI5's intention to arrest Wolkoff and he sought permission to search Kent's London flat. After this was obtained, Knight led the search party, discovered 'masses' of Embassy documents among a variety of other incriminating material that Wolkoff and her associates had entrusted to Kent's care, in the mistaken belief that his diplomatic immunity had put them out-of-reach of the British authorities.

Among the trophies was a red leather-bound accounting ledger that was protected from casual inspection by a small brass lock. It was the Membership Book of the Right Club in which Ramsay had listed some 250 names, although most including Wolkoff had not paid any subscription.

Miller romanticised about her relationship with Knight and even claimed that she had beaten him to the Registry Office before he made his third entry in the marriage stakes. This supported her story that she had given him the brush off but, in fact, Knight married Susan Barnes on 18 November 1944, whereas Miller did not wed her first husband Lieutenant Commander Thomas Kinloch Jones of the Royal Navy until 29 December 1945. For the purposes of her book, Miller brought the date of her own marriage forward to 19 June 1943[15] and then claimed that 'having deprived M of my own personal services', she had found Susan for him as 'a suitable replacement'.

Despite the supposed closeness of her relationship with Knight, she admitted that it had never been consummated. This is not surprising because Knight was 'completely impotent' and throughout his three marriages he had never fathered any children. After his second marriage was annulled, his former bride produced two children from a more productive relationship.

---

[15] Miller had changed her surname to 'Jones' by Deed Poll some time prior to her first marriage to Thomas Kinloch Jones. Towards the end of her life, she was known as Joanna Phipps.

Miller dramatised the death of Knight's first wife Gwladys by claiming that she had committed suicide after 'an occult experience with the notorious Aleister Crowley'[16] but this is demonstrably false. Gwladys Knight died in 1936 at the age of 37 and a Coroner's Inquest concluded that her death was due to 'poisoning by a barbiturate and hypnotic probably Soneryl and there is insufficient evidence as to circumstances. Open Verdict.'

Gwladys had been suffering from sciatica, which can be very painful and she had been prescribed a barbiturate to relieve the pain. This was standard practice in those days but drugs like Soneryl™ are now considered highly dangerous because there is only a small difference between the normal dose and an overdose. But any drug, even aspirin, can produce a fatal reaction.

Miller also claimed that Knight was homosexual but her evidence was decidedly flimsy and her claim was contradictory because elsewhere she had reported that he had an aversion to homosexuals. Contemporaries of Knight's believe her claim to be false, but true or false it certainly spiced up her story and Miller's allegation is now firmly embedded whenever Knight's name appears.

Miller even lied about her last meeting with Knight 'towards the end of 1945' which provided her tale with a suitably dramatic ending. In fact, Knight was the godfather of her daughter Jonquil who was born on 22 May 1948, long after the fictitious incident.

Miller's 'revelations' have successfully fooled many commentators over the years and her fabrications have often been recounted as if they were true even though she evidently did not know much about the Right Club case, except from her own rather modest involvement and from what she had gleaned from previously published sources. Consequently, she had to fill in many gaps in her knowledge with guesswork; and her guesswork was often very wide of the mark.

---

[16] Aleister Crowley (1875-1947) was Britain's leading exponent of black magic and considered himself 'the wickedest man in the world'. Maxwell Knight met him on at least one occasion.

Nevertheless, she had clearly known Knight personally and was able to provide an accurate description. According to Miller, Knight was rather tall and lanky with a big nose, which he referred to as 'my limb'. He always dressed in stylishly shabby tweeds and smoked long, hand-made cigarettes. He had charm of a rare and formidable order with a voice that Miller described as 'hypnotic'. Another woman[17] who met Knight in the Thirties and had often seen him on post-war television has also recalled his 'marvellous voice'.

So why did Whitehall ban Miller's book which was largely a fictionalised reworking of previously published material?

In part, it was probably because Miller had named names and with so many former officers and agents still alive, this was strictly taboo. She had even revealed the name of the hitherto mysterious 'Miss X', one of Knight's agents, who had successfully infiltrated the 'Friends of the Soviet Union'. Based on information provided by Miss X, four Communist spies were tried for espionage in 1938 in what became known as the Woolwich Arsenal Secrets Case. Unlike the Kent and Wolkoff trials that were held entirely *in camera* under wartime Emergency Regulations, the four Communists were tried partly in open court where Knight's agent was allowed to testify as Miss X. This had evidently influenced Miller in her belief that this was standard practice.

Anthony Masters had not only revealed the identity of Miss X in his biography of Maxwell Knight *The Man Who Was M* (1984) but he had even managed to track her down to a suburb in Toronto and obtain both a long interview and a photograph from her younger days. Masters named her as the former Olga Gray[18] who having been born in 1906, was then in her late seventies. As Joan Miller had been one of his sources[19], a link could be made

---

[17] Heather Iandolo née Joyce, William Joyce's elder daughter.
[18] Masters did not reveal Olga's married name.
[19] Masters reported that Miller had entertained him with 'gin and smoked salmon in great quantities'.

and this was precisely the sort of disclosure that MI5 would have deplored.

Miller stopped short of naming another of Knight's agents, a German Jew whom she described as having 'been in England since the early thirties ... his father was a judge ... who had decided that his son would be better off abroad'. However, when taken together with other titbits, she had revealed enough to identify Ferdy Mayne[20] (1916-1998) who had become a well-known actor and was then still alive.

But, undoubtedly, the main reason for Miller's book being banned was because of the sting operation that MI5 had set up to get Anna Wolkoff categorised as a 'foreign agent'. This was the key to getting at Tyler Kent and with Kent still alive, it was possible that he might have been able to make something out of Miller's claims.

Having previously participated in a colossal cover-up on both sides of the Atlantic that included lots of spin and several colourful cover stories, the British Government could only have been embarrassed by Miller's book and they took the sensible course of action.

The material on Kent in the Washington National Archives was made publicly available again on 13 August 1989. Around the same time, Whitehall lifted its ban on Miller's book. So, whatever matters had concerned the authorities on both sides of the Atlantic, these had evidently been resolved by the deaths of Joan Miller in June 1984 and Tyler Kent on 11 November 1988.

---

[20] Born Ferdinand Philip Mayer-Horckel, he would make over 70 films, having started with an uncredited part as a Prussian Student in *The Life and Death of Colonel Blimp* (1943). He was a witness at Miller's wedding in 1945 and he signed under his stage name of Ferdy Mayne.

# 2: News Management

Although Captain Ramsay's connections with Tyler Kent and Anna Wolkoff were not mentioned, the first allusion to 'the Affair' appeared in the British press on 24 May 1940 when *The Times* reported:

### MP DETAINED

### HOME SECRETARY'S LETTER

The SPEAKER said: I have to inform the House that I have received the following letter from the Home Secretary: -

May 23, 1940

Sir, - I have to inform you that I have found it my duty in the exercise of my powers under Regulation 18B of the Defence Regulations 1939 to direct that Captain Archibald Henry Maule Ramsay, Member of Parliament, be detained. Captain Ramsay was accordingly taken into custody this morning and is at present lodged in Brixton Prison. I am, Sir, your obedient servant,

(Signed) JOHN ANDERSON

Mr. THORNE (Plaistow, Lab.), whose rising caused protests from all parts of the House, asked if the Home Secretary was prepared to give information as to the reason why the hon. Member had been arrested.

THE SPEAKER, - Not at this stage.

The fact that the 'rising' of a hon. Member should have caused protests before he had had any chance to speak suggests that all the other hon. Members had already been briefed on the circumstances that had led to Ramsay's arrest. But, had it not been wartime with the press closely censored, the arrest of any hon. Member would have certainly given rise to further comment, even in the strait-laced *Times*.

In 1940, the United States had not yet entered the war but the American Press was generally sympathetic to British attempts to counter the Nazi menace and it was fully prepared to publish State-generated propaganda. One series of articles that was widely disseminated by the US Cabinet 'to warn the public of the dangers of the Fifth Column' was based on a fact-finding mission to Britain that had been undertaken by Colonel 'Wild Bill' Donovan, an emissary of President Roosevelt's.

Although Donovan may have arranged the distribution, it is now known that Somerset Maugham had actually written the articles having been briefed by Guy Liddell[1] prior to visiting Washington. Over lunch on 9 August 1940, Maugham told Liddell that his task was difficult because 'he wanted to arouse Americans to a sense of danger but without giving the impression that the position was hopeless'[2].

Most newspapers printed Maugham's articles verbatim but as well as running the articles during the period 20 to 23 August 1940 the *New York Times* also featured the story in its 'News of the Week Review'. On this occasion, Raymond Daniels, one of its staffers, spiced it up so that its Sunday edition on 25 August 1940 included a reference to Captain Ramsay:

> A car from Brixton Prison drew up last week at the British House of Commons. Waiting was the Sergeant-at-Arms … He took from the police custody of Captain Archibald Ramsay MP, a World War veteran of the Coldstream Guards. The captain, arrested last May under the Defence Regulations had been brought to Westminster to argue that the detention violated his traditional Parliamentary rights of immunity.
>
> Captain Ramsay, a man of medium height, a Roman nose above his trim, black moustache, was educated at Eton and Sandhurst … He has been an

---

[1] Guy Liddell was the director of 'B' Division, which handled the whole spectrum of counter-espionage. He was Maxwell Knight's immediate boss.
[2] KV 4/186, page 559

MP since 1931 for ... Peebles. Before the war, he was strongly pro-Hitler.

Though no specific charges were brought against him on his arrest - Defence Regulations allow that - informed American sources said that he had sent to the German legation in Dublin treasonable information given him by Tyler Kent, clerk to the American Embassy in London ...

Unfortunately for the *New York Times*, although it only had a small circulation in Britain, the article came to Ramsay's attention in his cell in Brixton jail. Even more unfortunately, the 'informed source' had been misinformed: Ramsay had not sent any treasonable information given to him by Tyler Kent anywhere. Worse, there was absolutely no evidence that Ramsay had even visited Dublin.

Ramsay therefore decided that he had been libelled and he brought actions against both the *New York Times* and its London distributor. However, the actions would not be heard until 17 July 1941, several months after the Kent and Wolkoff trials had taken place and after Roosevelt had been re-elected President for an unprecedented third term.

Kent and Wolkoff were sent for trial at the Old Bailey, London's Central Criminal Court, in October 1940. They were tried *in camera* before a seven-man jury, as permitted by wartime emergency regulations. Mr. Justice Tucker heard the case.

Kent's Counsel requested that he should be tried separately. This was agreed and Kent was tried first. On the fourth day, the Judge sent the Jury to consider its verdict and twenty-five minutes later Kent was found guilty of five counts under the Official Secrets Act and one count of Larceny. The jury was then dismissed and a new jury sworn in for Wolkoff's trial. She was found guilty of two charges under the Official Secrets Act and one charge against the Defence (General) Regulations.

They were both sentenced in open court on 7 November 1940. Kent was handed down seven years on each of the five charges under the Official Secrets Act and twelve months against the Larceny charge. Wolkoff was sentenced to five years on each of the two charges under the Official Secrets Act and ten years for her 'still more serious offence' against the Defence (General) Regulations. All the sentences were to run concurrently.

The judge's comments on Wolkoff's 'still more serious offence' were widely reported in the press:

> An act which was likely to assist the enemy in that by secret means you attempted to send a letter in code to one Joyce in Berlin. Now what you did - you, a Russian subject who in 1935 became a naturalised British subject - was done at a time when this country was fighting for her very life and existence. You sent a document to a traitor who broadcasts from Germany for the purpose of weakening the war effort of this country.

The man that the judge had branded a traitor was William Joyce. He had been a prominent member of Sir Oswald Mosley's Fascist party and then the National Socialist League but he had fled to Germany shortly before the war, after having been tipped off that he had been listed for internment if he stayed in Britain.

Joyce had also been a member of Captain Ramsay's Right Club and both he and Ramsay had been prominently associated with the Nordic League, another secret anti-Jewish organisation whose members greeted each other with 'PJ', the slogan of several anti-Jewish groups. It stood for 'Perish Judah', a clear echo of 'Juda Verrecke', the battle cry of the marching SA and SS.

As 'Lord Haw-Haw', Joyce had become the most notorious of the Nazi propaganda broadcasters. After the war he was tried for High Treason and, controversially, he was sent to the scaffold even though he was an American by birth and he had acquired German nationality before America had entered the war.

Captain Ramsay's libel actions against the *New York Times* and its London distributor started on 17 July 1941. Prior to the action, lawyers acting for the defendants had visited Kent in London's Wandsworth Prison. They found him in the prison hospital, recuperating after being on hunger strike and possibly also from a nervous breakdown. They sought his help in defending the newspaper. After reading the article, Kent denounced it as 'a tissue of lies' and refused to help.

For his part, Ramsay had requested copies of the transcripts of the Kent and Wolkoff trials[3]. Of course, the British authorities weren't going to fall for that and they refused his request by explaining that transcripts could only be provided to those who had been parties to a trial. Consequently, Ramsay's libel actions proceeded without the benefit (or otherwise) of either transcript.

But notwithstanding such legal niceties, the British authorities did everything they possibly could to help the defendants, who were evidently given access to material that could only have been provided by MI5.

In addition, one of MI5's legal gurus visited Sir William Jowitt, the Solicitor General, on 28 April 1941. According to the MI5 report, Jowitt (who had led for the Prosecution at the trials) took the view that it would be 'tragic for the Americans to get the impression that we were not co-operating' but he was shocked that 'Colonel Donovan should have given the impression that Ramsay had transmitted information to Germany when such was not the case'[4].

Jowitt considered that the best plan was for someone to talk to the defendants' solicitors privately, inform them that there was no truth in the allegation but suggesting that they should admit the libel, pay a token payment into Court and plead mitigation in respect of damages. In Jowitt's opinion this might only be 'an infinitesimal sum'.

As was its custom in those days, *The Times* published details of Ramsay's case in its Law Reports.

On Day One the 17 July 1941, Ramsay rejected a description of himself as anti-Semitic because the expression 'Semitic' included the Arabs and he was not anti-Arab. However, he

---

[3] Ramsay had appeared as a Defence Witness at Wolkoff's Trial.
[4] KV 2/543 (45x)

admitted that he believed that the Jews were the enemies of England. He said that he had never been to Germany and knew very little about it. Moreover, what he knew of Nazism he didn't approve of. His only point of contact with Nazism was its anti-Jewish policy although he strongly disapproved of the cruelty inflicted by it on innocent Jews.

Ramsay also said that he had nothing to do with the British Union of Fascists (although he wasn't a member, this wasn't strictly true and he had certainly attended some 'secret meetings' with Mosley and others) or an organisation known as The Link (this was a downright lie).

Ramsay said that he had first met Tyler Kent early in 1940 and that Anna Wolkoff had introduced them. He confirmed that he knew that Kent worked at the American Embassy and that Kent had shown him some documents, and that he had intended to 'inform Mr. Chamberlain of anything which I might find out'. (Chamberlain had been Prime Minister up to 10 May 1940, when he was replaced by Churchill.)

Replying to 'His Lordship' (Mr. Justice Atkinson), Ramsay said that 'on the true facts' Hitler was largely justified in the seizure of Czechoslovakia; he was pro-Hitler on the question of Danzig; and he was pro-Hitler on the revision of the Versailles Treaty. The judge remarked, 'Then there were many respects in which you were pro-Hitler?' Ramsay replied, 'If the word is used apart from the interests of this country'.

On Day Two the 18 July 1941, Ramsay described the Right Club which he had formed in May 1939 and said that it had ceased to function on the outbreak of war. He agreed that Anna Wolkoff had been a member 'from early on'. Under cross-examination, he was asked why he had entrusted the locked book containing the names of members of the Right Club to Tyler Kent. He replied that he suspected that Jews might cause his own house to be burgled in order to get possession of it because they wanted to know the names in it. Ramsay was also asked about a number of anti-Semitic cartoons with adhesive backs that had been found in his house when he was arrested.

Nothing much happened on Days Three or Four the 23 and 24 July 1941 but on Day Five the 25 July 1941, Ramsay's Counsel argued that there was no justification for calling Ramsay a 'fifth columnist' because he had a slight knowledge of William Joyce (Lord Haw-Haw) before the war. Captain Ramsay, he explained, did not know when Joyce was made a member of the Right Club that he was going to Germany to broadcast and his client had had nothing to do with this 'phenomenon'.

On Day Six the 28 July 1941, Ramsay called the MP for Forfar, Thomas Shaw, as a witness and Shaw testified that to his knowledge Ramsay's anti-Jewish views stretched back to 1932, as long as he had known him. In his final speech, Ramsay's Counsel advised that 'other educated people took as strong a view on this [Jewish] question as Captain Ramsay and he referred to the writings of a professor of theology which had received the imprimatur of the Catholic Church[5]. Additionally, he then trotted out some of the conspiracy theories propagated in the writings of Mrs. Nesta H. Webster, Britain's leading conspiracy theorist of the Twenties and Thirties.

Day Seven the 31 July 1941 was the Day of Judgement and His Lordship noted that Ramsay had formed a secret society called the Right Club that consisted of 100 men and 150 women. Among the earliest members was Joyce and there were the convicts Anna Wolkoff and Tyler Kent. He then summarised the judgements in their cases.

He also referred to a letter from a Miss Taylor (sic)[6] that had been found in his house at the time of his arrest. In the letter, Miss Taylor described how she and others had hissed Mr. Churchill at a news theatre when a film was shown of him addressing members of the crew of the Hardy. Then, the police found adhesive copies of a cartoon representing three wealthy Jews made to look as repulsive as possible under the heading

---

[5] This was probably a reference to *The Rulers of Russia* by Rev. Denis Fahey, a booklet published by the Archbishop of Dublin on 26 March 1938.
[6] This would have been Fay Taylour, a famous racing driver, who had won the Ladies' Race at Brooklands in 1931, after clocking 98 mph. A member of Ramsay's Right Club and the BUF, she was detained.

'Onward Christian Soldiers'. Another pamphlet found at his house had contained a parody of 'Land of Hope and Glory':

> Land of Dope and Jewry
> Land that once was free
> All the Jew boys praise thee
> Whilst they plunder thee
> Poorer still and poorer
> Grow thy true-born sons
> Faster still and faster
> They're sent to feed the guns[7].

The Judge then asked, 'How could anyone, in the middle of this war, regard the Jews as a greater enemy of this country than Germany?' Obviously not expecting an answer, His Lordship then gave judgement for Ramsay but declared that 'No jury would have given Captain Ramsay more than a farthing damages'.

In peacetime, the jury would have determined the damages but as there was no jury[8], the judge was allowed to determine the damages, which he assessed at a farthing each against the two defendants.

At this point, the Defence Counsel stated that sums of £50 and £25 had been paid into Court, with denials of liability by both defendants. Costs usually 'go with the verdict' but they are always a matter for the judge's discretion and on this occasion, His Lordship exercised his discretion by ordering that Captain Ramsay should pay the defendants' costs as from the time of the payment in. So everything worked out satisfactorily for the defendants who were only required to pay 'an infinitesimal' sum as damages, exactly as Sir William Jowitt had predicted.

The publicity given to Ramsay's libel actions had one immediate effect; his constituents asked him to resign as their MP. He refused but they reiterated their request when he was released on 26 September 1944. He again refused and duly

---

[7] It would later be discovered that Ramsay had penned the words himself on House of Commons notepaper, apparently the day after the declaration of war.
[8] A wartime Emergency Measure.

resumed his seat in the House of Commons until the next election on 5 July 1945.

He was never again invited to contest the seat.

With Britain under strict censorship, another wartime emergency measure, there were no newspaper splashes nor scoops and several North American journalists who sensed a good story discovered that it wasn't a good idea to enquire into the Kent-Wolkoff Affair. Two Canadians who made this mistake were incarcerated in the Peveril Camp in Peel on the Isle of Man, one of several internment camps on the island.

John Charnley, a Mosleyite who had been detained at Peveril Camp, wrote:

> There was one man whose name I will not disclose. I recently supplied what background recollections I had to his daughter. She had been making enquiries about her father's detention while in England ... He was a Canadian journalist and in the early months of the war was on assignment to the American magazine *Time*. He knew a great deal about the Tyler Kent-Anna Wolkoff story and his detention was the result of official fears that he might splash the story in the American press to the mutual embarrassment of the British and American governments. He remained very secretive throughout the whole period of his detention and after the war until his death, even within his own family.[9]

The Canadian journalist has since been identified as Erland Echlin and whatever Echlin may have known about the Kent-Wolkoff story, little is known about Echlin himself. He had been the London correspondent for a number of Canadian papers and at some time for *Time* and *Newsweek*. His name appears on a list of detainees in the National Archives with the notation 'AP'

---

[9] *Blackshirts and Roses* by John Charnley, page 133.

alongside[10]. This indicates that he had been incarcerated for having committed 'Acts Prejudicial'.

During internment, Echlin is reported having attended a 'religious meeting' held by fellow internee Captain T.G. St. Barbe Baker in April 1942, in which Baker preached that Jesus was the first National Socialist and that Hitler had been sent by Christ to fight the evils of the International Jewish money racket[11].

Guy Liddell also mentioned Echlin in his diary on 16 August 1942 as 'still being an admirer of Hitler'[12].

According to Brian Simpson, Echlin was detained from March 1941 to September 1943[13] and 'on release he was required to live in London. It seems likely that he fell foul of the authorities through attempts to get to the bottom of the Kent affair'[14]. He died in 1951.

Echlin's daughter Mrs. Beverley Staples of Toronto, who had visited England shortly before John Charnley's death on 27 December 1988, knew that her father had worked for *Newsweek*, that he had made broadcasts to Canada and that he had been 'on a spat with Ed Murrow', the famous American commentator. She also knew that her father's secretary, Miss W. Hooton, had been interned.

Beverley Staples did not turn up any new information but after she had returned to Canada, McNeil Sloane, another Mosleyite who had been detained at Peveril Camp, recalled that a second Canadian journalist had also been at the camp.

Sloane, who had spent most of his time in detention digging escape tunnels to no avail, identified him as Jimmy Green, a

---

[10] HO 45/25115. The document is undated but it was filed near another dated 30 November 1941.

[11] HO 214/45

[12] KV 4/190

[13] Echlin was released on 10 September 1943, according to an intercepted letter sent by Admiral Wolkoff (Prisoner No 3293) in Brixton Prison to 'Bertie' Mills, a former member of the Right Club who had already been released. KV 2/1213.

[14] *In the Highest Degree Odious* by Brian Simpson.

reporter on the *Toronto Daily News*, but even though they'd had 'lots of conversations', Green had been very tight-lipped about the reason for his detention.

However, Green did tell Sloane that he had been a colleague of Echlin's and that before the war they had been correspondents for the Balkans, working out of Vienna.

Meanwhile in Washington, Tyler Kent's widowed mother Ann was becoming increasingly anxious about the fate of her son. Prior to his arrest, they had communicated every few weeks or so through the State Department mailbag but apart from learning of his arrest, she had since been left in the dark.

Then in May 1941, she learned from Robert Scott, a newspaperman who had worked on the *Washington Post*, that her son was somehow involved because of having seen some secret cables that had been exchanged between Roosevelt and Churchill.

These secret cables had supposedly included plans for Anglo-American cooperation and specifically the 'Lend-Lease formula'[15]. For his part, so the story went, Churchill had undertaken that should he become Prime Minister he would provide British propaganda services in support of Roosevelt's re-election campaign. (Roosevelt was coming up for re-election in November 1940 and, according to received history, the concept of Lend-Lease did not occur to him until 16 December 1940 some six weeks after he had been re-elected for an unprecedented third term.)

Scott implied that newspapermen in London and Washington generally accepted the truth of these stories but that they were afraid to publish. In fact, only one newspaper, the *Washington Times-Herald*, did run the story by Arthur Sears Henning on 12 November 1941 but no other newspaper picked it up.

Mrs. Kent, who had been refused a passport that would have enabled her to visit her son, then persuaded Ian Ross MacFarlane

---

[15] 'Lend-Lease' provided the funding that enabled Britain to continue the fight against Germany. It was eventually extended to 38 nations and totalled some $50 billion of which the British Commonwealth received $31 billion.

to act on her behalf. MacFarlane, who described himself as a Wireless Commentator, took up the challenge and arrived in England in March 1942.

Evidently, MacFarlane was not working exclusively for Mrs. Kent because while in England he did an eight-minute radio commentary on 'A Description of the Bombing of Bremen'. It was broadcast by short wave on 23 June 1942.

Surprisingly, MacFarlane did manage an interview with Kent on 8 August 1942 and even more surprisingly, the prison authorities at Camp Hill Prison at Newport on the Isle of Wight failed to take any record of their conversations. Over two years later in September 1944, the Prison Commission gave MI5 the lame explanation that 'it can be assumed that nothing transpired at these visits which aroused the suspicions of the Officer supervising them.'

MacFarlane left England by plane to Newfoundland in September 1942 and then took a boat to New York. He had struck up an acquaintance with a fellow passenger John Bryan Owen who, following a spell in prison, was being deported as an undesirable alien. Owen was a freelance writer who, after learning of the Tyler Kent Affair from MacFarlane, declared that 'It will be my life's work to expose all this'.

Owen was found dead in his New York apartment on 2 January 1943. The medical examiner who performed the autopsy, attributed his death to natural causes and Owen's sister, who had identified the body, went along with this and signed a statement to that effect.

However, there would be other versions of how Owen had met his death. According to an unnamed member of the police, it was 'suicide following the consumption of a large dose of veronal' and according to an unnamed member of US Naval Intelligence 'he was murdered because he had been talking about these matters'.

They couldn't all be right but natural causes or not, MacFarlane was reported as having then lost interest in the Kent affair and was 'very nervous' whenever he was approached to discuss the case[16].

MacFarlane was a very adventurous soul who had travelled extensively before succumbing to illness in the Syrian Desert. This affected his sight and left him nearly blind. Nevertheless, he continued broadcasting, despite an inability to read scripts. He did not seem the sort of person who would readily give in to threats, if indeed any were made. However, he had a wife and five children to consider. For the last three years of his life he suffered poor health after contracting hepatitis in Africa. He died in Baltimore in 1962 at the age of 60.

Regardless of whether or not Owen and MacFarlane were 'silenced', the incarcerations of Erland Echlin, Jimmy Green and their secretary Miss W. Hooton provide compelling evidence that 'the authorities' on both sides of the Atlantic had something that they wanted to hide.

---

[16] *The Case of Tyler Kent* by John Howland Snow.

# 3: The Official Statement
(American spellings retained.)

Tyler Kent's mother, Ann, always believed in her son's innocence and she was a great champion of his cause. She had written to everyone whom she perceived might be able to help and Senator Henrik Shipstead, a prominent isolationist, had raised the matter in Congress on 19 June 1944 and called for more information. Mrs. Kent also wrote to President Roosevelt on 21 July 1944. The net result of her endeavours was a carefully worded press release from the Department of State dated 2 September 1944.

Department of State,
September 2, 1944.

(For the press)                                 No.405.

The Department of State has taken note of recent inquiries and newspaper reports regarding the case of Tyler Kent, formerly employee of the American Embassy at London, and the Office of Foreign Service Administration has been instructed to review the matter thoroughly and prepare a comprehensive report. The following is the text of the report:

Tyler Kent, American citizen, an employee of the American Foreign Service assigned to London, was tried and convicted under the Official Secrets Act (1911) of Great Britain before the Central Criminal Court at the Old Bailey, London, in October, 1940. The charges against him were the obtaining and delivering to an agent of a foreign country (Germany) copies or abstracts of documents which might have been directly or indirectly useful to the enemy, and which were, at the same time, prejudicial to the safety of interests of Great Britain. Incidental to the proceedings against him, it was brought out that he had violated the Larceny Act of 1916 of Great Britain by the theft of documents which were the property of the Government of the United States in the custody of the American Ambassador, London. The above mentioned were found proven by a jury on the basis of evidence produced during the trial. Kent had worked through a confederate who was allegedly anti-Jewish and pro-Nazi.

The background of the case and the circumstances leading up to Kent's arrest and trial were as follows: Kent, at the age of 22, had entered the Foreign Service as a clerk, his first assignment having been to the American Embassy at Moscow. He was later transferred to the American Embassy, London, arriving there in October 1939. He was assigned to the code room as a code clerk, where his duties were to encode and decode telegrams. Before entering the service he had attended Princeton University, the Sorbonne (Paris), the University of Madrid, and George Washington University. He had acquired several foreign languages, including Russian, French, German and Italian.

On May 18, 1940, a representative[1] of the London Police Headquarters at Scotland Yard called at the Embassy to report that Kent had become the object of attention by Scotland Yard through his association with a group of persons suspected of conducting pro-German activities under the cloak of anti-Jewish propaganda. Prominent in this group was Anna Wolkoff, a naturalized British subject of Russian origin, the daughter of a former admiral of the Imperial Russian Navy. Miss Wolkoff had resided in Great Britain since emigrating, with her father, from Russia following the Bolshevist revolution, had been hospitably received and had made a considerable circle of friends among Londoners of standing, some

---

[1] This was Maxwell Knight.

of whom had assisted in setting up the Wolkoff family in a small business. After the outbreak of the present war the British police had become interested in Miss Wolkoff's activities, believing that she was in sympathy with certain of Germany's objectives, that she and some of her associates were hostile to Britain's war effort, that she was involved in pro-German propaganda, that she had a channel of communication with Germany, and that she was making use of that channel of communication.

Kent had been observed by Scotland Yard as having been in frequent contact with Anna Wolkoff and in touch with others of a group known to her. Among other things, it had been noted that Kent and Miss Wolkoff were sharing an automobile and that Miss Wolkoff frequently drove the car, using gasoline allegedly supplied by Kent. Scotland Yard was now convinced that Anna Wolkoff was receiving confidential information from Kent, and stated that she would be arrested on May 20. The police added that on the same day they considered it highly desirable to search the rooms occupied by Kent. In reply to an inquiry made by the British authorities, Ambassador Kennedy, with the approval of the Department, informed such authorities of the waiver by this Government of the privilege of diplomatic immunity. Scotland Yard thereupon indicated that a search warrant would he issued and that Kent's rooms would be searched on May 20, 1940.

The possibility that an employee of the Embassy, having access to the confidential codes, was making improper use of the material entrusted to him in the course of his work was of the utmost concern to Ambassador Kennedy and to the Government of the United States. Preservation of the secrecy of this Government's means of communication with its establishments abroad is a matter of fundamental importance to the conduct of our foreign relations. In

53

the circumstances described it was imperative that Ambassador Kennedy ascertain, and ascertain immediately, whether Kent was guilty of a violation of trust. There was every reason, in the interest of the American Government, for the waiving of diplomatic immunity and for allowing the British authorities (who alone had the means of obtaining the evidence) to proceed in an effort to prove or disprove their suspicions. In this connection it may be noted that it is well established in international law that the so-called immunity of an employee of a diplomatic mission from criminal or civil processes may be renounced or waived by the sending state at any time.

The search of Kent's room was conducted according to plan, an officer of the Embassy being present throughout. It revealed that Kent had in his possession copies of Embassy material totaling more than 1,500 individual papers. He also had two newly made duplicate keys to the index bureau and the code room of the Embassy, these being unauthorized and in addition to the keys furnished him officially for his use as a code clerk. He explained that he had had these keys made so that in the event he should ever be transferred from code work to another section of the Embassy he would still have access to the code room. Also found in his possession were two photographic plates of Embassy documents believed to have been made by confederates for the purpose of endeavoring to transmit prints thereof to Germany, and certain printed propaganda material which was prejudicial to the British conduct of the war. The police also established that some of the papers found had been transmitted to an agent of a foreign power.

An examination of the documents found in his room indicated that Kent had begun classifying the material by subject, but this work was far from completed. They covered practically every subject on which the Embassy was carrying on correspondence

54

with the Department of State. As may be supposed,
they included copies of telegrams embodying
information collected by the Embassy which
otherwise would not have been permitted to leave
Great Britain without censorship. As may be likewise
supposed, they contained information which would
have been useful to Germany and which Great
Britain would not have permitted to reach Germany.
It is of interest to note, in this connection, that Kent
had, during his service in London, written to the
Chargé d'Affaires of the American Embassy in Berlin
asking his assistance in arranging for his (Kent's)
transfer to Berlin. When questioned as to what he
would have done with the documents in his
possession had he been transferred to Germany, Kent
replied that he could not state what he would have
done with them; he regarded the question as a
hypothetical one.

Regardless of the purpose for which Kent had
taken the material from the Embassy, he had done so
without authorization, in violation of the most
elementary principles governing the rules for the
preservation of the secrecy of the Government's
correspondence. By his own showing he had, while
occupying a very special position of confidence
within the Embassy, displayed a shocking disregard
for every principle of decency and honor so far as his
obligations toward the United States were concerned.
The removal of so large a number of documents from
the Embassy premises compromised the whole
confidential communications system of the United
States, bringing into question the security of the
secret ciphers. It was obviously impossible to
continue his services and Kent was dismissed from
the Government service as of May 20, 1940.
Thereafter the question of diplomatic immunity
naturally did not arise.

So far as the British police were concerned, the

evidence found in Kent's room was such as to convince them of the necessity of detaining him at Brixton prison pending investigation of the use he had made of the documents in his possession and the true implications of his connection with Anna Wolkoff. Ambassador Kennedy, with the consent of the Department of State, agreed to Kent's detention.

On May 28 a representative of Scotland Yard informed the Embassy that investigations were proceeding, that the case became progressively more complex, and that it could not be cleared up quickly. It was believed, however, that there would be a case for prosecution against Kent and Anna Wolkoff under the Official Secrets Act of the United Kingdom.

Kent's trial eventually commenced August 8, 1940[2], and was attended by the American Consul General. It was held in camera because of the harmful effects to British counterespionage efforts which were to be anticipated if certain of the evidence became public. Prior to the trial the American Consul General in London had called upon Kent (July 31,1940) at Brixton Prison. The Consul General informed him that he would be taken to court the following day and formally charged with offense under the Official Secrets Act of the United Kingdom, i.e. obtaining documents for a purpose prejudicial to the safety or interests of the United Kingdom which might be directly or indirectly useful to an enemy. The Consul General inquired whether Kent had a lawyer to represent him to which Kent replied that he had not, and that he had not given the matter any thought. The Consul General advised him

---

[2] This was the date when Kent went before the Bow Street Magistrates' Court. The case was then adjourned until 19 August 1940. Kent's trial before Judge and Jury at the Old Bailey (London's Central Criminal Court) started on 23 October 1940.

that he should he represented by a lawyer and agreed to assist in getting in touch with a suitable solicitor. Kent was subsequently placed in touch with a lawyer, whom he engaged to represent him during the trial.

On October 28, 1940, the jury found Kent guilty of violating the Official Secrets Act. The sentence was postponed until completion of the trial of Anna Wolkoff. On November 7, 1940, Kent was sentenced to 7 years' penal servitude and Anna Wolkoff was sentenced to 10 years. Kent's attorneys applied for permission to appeal. On February 5, 1941, this application was rejected by a panel of judges which included the Lord Chief Justice.

In reviewing the Kent case it is important to bear in mind the circumstances surrounding it. At the time of Kent's arrest and trial Great Britain was at war and the United States was not. The case involved a group of people suspected of subversive activities. The evidence relating to individuals of the group was inextricably mixed, and the activities of no single suspect could be separated from the activities of the others. The interest of Great Britain in such a case, at a time when it was fighting for its existence, was therefore pre-eminent. Deep as was the concern of the Government of the United States over a betrayal of trust by one of its employees, it is hardly conceivable that it would have been justified in asking the Government of Great Britain to waive jurisdiction over an American citizen in the circumstances described. Kent was within the jurisdiction of the British courts, and all the evidence, witnesses, etc., were available to the British courts. Moreover, it was, as has been mentioned, in the interest of the United States to have determined immediately on the spot, where the evidence was available, whether or not one of its employees in a position of trust was violating such trust. The question whether the United States will prefer additional charges against Kent will be decided after his release from imprisonment in Great Britain and he again comes under the jurisdiction of our courts.

*(End of the State Department official press release)*

The press release provided a great cover story because it made absolutely no mention of the exchanges between Churchill and Roosevelt, which were at the heart of the State Department's real concerns.

It correctly referred to 'photographic plates' having been found in Kent's possession although there were three plates, rather than two. There was no mention of any microfilm or microdots; these embellishments would be introduced later.

Contrary to the claim in the press release, there was absolutely no evidence that the photographic plates had been made for the purpose of 'endeavouring to transmit prints thereof to Germany'; they had been made at Captain Ramsay's request because he had intended to show these to Prime Minister Chamberlain, as evidence of the conspiracy that he believed was being conducted behind his back.

The claim that Kent had 'compromised the whole confidential communications system of the United States, bringing into question the security of the secret ciphers' was untrue and it cleverly switched the focus of the problem. But, as cover stories go, this was a class act.

# 4: First Spin Cycle

In the wake of the State Department's press statement, newspapermen started clamouring for more information and Henry J. Taylor, a Scripps-Howard reporter, had the bright idea of telephoning Joseph P. Kennedy who had been the American Ambassador at the time of Kent's arrest, an event that he had precipitated by waiving Kent's diplomatic privilege, thus allowing his flat to be searched, which led to his arrest.

Taylor found Kennedy in Cape Cod at his 19-room summer home in Hyannisport where he and his family were mourning the loss of his eldest son, Lt. Joseph P. Kennedy Jr. who had been killed on the 12th of the previous month when his 'heavily modified' B-24 exploded over England. It had been on a secret mission 'Project Aphrodite'.

The former Ambassador agreed to give a telephone interview and his comments were widely reported on 5 September 1944:

> Week by week during late 1939 and early 1940, British officials had given me detailed reports on the country's strength and we had to assume that week by week this same data went to Berlin by way of Kent.
>
> Explaining how and why had Kent sent the data, Kennedy claimed that Kent's reported friendliness with the Russian girl, Anna Wolkoff, had its place in his attitude but apparently she didn't have safe and regular channels into Germany, although both their trails led to a small London photographic studio where Anna Wolkoff had left two of Kent's decoded messages and where British agents found these reduced to microfilm by an employee proven to be in the German spy ring.
>
> Kent used the Italian Embassy to reach Berlin. For the most part he passed our secrets out of England in the Italian diplomatic pouch. Italy, you recall,

didn't enter the war until after Kent was arrested.

If we had been at war I wouldn't have favored turning Kent over to Scotland Yard or have sanctioned his imprisonment in England. I would have recommended that he be brought back to the United States and been shot.

While the British were searching Kent's flat, a telephone call to Kent from the Italian Embassy put us on the trail of his Italian outlet to Germany.

Kent had crippled the US government's confidential communications system. On the night of May 20, America's diplomatic blackout started all over the world.

I telephoned the President in Washington saying our most secret code was no good any place.

The result was that for weeks, right at the time of the fall of France, the United States Government closed its confidential communicating system and was blacked out from private contact with American embassies and legations everywhere. No private message could be sent or received.

This lasted from two weeks to a month and a half - until a new unbreakable code could be devised in Washington and carried by special couriers to our diplomatic representatives throughout the world.

Kennedy's indictment of Kent went far beyond the carefully worded official statement and his claim that there had been a complete blackout in communications was demonstrably false, as Richard Whalen had observed in his biography of Kennedy[1]. Whalen also pointed out that, had it been true, Kennedy would not have been able to communicate with Washington on 24 and 27 May 1940, as he evidently did.

Students of 'news management' would not have been surprised by the presentation. First, a bland official statement that

---

[1] Richard Whalen, *The Founding Father* (1964).

almost mirrors the truth, closely followed by a colourful 'cover story' designed to grab the headlines and switch the focus of attention in its entirety. In this case, from the real heart of the matter: the exchanges between Roosevelt and Churchill (which were never mentioned) to a much sexier version with intriguing references to 'a German spy ring', 'use of the Italian Diplomatic Pouch', 'microfilm', 'unbreakable codes' and the alarming 'communications blackout' at a critical time in world history.

A particularly clever touch was to ask Joseph Kennedy to put the cover story into circulation. Having been Ambassador at the time of Kent's arrest, he was able to give the story credibility. Also, having retired from diplomatic service, he was presumably free to speak his piece. Not surprisingly, it was Kennedy's version that attracted the attention of the newspaper editors with their instinct for selling stories, while the bland Official Statement got lost in the spin.

Kennedy had evidently taken little interest in Kent, after paving the way for his arrest in May 1940 and perhaps coincidentally, or perhaps not, he had left Britain shortly before Kent was put on trial on 23 October 1940, just before the Presidential Election.

Several events then followed in quick succession: Roosevelt was re-elected on 5 November 1940 for an unprecedented third term, Joseph Kennedy tendered his resignation as Ambassador on 6 November and Kent and Wolkoff were sentenced in 'open court' on 7 November.

It is now generally believed that Roosevelt fired Kennedy but tradition requires that high officials should always be given the opportunity of falling on their sword. Ten years later, Kennedy showed further interest in the Kent-Wolkoff Affair in a letter dated 28 November 1950 to his old friend Lord Beaverbrook[2]:

> The anti-Roosevelt press has always made something terribly diabolical about the Tyler Kent case and the only reason that it didn't make a smear against me was because I was able to smash

---

[2] Amanda Smith, *Hostage to Fortune* (2001).

back at Kent rather strongly. However, one of these days I've got to put the whole case out, and there are three or four things that would be of tremendous help to me if you could get them through your influences:

1. Minutes of the trials of Tyler Kent and Anna Wolkoff.
2. A pamphlet put out by Captain Ramsay in his own defence.
3. A List of members of the Right Club.
4. A Report of the Advisory Committee recommending the continued detention of Captain Ramsay.

Kennedy told Beaverbrook that he was unsure how he was going to use the information should he get it but he said that he felt he needed it 'for his own protection'. There is no evidence that Kennedy received either a response from Beaverbrook or the information that he was seeking.

It was decidedly strange that Kennedy should have sought to obtain details of the case ten years after the event. Evidently, he did not know much about the case, which suggests that words had been put in his mouth before he gave the telephone interview to Henry J. Taylor.

Tyler Kent was still in jail at the time of Kennedy's statement but his mother sent him a copy, which evidently evaded the Censors. As soon as he was able, Kent dismissed it as 'arrant lies'. It certainly went beyond the entry that Kennedy had made in his Diplomatic Memoir for the 20 May 1940. On that occasion, he noted that the search of Kent's flat had revealed 'two excellent photographic plates of two cables that I had sent containing messages from Churchill to Roosevelt'. There were, in fact, three photographic plates because the lengthier cable had run to two pages. However, there was no mention of any microfilm. Also, even though concern was expressed about the secrecy of 'our most secret code', there was no mention of the communication systems having been 'blacked out'. However, on that occasion Kennedy had also added:

> I was naturally distressed by the incident and by the failure (that I had no hesitation in commenting on) of the Scotland Yard Officials to bring their suspicions about Kent to our attention months before.

Evidently Kennedy was unaware that Guy Liddell had formally warned Herschel Johnson about a reported leak on the 7th February 1940. Johnson, the Counsellor at the Embassy, had been deputising for Kennedy, who was holidaying in the States at the time.

|  |  |
|---|---|
| SECRET | Box No. 500, |
|  | Parliament Street, B.O, |
| L.305.95.Dy.B | London, S.W.1. |
|  | 7th February 1940 |

**PERSONAL & CONFIDENTIAL**

Dear Johnson,

I think the following information may be of interest to the State Department.

I have heard from an informant whose statements have in other respects proved to be accurate, that at any rate just prior to the war and possibly still, the German Secret Service had been receiving American Embassy reports, at times two a day, which contained practically everything from Ambassador Kennedy's despatches to President Roosevelt, including reports of his interviews with British statesmen and officials. The source from which the German Secret Service got these documents is not definitely known, but is someone who is referred to as 'Doctor', and our informant, who is in a position to know, is of opinion that the 'Doctor' is employed in the American Embassy in Berlin.

> The above information, as you will realise, is
> extremely delicate and in any enquiries that you or
> the State Department think fit to make, we should
> be grateful if you would take every possible step
> to safeguard our informant.

The next day, Johnson passed this intelligence to Jimmy Dunn at
the State Department in Washington but evidently he never
shared it with Kennedy. But whatever the source of these leaks, it
couldn't have been Kent because he did not take up his
appointment in London until either the 5th or 6th October 1939, a
month after the declaration of war. And, even if Wolkoff had
been involved in some way, it could not have been from material
provided by Kent because they were not introduced until around
21st February 1940[3].

It is surprising that Churchill continued to use this
communication channel even after MI5 had reported the leaks;
while Roosevelt, who had mainly corresponded with Churchill
through 'the pouch', sent Churchill a telegram on 16 May 1940
just four days before Kent's arrest.

Churchill sent two more telegrams to Roosevelt, one on the 18
May, the day that MI5 had formally approached the American
Embassy about its wish to search Kent's flat and another on the
20 May, two hours after Kent's arrest.

Even more of a surprise, all their telegrams had been
transcribed in the 'Gray Code'[4], the lowest-grade code used in
the US State Department. It had been introduced in 1918 for the
express purpose of saving transmission costs and by 1924 the
State Department was aware that it had been compromised.

Moreover, Roosevelt knew it and during the Abyssinian crisis
he purposely used the Gray Code to send a message to the
American Embassy in Rome anticipating that Mussolini would

---

[3] At his trial, Kent testified that he thought that it was earlier but MI5
undercover agent Marjorie Mackie reported on 23 February 1940 that Wolkoff
had told her about meeting an interesting new contact from the American
Embassy.
[4] Some US Diplomatic Codes (like Red, Brown, Green and Gray) were named
after the colour of the cover in which they were first issued.

get to see it. Again, in December 1941 he sent a personal appeal for peace to the Emperor of Japan through the State Department. A handwritten note conveyed his instruction:

> Shoot this to Grew[5] - I think it can go in gray code
> saves time - I don't mind if it gets picked up[6].

Churchill was also fully aware of the vulnerability of the American diplomatic channels because British Intelligence routinely intercepted all telegraphic traffic passing through the foreign Embassies in London.

So what had these two been up to?

---

[5] Joseph C. Grew, American Ambassador to Japan.
[6] David Kahn, *The Codebreakers* (1966).

# 5: Cause Célèbre

The war was coming to an end before news of Tyler Kent's incarceration seeped through to the American public. It then generated divergent opinions as to whether he was hero or villain.

First off the mark was Gerald L.K. Smith[1] a former acolyte of Huey Long and a dedicated isolationist who published a six-page typewritten pamphlet *The Story of Tyler Kent* around September 1944[2]. Billed as 'the most sensational story of the century', he had based his story on 'numerous interviews' with Kent's widowed mother. It was then priced at 25 cents and is still in print.

Smith told the story as he had heard it in twenty-four numbered paragraphs:

1 Kent's diplomatic immunity should not have been withdrawn; he should have been sent to the US for trial.

2 During Churchill's first week in office about 600 prominent British subjects, among them Captain Archibald Ramsay, a Member of Parliament, were detained. Kent was not brought to trial until November 1940 and then his trial was held in secret.

(Churchill stepped up as Prime Minister on 10 May 1940 and his War Cabinet approved the mass roundup of the so-called Fifth Column on 22 May 1940. The trials of Kent and Wolkoff actually started on 23 October 1940 and the sentences were announced on 7 November 1940.)

3 Kent had been charged with 'something to do with the transmission of information to the enemy'. Yet the United

---

[1] A Preacher-Politician, Gerald L.K. Smith would run three times for President. He is now remembered for having organised the funding for 'The Christ of the Ozarks', a large statue.
[2] The reference to Ramsay having been released (24 September 1944) shows that Smith's booklet was published afterwards.

States did not have any enemies.

(It was Anna Wolkoff who had been charged with 'attempting to communicate with the enemy'.)

4   However that charge had 'failed' and one of larceny had been substituted.

(Two charges against the Larceny Act had been included from the outset but one was 'not pursued' by the Prosecution.)

5   Kent was later transferred to 'a political prison' on the Isle of Wight.

(It wasn't a 'political prison'; it was for long-term First Offenders.)

6   Kent had a record of 'brilliant service'.

(It was hardly 'brilliant'; Kent had got off to a sticky start and was nearly dismissed.)

7   All that was asked was that Kent should be brought home and tried under American law.

(Although he would have been tried in open court and probably could have mounted a more vigorous defence, this was not necessarily a good idea because Kent had made a statement[3] in which he had admitted having disclosed information learned during his employment.

Perhaps unwittingly, he had contravened the 'Yardley Act' that had been introduced in 1933 following embarrassing revelations by Herbert O. Yardley[4], a former cryptographer. For each offence, the Act prescribed a fine of up to $10,000 or imprisonment of up to ten years, or both, for State employees found guilty.

---

[3] Kent had signed the statement after having been duly 'cautioned' and his signature was properly witnessed.

[4] Herbert O. Yardley was the author of *The American Black Chamber* (1931).

Kent had accepted that he had disclosed 500 documents and if he were to be found guilty in an American court, he could have been jailed for the rest of his life.)

8   Ambassador Joseph P. Kennedy had on one occasion offered to procure Kent's release against an undertaking not to disclose the contents of certain cablegrams but Kent had refused the bribe.

(This has never been corroborated, not even by Kent.)

9   Smith picked up on the May 1941 story by Robert Scott, a former newspaperman for the *Washington Post*, that the cables contained details of the 'Lend-Lease' formula.

(Roosevelt only revealed the 'formula' after having been re-elected but Kent claimed to have seen correspondence that showed that it had been under discussion at least a year previously. Whether true or not, this allegation would have been very embarrassing for the Roosevelt administration in the run up to the Presidential Election in November 1940.)

10   Mrs. Kent had established that there had been 'secret cables' exchanged between Roosevelt and Churchill before Churchill had stepped up as Prime Minister.

(This was certainly true but contrary to speculation at the time, Churchill was evidently not acting behind the back of the Foreign Office.)

11   Smith reported that there had been questions asked in the House of Commons about the cables and the fact that the Home Secretary had declined to comment.

(This was true.)

12   Smith revisited the article by Arthur Sears Henning published in the *Washington Times-Herald* on 12 November 1941 but he wrongly claimed that it had been pulled from later editions.

(Mrs. Kent had sent a copy of the article to her son while he was in jail and in May 1944 he had replied that it was 'Essentially correct'.)

13   Smith reported on Ian Ross MacFarlane's visit to see Kent in his British jail.

(This was true and prior to Smith's disclosure, MI5 was not even aware that MacFarlane had interviewed Kent on 8 August 1942.)

14   According to Ian Ross MacFarlane, the messages between Roosevelt and Churchill had passed 'at rapid intervals' and sometimes several in one day. Kent had told MacFarlane that the first message had been from Churchill and was something to the effect that:

> I am half American and the natural person to work with you. It is evident that we see eye to eye. Were I to become Prime Minister we could conquer the world.

(The style is not instantly recognisable as Churchill's and there is no evidence that Roosevelt helped Churchill in the way suggested. On the contrary, Roosevelt did not initially consider Churchill to be a good choice.)

15   Smith claimed that Wendell Wilkie (Roosevelt's opponent in the 1940 Presidential Election) had heard that the Lend-Lease formula had been pre-arranged by Roosevelt and Churchill.

16   Smith speculated that the Russian Secret Service might have obtained copies of the secret exchanges.

(This was highly likely.)

17   Smith described the mysterious death of John Bryan Owen.

18   Questions had been asked in the House of Commons concerning the fate of Captain Ramsay while he was still

imprisoned.

19  Oliver Lyttleton the British Minister of War Production was quoted as having claimed in a speech that America had provoked the Japanese attack on Pearl Harbor.

20  Mrs. Kent had sent her son a copy of the *Washington Times-Herald* article by Arthur Sears Henning published on 12 November 1941 and had asked him to comment. Kent duly confirmed that the Lend-Lease formula was being discussed between Roosevelt and Churchill 'at least a year before the American people heard of it'.

(Even if this were true, then neither the American nor the British Governments would have been likely to admit it and obviously all documentary proof would have been destroyed.)

21  Smith argued that Kent had committed no crime against the American Government.

(This was not true. Evidently, Smith was not aware of the Yardley Act.)

22  Smith reported that an American observer at the trial (Consul General John G. Erhardt) had told Mrs. Kent that her son had done 'nothing reprehensible' and Ambassador Kennedy (who had left England shortly before the trial started) was reported as having said 'I am very much ashamed of the part I played in the Kent case, I lost my head'.

23  On being shown a copy of the remarks made by Kennedy in the wake of the State Department Press Statement, Kent had said that 'Kennedy's statement is false'.

24  According to Smith, 'The last chapter in this fantastic case occurred on September 26, 1944 when Captain Ramsay was released'.

Smith was decidedly (and understandably) weak on the legality of whether or not Kent should have had his diplomatic immunity withdrawn and if he should have been sent for secret trial in a British court but the bottom line was whether or not Roosevelt and Churchill had been conspiring to bring about the Lend-Lease formula 'at least a year before the American people heard of it.'

In Smith's view, Kent was a hero who had tried to expose the politicians who were conniving to bring America into the war and he was now paying a heavy price for his public-spirited act. The question that he might have been a spy was never an issue.

Mrs. Ann Kent never doubted her son's innocence and on 1 October 1944 she petitioned Congress for the release of her son who 'for four long years has been held prisoner without due cause in a foreign land by a government with which we are at peace'. She had supported her petition with all the usual attachments that Smith had referred to in his pamphlet.

She also issued a writ of mandamus[5] on the Supreme Court asking that the President be directed to secure her son's release and for his return home. On the 16 October 1944, the Court denied the motion without comment.

In the event, Tyler Kent would have to wait over a year before he was released, by which time both Germany (7 May 1945) and Japan (15 August 1945) had surrendered. On 23 September 1945, he was transferred to London's Brixton Prison to await a suitable vessel. He set sail for home on 21 November and his ship docked at Hoboken on 4 December. Kent disembarked to face his mother and a large crowd of reporters and photographers.

Kent disappointed the waiting newsmen by saying nothing of any significance. There had been times while he was in jail when he had feared for his life and whether or not this was a factor, he was the soul of discretion. It is unlikely that his reticence was caused by a fear of prosecution under the Yardley Act because

---

[5] Latin for 'we enjoin': a writ issued by a superior court commanding the performance of a specified official act or duty.

the possibility for action had become statute barred but, of course, he may not have realised this.

Nevertheless, Kent sued the United States for 'his salary at the rate of $2,250 p.a. from 20 May 1940 down to the present time plus travel expense from London to his residence in the United States on the ground that his dismissal was illegal and of no effect'.

The Court of Claims dismissed Kent's petition on 7 January 1946, having decided that he was not a Foreign Service Officer but merely a Junior Clerk Class 3, which was at the very bottom of the pecking order. His salary reflected the lowliness of his position but, in any event, the Court concluded that the Ambassador was perfectly in his rights to have dismissed Kent because he had been charged with 'malfeasance in office'. In fact, Kent had never been 'charged' with any offence under American law.

This setback failed to prevent Kent from becoming a minor celebrity in rightwing and isolationist circles and he soon renewed the acquaintance of a wealthy woman Clara Hunter Hyatt, heiress to the Carter's Little Liver Pills fortune. She was 48, thirteen years his senior. They were married in Mexico in 1946 either on 13 June at Nuevo Laredo (according to the formal announcement circulated by Clara's mother at the time) or during the Fourth of July weekend at Juarez (according to Clara's memory after she had turned 90).

And they both lived happily ever after. Well, they remained together until the day he died, by which time Kent had helped Clara to spend most of her fortune.


Notwithstanding their happy ending, John Howland Snow produced a 60-page booklet *The Case of Tyler Kent* in 1946. It is full of righteous indignation and quotes from famous statesmen including George Washington who once wrote 'Integrity and firmness are all I can promise'. It is still in print.

Snow then introduced his hero. 'In October 1939, Kent was transferred to our Embassy in Grosvenor Square London and placed in a position of the highest trust and confidence, the code room. Almost immediately he encountered the amazing secret messages which are the key to the whole affair.' However, Snow's 60-page booklet revealed nothing new and was essentially a rehash of Gerald L.K. Smith's six-page pamphlet. Kent had a low opinion of Snow's effort that he considered 'about 75% reliable'[6].

Despite Mrs. Kent's best efforts, there would be several other stories published that condemned Tyler Kent either as a spy or a traitor. Traitor he was not and he successfully sued those who dared to print the allegation. However, Kent did nothing to counter the stories that he had been a spy until he finally spoke his piece in 1982.

Perhaps by then he had given up caring about whatever had caused him to keep his silence and maybe he had wanted to set the record straight before going to meet his Maker. Of course, by the time he finally broke his silence, few listened and even fewer believed what he had to say.

The conviction by an English court of an American diplomat for spying would eventually become a cause célèbre in the United States and many Americans believed that it must have been for something Tyler Kent knew rather than for what he did, a view that had been stirred up by his mother who, having been married to a diplomat, knew a bit about these things.

---

[6] Cited by Andrew Lownie in *Tyler Kent: Isolationist or Spy?* (1991).

# 6: Second Spin Cycle

In line with best practice, 'cover stories' then appeared on both sides of the Atlantic. A common characteristic of the genre is that the degree of reliability is always in inverse proportion to the claims for authenticity.

Kurt Singer was the first to get into the act, by devoting a chapter to Tyler Kent in his book *Spies and Traitors of World War II*. Priced at $2.25 it was published in July 1945 while Kent was still in jail and it quickly went into several reprints.

Singer mainly devoted his book to the exploits of Admiral Canaris whom he castigated as an evil genius, obviously not realising that Canaris and his close colleagues had secretly opposed Hitler and that they had been helping the Allies to the best of their abilities. Singer reported that Canaris had visited London on 21 March 1938, so that he could meet up with Percy Glading, one of his agents.

Having regard for Ian Ross MacFarlane's interview with Tyler Kent while he was in jail, anything seems possible but it seems highly unlikely that Canaris would have risked visiting Glading while he was languishing in jail. Glading was a committed Communist who had been arrested on 21 January 1938 for his part in masterminding what has become known as the Woolwich Arsenal Secrets Case. In the unlikely event that Canaris had introduced himself to Glading, the probability is that Glading would have denounced him as a German spy.

Glading was eventually brought to account by Maxwell Knight as a result of work by one of his undercover agents, Olga Gray. Gray was a mole who had worked for MI5 since 1931 worming her way into the confidences of senior members of the 'Friends of the Soviet Union'. The dénouement came in 1938 and after being tried under the Official Secrets Act, Glading was handed down a sentence of six years' penal servitude.

Of course, in 1945 Soviet Russia was still seen as the staunch wartime ally with Germany the sworn enemy and stories had to be re-worked to suit the political climate of the time.

According to Singer, Kent had attended meetings of the Mosley Fascists (he had certainly attended a public lunch) and Wolkoff had also worked with them (she had never 'worked' with them although, like Kent, she had attended a public lunch). And rather than sharing the secret correspondence with Captain Ramsay (who after all was a Member of Parliament) Kent had been sending it to the Axis. This was complete invention.

Edward Spiro (1903-1979) then took up Kurt Singer's theme in *Secrets of the British Secret Service* published in Britain in 1948 under the penname of E.H. Cookridge[1]. Whether or not Singer and Spiro knew each other, they shared similar backgrounds. Both had been born in Vienna and both were prolific authors.

It has been reported that Spiro served with British Military Intelligence during the war but according to an obituary provided by the Helvetia Philatelic Society that he founded in 1946, he was of Czech origin and a survivor of Dachau Concentration Camp. After arriving in Britain, he adopted the name of Cookridge from the village that had sponsored him.

Following an encounter with Ernest Bevin, the Labour Minister, Spiro became a foreign radio monitor where his knowledge of European languages and politics were considered useful. Later, he became a political correspondent at Westminster and he wrote a number of books on intelligence and counter-espionage mostly published in America plus articles for the *Sunday Telegraph Magazine*. 'Despite severe disabilities', Spiro maintained an active interest in the Helvetia Philatelic Society to the end of his life.

---

[1] Spiro, who had been born in Vienna, dedicated his book 'to the Memory of My Mother who suffered and died in France and to the Memory of the millions of victims of *Furor Teutonicus*'. Spiro's parents were Paul and Rosa Cookridge Spiro.

Curiously, in an Appendix to his book, Cookridge listed some of the 2,300 names that had appeared on the 'Informationsheft GB' (Special Wanted List GB) produced by the Gestapo in anticipation of their occupation of Britain. The name of Mr. Edward Spiro was included in his list without comment but Spiro does not feature in any of the lists published elsewhere[2].

In introducing his book, Cookridge claimed that he had 'tried to avoid the false romanticism' and thought it better to rely upon 'careful investigation and official documentation rather than vivid imagination'. He thanked the Foreign Office, the War Office, the Home Office and the Lord Chief Justice's Office for their assistance that allowed him to check some of the facts. In other words, Cookridge's version was absolutely authentic.

However, despite these assurances, Cookridge's book was totally unreliable. This can be judged from Chapter 2 'The Spycatchers'. According to Cookridge, the chief of the German Intelligence, Admiral Canaris, came over to London in January 1938 'to see how his henchmen were getting on'. He arrived, 'travelling incognito, of course, because he wanted an interview with one of his chief agents in Woolwich Arsenal, a man named Percy Glading ...'

So although both Spiro and Singer picked up on Canaris's supposed visit to Percy Glading, they did not agree on the date. Of course, if Canaris had travelled incognito, how was Spiro able to penetrate his disguise? There have never been any other reports in the Press or anywhere else.

Cookridge also questioned Canaris's 'death' in 1944 (sic) by claiming that French agents had discovered him in Argentina in 1947 living under an assumed name. According to Cookridge, it was one of the 'many bold bluffs of his adventurous life' but there is compelling evidence that Canaris had been executed on 9 April 1945, after having fallen into disfavour with Hitler.

The thrust of Cookridge's take on the Kent-Wolkoff Affair is evident from his chapter entitled 'The Stolen Code' in which it transpired that Kent's greatest sin was having jeopardised his

---

[2] See *Invasion 1940* by Walter Schellenberg.

country's 'unbreakable code'. This was untrue and now seems ludicrous but there was considerable mystique about codes and ciphers in those days and so the story was developed accordingly.

Despite his careful checking, Cookridge reported that Kent had joined the American Diplomatic Service early in 1939 (actually 1934) and was destined for a brilliant career. (Hardly, he had got off to a sticky start in Moscow and was almost sacked.)

According to Cookridge, the 23 year-old Kent (actually 28) was posted to London in 1939 and soon after his arrival 'the Canaris[3] war machine began to work smoothly and quietly'. One day Kent was introduced to the Baroness Wolkoff, 'a charming woman who although much older had all the sophisticated attractions of an experienced lady of the social set' who could 'certainly turn the head of a callow American youngster'. (Kent, a bachelor who always fancied himself as a 'ladies man', was already in a relationship with Irene Danischewsky, an attractive married woman. He was certainly no 'callow youngster'. During adulthood Wolkoff called herself 'de Wolkoff' but she was not a baroness.)

Before 1917, Wolkoff's father had been an admiral of the Russian Imperial Fleet who had 'fled to London from the Bolshevist Revolution'. (Actually, he had been the Naval Attaché at the Russian Embassy in London and he had opted to remain in England). And the Baroness had 'been a British subject since childhood'. (She became a British subject in August 1935, two months before reaching 33).

Wolkoff ran an exclusive dress shop where 'she presided over comely assistants and was never seen without a magnificent ginger cat wearing a solid gold collar'. (Her business Anna de Wolkoff Ltd that had run a dress shop in Mayfair had gone into receivership and was wound up in February 1939 leaving a trail of unpaid creditors.)

---

[3] Admiral Wilhelm Canaris was the Head of Abwehr, German Military Intelligence. According to Ladislas Farago, the Abwehr played no part in the Tyler Kent Affair. See *The Game of the Foxes*.

Cookridge had lifted the bit about the ginger cat with a solid gold collar from the *Sunday Dispatch* that ran a story on 10 September 1944 headlined 'The Secret Lives of Tyler Kent and Anna Wolkoff'. Despite the headline, the story had absolutely nothing to do with Anna but concerned Kent's alleged relationship with an unnamed woman who owned such an animal, reportedly called George.

The unnamed woman was actually Mrs. June Huntley the American-born wife of the actor Raymond Huntley. MI5 had thoroughly investigated Mrs. Huntley and found that her relationship with Kent was purely social and entirely innocent. The *Sunday Dispatch* published an apology on 29 October 1944.

Cookridge was correct, however, in claiming that 'In her spare time, Wolkoff painted pretty little water colours which she exhibited in the salons of her friends'. But, he quickly reverted to fantasy by continuing 'not even the Baroness's closest friends suspected her of being one of Canaris's most efficient agents'. (Cookridge was obsessed with Canaris and his claim that Wolkoff was a Canaris agent hasn't stood the test of time.) Soon Kent was 'head over heels in love' with the Baroness. It didn't take her long to persuade her young lover to succumb to her fiendish plans. (Although they became close friends, it is highly unlikely that they were lovers[4].)

The task that she outlined to him was simple. Was he not holding the most closely guarded secrets of the discussions between the statesmen of Downing Street and the White House? Was it not a fact that every message that Neville Chamberlain or Winston Churchill sent to President Roosevelt and every reply from the President to the British leaders had to go through the cipher room of the American Embassy? (This was not a fact; so far as is known Chamberlain had never used this route.)

'There can be no better authority to quote on the activities of the couple', proclaimed the author, 'than that of Kent's direct superior, the US Ambassador Mr. Joseph Patrick Kennedy'.

---

[4] See *Ten Days to Destiny* in which John Costello cited his interview with Kent. This opinion is corroborated by other sources.

(Kennedy was not 'Kent's direct superior'; Kent was only a junior clerk among some 200 staff.)

Joseph Kennedy, it was reported, 'had telephoned the President in Washington, saying that our most secret code was no good anymore. The Germans and Italians and presumably also the Japanese had possessed a full picture of the problems and decisions and everything else sent in and out of the White House and the State department for the previous eight months, at as critical a period as any in the history of the war.'

Cookridge reported Kennedy accurately but although Kent had been employed at the American Embassy in London since the 5th or 6th of October 1939, he didn't meet Anna Wolkoff until on or around the 21st February 1940[5]. Nevertheless, Kennedy understated the period during which German Intelligence had been obtaining copies of the Embassy's communications. The leaks had actually started before the war, before Kent had taken up his appointment. Whatever he may have done, Kent could not have been the exclusive source for German Intelligence. Similarly, Wolkoff could not possibly have been Kent's conduit before they met.

Cookridge elaborated by explaining that 'from the early days of the war until Kent's arrest on 18 May 1940 (it was actually 20 May 1940), the Nachrichtendienst had been kept informed of every single message sent by the British Government to Washington, including the most secret statistics of British land, sea and air forces, their dispositions and reserves, the food and oils stocks held in Britain and the Commonwealth and the strategic plans for the future. In brief, the conferences of the High Command in Berlin had much the same quality of information as Field-Marshal Ironside and Lord Gort at their meetings with the War Cabinet in Whitehall'. (The Germans were apparently getting the intelligence cited but they certainly could not have been getting all their information from Kent, if any. Moreover

---

[5] Kent testified at his trial that he thought that it was either late January or early February but Marjorie Amor reported on 24 February that 'a man employed in the American Embassy was a new contact'.

Ironside was only a General at the time and he wasn't promoted Field Marshal until after he had been sacked on 29 July 1940.)

'It is not too much to say … that without Kent's daily reports the Nazis might never have risked taking the breathing space during the winter of 1939-40 which permitted them to plan without interference for the blitzkrieg of the spring'. (This was more rubbish. There had been a string of peace initiatives that eventually came to naught and they had also waited for better weather.)

'Altogether Kent and his mistress copied more than 1,500 cipher messages by making microfilm copies of the documents which he purloined from the cabinets as he went off duty, returning them on the following day.' (Kent admitted taking copies of numerous Embassy documents but they were mainly carbon copies. The number of documents varied with each re-telling: 500 were mentioned at Kent's trial, 1,500 in the State Department Press Release and 1,929 in a later account. In fact, only four documents were introduced as evidence at Kent's trial. These had been selected because of their British sources, because it could be claimed that they represented 'official secrets' and because the Americans had refused permission for any of their own documents to be introduced as evidence.)

'Everything went so smoothly', claimed Cookridge, 'that the couple became a little careless. Instead of messing about with the photographic material themselves, they decided to entrust the copying to a professional photographer … [and] … Kent found a little studio near Fleet Street …' (The photographer was Nicolas Eugenovitch Smirnoff who before the 1917 revolution had worked in the Financial Department of the Russian Embassy in London where he had known Admiral Wolkoff. In April 1940 he was working as an Examiner in the Censorship Department. Anna Wolkoff actually contacted him at his home at 32d Penywern Road, Earls Court. This is close to the Wolkoff's basement flat in Roland Gardens, South Kensington. Fleet Street is on the other side of London, miles away.)

'This development in the Kent story proves, if anything can, that truth can be stranger than fiction,' argued Cookridge, trying to substantiate his imaginative offering. Anyhow, although the Baroness 'had been watched by the Secret Service for a considerable time', their regular reports had contained 'no blemish' and she emerged from a routine screening 'unscathed'.

Then a Special Branch man reported to Chief Constable Canning[6] that the love affair seemed to have an unusual angle. The meetings in her flat were not followed by an excursion to the nightclub or theatre but frequently involved a trip to the Fleet Street photographic studio. A detective then visited the studio and after making a few enquiries the startled detective was soon gazing at a strip of celluloid showing pictures of some documents marked 'Very Secret'. (The startled detective must have had amazing eyesight to read anything by simply 'gazing' at a strip of microfilm. Most folk would have needed a microfilm reader. Actually only three glass negatives containing images of two documents were introduced in evidence as a result of one visit to Smirnoff's home on 13 April 1940 to have the photographs taken and a second visit on 16 April 1940 to collect the prints and the negatives. Moreover, Wolkoff went alone and without Kent's knowledge. Smirnoff testified at Kent's trial that he had never met Kent.)

'That night', announced Cookridge, 'Members of the Cabinet, and Chiefs of the Foreign Office, the Secret Service and Military Intelligence attended a conference that had been hurriedly called at 10 Downing Street.' Apparently Cookridge's informant missed the conference because Cookridge next advised that 'years later, after he had retired from the diplomatic service, Mr. Kennedy revealed some more details of that sensational affair'.

'Kent was in charge of the unbreakable code of the US State Department. Because of his treachery, all diplomatic communications of the American diplomatic service were blacked-out following his arrest at a most terrible moment in history, during the days of Dunkirk and the fall of France. The blackout, which concerned the American Embassies and missions

---

[6] Albert Canning was in charge of Special Branch but there is some doubt as to whether or not he held the rank of Chief Constable.

throughout the world, lasted from two to six weeks until scores of special couriers had reached the Embassies with new codes from Washington'. (Cookridge quoted Kennedy accurately but the Gray Code that was used in transcribing the telegrams was certainly not 'unbreakable' although this was largely irrelevant because Kent had access to the messages in 'plain text'.)

According to Cookridge, Kent and the Baroness had given the microfilm to an official of the Italian Embassy in London who worked for German espionage. In the opinion of Mr. Kennedy, Italy had been 'ordered to stay out of the war for ten months, partly at least because of the usefulness to Germany of the transmission channel of Kent's information through the Italian Embassy in London'. (There was never any microfilm and Hitler had actually been urging Mussolini to enter the fray.)

Kennedy is accurately quoted as saying 'If America had been at war I would have recommended that he be sent back to America and shot as a traitor. But in the circumstances prevailing we had to leave it to British justice'.

Cookridge reported that Kent was sentenced in November 1940 to seven years penal servitude and that Baroness Wolkoff received ten years. He also added his own observation that 'British justice was very lenient indeed' which was fair comment based on his own description of their activities. He revealed that Wolkoff had served her sentence in Aylesbury Prison and that she had been released in June 1946 (actually June 1947), after having served 5½ years of her sentence (actually over 6½ years[7]).

In a concluding remark, Cookridge mentioned the 'special investigator' who had been hired and sent to Britain 'where he received every facility to examine the irrefutable evidence'. He named Ian Ross MacFarlane who entirely on his own initiative had managed to interview Kent while in prison. MacFarlane had been given absolutely no facility to examine any evidence and MI5 didn't even find out about his visit until they learned of his enterprise from Gerald L.K. Smith's pamphlet. If MacFarlane

---

[7] Her time in prison before the trial would not necessarily have been 'taken into account'.

had requested permission then undoubtedly it would have been refused.

So, although Cookridge called his book *Secrets of the British Secret Service*, he not only failed to reveal any secrets, he had also distorted the facts.

Stanley Firmin, who described himself as 'Correspondent of the *Daily Telegraph* accredited to Scotland Yard', introduced his book *They Came to Spy* (1950) by promising 'the first full authentic account of how, from London, the wide-flung moves of the German Secret Service were met and checkmated'.

The sixth of his twenty-two chapters was entitled 'Dossier for Invasion' and despite the misleading title, it largely covered the Kent-Wolkoff Affair. Consistent with his promise to provide 'a full authentic account' Firmin departed from Cookridge's fable and, in his version, Colonel Karl Buchs had replaced Admiral Canaris as the Nazi spymaster. Or maybe Buchs was Canaris's boss because, according to Firmin, 'he was the Supreme Commander and answerable to only one man, Hitler'. Firmin explained that 'Buchs was a man of whom the world has heard very little, if anything'. This was perfectly true and nothing has changed over the last fifty years.

He provided some completely new takes by claiming that Wolkoff first met Kent at the Right Club where they were fellow members. In fact, Wolkoff had joined the Right Club before the war and Kent only joined in May 1940, after Wolkoff had introduced him to Captain Ramsay.

According to Firmin, Wolkoff was 'anxious to get information to Germany' and she had used Kent as her conduit to put envelopes into the American diplomatic pouch for Italy because this was 'the safest and surest method'. This was a clever twist making Wolkoff the spy and Kent her conduit but, unfortunately, Firmin failed to reveal how Wolkoff had been getting her information.

'Kent and Wolkoff had managed to carry out their little game for nearly eight months before they were caught' as a result of 'a lucky accident' when officers of British Intelligence had got onto the track of an expert photographer. When they raided his place, they discovered 'four tiny films' reduced to the size of a full stop. On examination, the investigators found that they contained 'two messages in code' that were eventually introduced into evidence at their trial.

It must have been extremely difficult for British Intelligence to find something as small and as well disguised as a full stop. It would certainly have been impossible for Nicolas Smirnoff to produce any microdots. Not possessing an enlarger, he was unable to produce readable prints from the quarter-plate negatives that he had taken. Also, it would have been a technological breakthrough at that time because MI5 didn't discover that the Germans had been using microdots until 6 August 1941[8].

Firmin concluded his ludicrous story by claiming that 'their trial proved to be the biggest and perhaps the most sensational of its kind of the whole war'. Having been held *in camera*, their trials were anything but sensational. They were non-events that were deliberately kept low-key.


Kurt Singer revisited the case in *The World's Greatest Women Spies* (1951) by which time he had dropped his previous references to Admiral Canaris but he failed to report for whom Anna Wolkoff was working, simply claiming that she 'would find ways and means to forward them to the appropriate quarters'. Singer's revised take bore striking similarities to Cookridge's offering. He now represented Anna as a Baroness and he even repeated the discredited claim that 'she was never seen without a magnificent ginger cat wearing a solid gold collar'.

As to Kent, he was reported to have been 'arrogant at his trial and shouted abuse at the office of Mr. Churchill and the other Jewish lackeys in Britain'.

As before, few of Singer's claims can be corroborated but, surprisingly, he now asserted that the correspondence that Kent

---

[8] KV 4/188.

had taken from the American Embassy included 'memoranda concerning plans for American Lend-Lease'. This was certainly a revelation.

Hungarian-born Ladislas Farago also known as László Faragó (1906-1980) was next on the case. He had become a naturalised American and in *The Game of the Foxes* (1971) he claimed that he was able to supply the 'missing link' because he was able to confirm that information from the American Embassy in London had been reaching the Abwehr (German Military Intelligence).

Farago's source was a large cache of microfilm records that he had discovered in 1967 in a loft in the National Archives in Washington. On investigation, these were found to relate to the Hamburg and Bremen branches of the Abwehr, the two branches that specialised in coverage of Britain and the United States. These had been captured in 1945 but having been misplaced, were presumed destroyed.

Farago was jubilant because he claimed that his cache included some important new information on the Tyler Kent Affair that he considered to be 'one of the most serious breaches of security in World War II'. He was able to add considerable unpublished information in rounding out the evidence and placing the case in its perspective.

Farago then painted an accurate portrait of Tyler Kent through to his posting to the American Embassy in London when 'a new super-secret batch of telegrams was added to the traffic handled by the Code Room'. He then accurately quoted the letter from Roosevelt to Churchill dated 11 September 1939 which heralded the start of their correspondence.

Mr. Churchill had responded 'with alacrity', reported Farago, using the signature 'Naval Person' but events were moving too fast, the pouches too slow and soon the impetuous Naval Person began to bombard Mr. Roosevelt with telegrams that he handed directly to Ambassador Kennedy for transmission to the President. (Minions always delivered the telegrams and Kennedy was not always at the Embassy. However, Farago had transgressed the official line, by claiming that the 'impetuous Naval Person began to bombard Mr. Roosevelt with telegrams'. The official line was that the totality of the exchanges between the two men had only amounted to fifteen items over nearly eight months prior to Kent's arrest. This could hardly be described as 'a bombardment'.)

The American Embassy merely processed them, enciphering the texts in the so-called 'Gray Code' that was classified as top secret and was, at the time, believed to be 'unbreakable'. The encrypted messages were then radioed to Washington directly for the President, avoiding State Department channels. (Farago was wrong: the Gray Code was not classified 'top secret', it was certainly not considered unbreakable and the messages in question certainly did go through the State Department.)

Without the slightest evidence, Farago then asserted that 'The British cryptographic establishment had of course been monitoring much of the diplomatic traffic, reading the cables of the chanceries of the world' and 'shortly after the Roosevelt-Churchill arrangement had been made, they stumbled upon a series of cables from Hans Mackensen the German Ambassador in Rome to his Foreign Minister in Berlin'.

(Farago was making this up. British code breaking had been in the doldrums since WWI, whereas the Germans had introduced machine-based systems such as Enigma, among others. None of the Germany systems was a pushover and the Bletchley Park initiative did not really start to bear fruit until the spring of 1941. Nevertheless, it made a good story that would be taken on board by several later commentators.)

Farago then went on to claim that 'When the transcripts were examined in the Foreign Office, it was found that Mackensen was apparently privy to information of an exceptionally confidential nature, some of it known only on the level of Roosevelt and the First Lord ... [and] ... in one of his reports in January 1940, Mackensen was able to warn his home office that an order had been issued to the Fleet that no American ship should be diverted into the combat zone round the British Isles declared by the President'.

Farago had clearly lifted this snippet from the telegram dated 29 January 1940 produced in evidence at Kent's trial. Having been encoded in the Gray Code, it could not possibly have been 'of an exceptionally confidential nature'. He also failed to show how he could have obtained this from his Abwehr material. Farago seemed uncertain himself because he then revealed that the tip-off had come from another channel, an Italian journalist with 'influential friends in Rome, among them Foreign Ministry officials, who freely discussed with him the fantastic influx of the American documents from London'.

According to Farago, 'the journalist pinpointed the American Embassy as the gaping hole through which classified documents were pouring to the Italian secret service at so massive a rate that sometimes it needed a laundry basket to carry even a single week's shipment'. Naturally, Farago failed to name the journalist in question but he may have had Virgilio Scattolini in mind. The enterprising Scattolini had made a small fortune during the war from fabricating lurid stories and selling them to various newspapers and Intelligence Agencies[9].

Farago continued by explaining that 'the examination of Mackensen's scattered references convinced the British authorities that there was a serious leak somewhere and it was obvious that he was relaying intelligence given him by the Italians'.

Although it may have been obvious to Farago, he didn't make it obvious to his readers and he continued by saying that 'the surveillance of the Italian diplomats was intensified ... the Duke of del Monte[10] was an occasional guest at the Russian Tea Rooms ... he was a friend of Anna Wolkoff ... [and] ... while under surveillance, Miss Wolkoff was trailed to the studio of a photographer named Nicholas E. Smirnoff where it was found she would rendezvous with her noble Italian friend'. (Certainly, Anna Wolkoff had dined with the Italian but Farago is unique in

---

[9] David Alvarez & Robert A. Graham *Nothing Sacred* (1997).
[10] Colonel Francisco Marigliano, Duke del Monte, was the Assistant Military Attaché at the Italian Embassy in London.

claiming that they ever met at Smirnoff's or that the Duke had ever visited the Russian Tea Rooms.)

Farago also stated that 'Wolkoff was <u>regularly</u> corresponding with William Joyce, the Nazi's British mouthpiece in Berlin' and using both the Duke of del Monte <u>and</u> an acquaintance at the Rumanian legation as channels of correspondence with William Joyce'.

So there it was; a further rehash of the supposed events with some added speculation before Farago revealed the fruits of his own research. It was, he declared, 'the missing link' which he discovered from the top-secret files: Mackensen's transmission of intelligence began in January 1940, shortly after Kent had started supplying documents to Anna Wolkoff and it ended on 23 May 1940, three days after Kent's arrest. (Well, if the transmissions had begun in January 1940 then it couldn't have been via Anna Wolkoff because she and Kent were not introduced until around 21 February 1940.)

Notwithstanding the cache of microfilm obtained from the Hamburg and Bremen branches of the Abwehr, Farago concluded that the Abwehr had 'absolutely nothing to do with the case, as somehow the entire operation had eluded the secret services'.

In other words, Farago had absolutely no new information and he was merely elaborating on previous cover stories culled from published sources.

Although *The Game of the Foxes* became popular, informed critics dismissed it for its 'controversial claims and questionable conclusions' and as 'misleading'. One critic also noted Farago's 'penchant for the dramatic and for exaggeration'.

But worse was to come from Farago. In his 1974 book *Aftermath*, he claimed to have met Hitler's deputy Martin Bormann, having discovered him hiding in Southern Bolivia in February 1973. The wealth of detail was impressive but Farago's 'research' flew in the face of forensic evidence.

Skeletons of two men had been dug up in December 1972 near the Reichstag in West Berlin. It was believed that they had been found by a Russian soldier and had taken cyanide. A West

German forensic expert used dental records to determine that one of the skeletons was almost certainly that of Bormann. In April 1973, a West German court formally pronounced him dead. The following month, the DNA was matched to that of an 83-year old relative of Bormann. The other skeleton was identified as Hitler's doctor, Ludwig Stumfegger.

Farago's 'research' into the Kent-Wolkoff Affair had also flown in the face of an altogether more accurate account by the Earl Jowitt that had already been published in Britain and, surprisingly, Farago even listed Jowitt's book *Some Were Spies* (1954) in his bibliography. Jowitt had reproduced the same Churchill-Roosevelt telegram dated 29 January 1940 that Farago had discovered among Hans Mackensen's January reports ... some three weeks before Kent and Wolkoff had been introduced.

# 7: Third Spin Cycle

When published in 1954, *Some Were Spies* by the Earl Jowitt provided the fullest and most accurate account of the Kent-Wolkoff Affair but as more reliable information has become available, Jowitt's version can now be seen as highly selective and not strictly truthful. It had been given 'spin' but coming from the pen of a former politician, this was hardly surprising.

In 1940, the author then known as Sir William Jowitt had been the Solicitor-General and he had led for the Prosecution at the Kent and Wolkoff trials. The following year, the *New York Times* had benefited from his advice after Captain Ramsay had sued for a libel that had stemmed out of the Affair.

William Jowitt (1885-1957) had been called to the Bar in 1909 and he took Silk in 1922. He served as a Liberal MP from 1922-1924 and as a Labour MP from 1929. Changing his political allegiance was a good career move because he stepped into the job of Attorney General in the Labour Government of 1929 and collected a Knighthood. He became Solicitor-General in 1940 in Churchill's Wartime Coalition and when Labour came to power after the War, he landed the top job of Lord Chancellor.

Jowitt's book ran to fifteen chapters. Two covered the Kent and Wolkoff trials in commendable detail but before delving into the main course, he had summarised the activities of seven would-be spies: Charles van den Kieboom, Sjoerd Pons, Karl Meier, José Waldberg, Karl Drueke, Werner Walti and a woman 'passing under the name of Madame Erikson'. All seven had been arrested in September 1940, shortly after their arrival. The first four had landed in pairs in Kent after a trawler had offloaded them into two rowing boats. The other three had landed in Scotland from a rubber dinghy after being dropped by seaplane[1].

In each case, Jowitt provided a short summary of the events that led to their arrests but he had little to say about the trials

---

[1] KV 4/188.

except that five had been found guilty; that Pons had been interned after having been acquitted; and that Madame Erikson had been interned after it had been 'decided to take no proceedings against her'. However, he failed to cite under what legislation they had been charged and what sentences had been prescribed. These were extraordinary omissions and considering that the author was a former Lord Chancellor, they must have been deliberate.

In fact, the six men had been charged under the Treachery Act of 1940 that carried a mandatory death sentence. The five who were found guilty were duly executed with Karl Meier and José Waldberg having the distinction of being the first spies to have been executed in Britain during WWII. They went to the scaffold on 10 December 1940. The other three appealed and Charles van den Kieboom met the hangman a week later, after withdrawing his appeal[2]. Drueke and Walti eventually lost their appeals and were executed on 6 August 1941.

Jowitt had prudently omitted stating their sentences because if five would-be spies had been executed even though they had been arrested before they had any chance of carrying out any espionage, this would have demonstrated the inappropriateness of the sentences handed down to Kent and Wolkoff (7 and 10 years) after having carried out some supposedly damaging espionage over several months.

The sentences imposed on Kent and Wolkoff were absurdly inappropriate given the gravity of their offences and it is significant that neither Kent nor Wolkoff was charged with any offences under the Treachery Act. It is also significant that neither was sent to Latchmere House, MI5's Interrogation Centre at Ham Common, where suspected spies were routinely debriefed using psychological methods and inducements that were considered appropriate. Several spies avoided the death sentence by accepting an offer that they couldn't refuse.

Understandably, Jowitt failed to explain that one of the German spies, Vera Erikson, a 27-year-old woman with several

---

[2] See Nigel West, *MI5: British Security Service Operations 1909-1945* (1981).

aliases[3], had avoided trial by her willingness to cooperate. Having worked for Russian and then German Intelligence and following a stay at Latchmere House, she named names and was potentially too valuable to waste on the scaffold, even though MI5's graphologist had given her a negative reading[4].

It is likely that Jowitt's book was published with one eye on the United States where official files are normally released into the public domain after fifteen years. Possibly it was intended to deflect any possible comment in the eventuality that a copy of Kent's trial transcript should become available to the public.

Two copies of the transcript did eventually become publicly available. One provided to the American Embassy in London was released in due course and the other now forms part of the 'Tyler Kent Collection' assembled by Charles Parsons, one of Kent's wealthy supporters. It is not known how or when Parsons obtained his copy but presumably Kent would have had to participate in the exercise. It was presented to the Yale University Library in November 1970.

The Yale copy is a curious document because the Index shows two sets of Page Numbers side-by-side. The first set is headed 'In Original Document' and indexes up to Page 166 and the second set is headed 'In This Copy' and indexes up to Page 200, an increase of 20%. Strangely, the percentage increase is not consistent throughout the Index. Surely, it would have been easier to copy-type a further document from an original? Or maybe, it was considered that the original contained some politically sensitive comments that needed editing out for public consumption?

This was a Machiavellian twist. Who would have imagined that a trial transcript would have been edited before release?

The FBI requested a copy of the trial transcript and on 16 April 1941 Maxwell Knight advised Guy Liddell that 'there are three in existence: one is at the American Embassy, one is at the

---

[3] Including Vera Schalberg and Vera de Cottami Chalburg. KV 2/14, KV 2/15, KV 2/16.
[4] KV 2/15.

Office of the DPP[5] and the other in the Records at the Old Bailey
… I do not think that it would matter in the least if the FBI had a
full transcript'.[6] A 'full' transcript? Knight's comment suggests
that it may not have been unusual to provide edited transcripts.

The publication of information on *in camera* trials had been
prohibited by Court Orders under Section 6 of the Emergency
Powers (Defence) Act. However, following the end of the war,
the implications of the expiry of the Act had to be considered. At
a meeting at the Home Office on 30 August 1945[7], Frank
Newsam, the chairman, advised that after the expiry of the Act,
the Orders would remain in place but that they would be
unenforceable in proceedings for contempt of court.

Newsam also referred to the request from Kent's solicitors for
permission to communicate the transcript of the proceedings at
his trial to persons in America with the possibility that the
transcript might be published in the United States. He suggested
that the 'proposed new arrangement' ought to cover publication.
This was agreed.

Of course, that was before the Freedom of Information Act
arrived in the United States in 1967 and in the UK in 2001. These
put a new complexion on matters.

Not surprisingly, Jowitt made no reference to any material
contained in *Secrets of the Secret Service* but like
Spiro/Cookridge, he also prefaced his book with some fine
sentiments:

> Occasionally, the interests of the State make it
> necessary that cases be heard *in camera*; but I
> believe that even here the facts should be known
> when the reason for secrecy no longer applies. I do
> not think that the revelation of the facts of such cases
> is, in the long run, harmful even to those who have
> been chiefly concerned. It is, of course, natural that

[5] Director of Public Prosecutions.
[6] KV 2/544 (50y).
[7] FO 371/44628, (65).

they should shrink from a wider publicity; but they should remember that without such a revelation they are at the mercy of rumour, and rumour is generally less charitable than the truth.

In reviewing the Kent and Wolkoff cases, Jowitt scrupulously avoided making any reference to MI5. This was accepted practice in those days when its existence was never officially acknowledged. However, he did get close at one point by revealing that one undercover agent, a Miss 'A', was working for 'our own secret service'. Nevertheless, he didn't reveal her real name or that of any other prosecution witness. Consequently, readers were left in the dark about the various personalities who had testified and this opened the door for Joan Miller to make false claims about her own role in the Affair.

The trial transcript shows that several MI5 Officers stepped into the witness box and although they gave their real names, they all avoided naming MI5 itself.

Major Maxwell Knight, who had run the Kent-Wolkoff case throughout, was apparently the most senior of those who testified but he had only been given the temporary rank of Major on 1 October 1940, shortly before the trials.

Knight had problems remembering for whom he was supposed to be working. On the First Day, he testified that he worked 'in the Diplomatic Service' but when he was recalled on the Second Day, he said that he was 'a member of the general staff attached to the Military Intelligence Department'. Earlier, when he had interviewed Tyler Kent after his arrest on 20 May 1940, he had been described as being with the 'Military Intelligence Branch of Scotland Yard'. In fact, he was the Head of Section B5b that countered Political Subversion and his forte was placing and running 'moles' in extreme political organisations.

Knight's boss, Captain Guy Liddell, also appeared and he described himself as being 'a Civilian Assistant on the General Staff of the War Office'. In truth, he was the Director of the 'B' Division with responsibility for the entire spectrum of Counter Espionage including Double Agents. Captain Thomas Argyll

Robertson who was the Head of the Double Agents section also testified. He got closer to the truth by saying that he was on the General Staff attached to the Military Intelligence of the War Office.

Jowitt misrepresented some of the facts that appeared in the trial transcript. For example, by asserting that 'Soon after his arrival in London, Kent met one Anna Wolkoff ...' The trial transcript shows that Kent arrived in London on either the 5th or 6th October 1939 and that he was introduced to Anna Wolkoff during the first week of February 1940. In fact, Marjorie Mackie an MI5 undercover agent who was diarising events reported that Kent and Wolkoff became acquainted around the end of February 1940.

Jowitt's implication that they had met at an earlier date gave credence to the allegation that they had been carrying out their espionage for very much longer than could have possibly been the case.

A comparison of the trial transcript with other contemporary material suggests that two of the Prosecution Witnesses may have strayed from the truth.

The first was Franklin Crosbie Gowen, the Second Secretary of the American Embassy in London. On the First Day (23 October 1940), when the Judge was considering whether or not Kent's diplomatic privilege had been properly waived, Gowen explained that Ambassador Kennedy was not in Court to testify because 'I saw him off this morning a few minutes before 7 o'clock'. However, according to Kennedy's Diplomatic Memoir, he left London after lunch on Monday 21 October and 'had a nice ride down to Bournemouth' where he spent the night in order to catch the Clipper the following day[8]. It is possible that Amanda Smith (Kennedy's granddaughter) who had edited his material may have misinterpreted but there is less room for doubt about Maxwell Knight's testimony.

---

[8] *Hostage to Fortune: The Letters of Joseph P Kennedy*, edited by Amanda Smith (his granddaughter).

Knight had testified that he was on the search party that had raided Kent's flat on the 20 May 1940 and that later he had taken a Statement from Kent. He also testified that he had been accompanied by: Inspector Keeble[9] who had the search warrant, another officer and Franklin Gowen.

This did not agree with Gowen's own 13-page report to his Embassy dated 28 May 1940. According to Gowen, it was Inspector Pearson who went on the search party and who had the search warrant. Inspector J.W. Pearson also made a three-page Statement dated 22 May 1940 in which he described the search and subsequent events in great detail[10]. An extract from Pearson's Statement was passed to the US Embassy on 11 June 1940[11].

On 30 August 1944, Knight introduced 'Minute 88' into Kent's file[12]. It was handwritten, signed and dated. On that occasion, Knight had written 'Irene Danischewsky was in Tyler Kent's room when we arrested him. She was subsequently interviewed by Inspector Pearson of Special Branch who came with us on the day of the search of Kent's rooms'.

Possibly, Pearson had been indisposed when the case came to trial but whether it was Keeble or Pearson did not affect the strength of the case because, after having given the required 'caution', Knight had obtained a Statement from Kent in which he had admitted having taken copies of the Embassy documents and of having shown these to Captain Ramsay and Anna Wolkoff.

In the Statement, which was signed and witnessed, Kent also admitted that Wolkoff had taken two documents from his

---

[9] Detective Inspector Harold Keeble was in Court but he was not called to testify about the search of Kent's flat; he was called on the Third Day, as the last witness for the Prosecution. He testified that he had found some documents at an unoccupied address but when the Judge questioned the relevance, the Prosecution decided not to 'trouble further with it'. These documents were later produced at Anna Wolkoff's trial.
[10] KV 2/840.
[11] KV 2/543.
[12] KV 2/544.

collection. She had returned these later and later still, she had left glass negatives with images of the two documents in his flat. The glass negatives that had been discovered by the search party were introduced into evidence; they held images of two telegrams that Churchill had sent to Roosevelt via the American Embassy.

Jowitt provided an overview of the events that had led to the prosecutions and he made reference to the correspondence between Churchill and Roosevelt but falsely claimed that:

> This latter correspondence was made available to our authorities by the Americans, and provided the material on which the prosecution was based. The rest of the documents found in Kent's flat were taken possession of by the American authorities, and their contents were naturally enough not revealed.

In fact, the American authorities had resolutely refused to allow any of their correspondence to be used in evidence and reliance was therefore placed entirely on four documents that had originated from British sources[13]. Consequently, the documentary evidence comprised two letters from Guy Liddell, together with the two telegrams from Churchill to Roosevelt.

Jowitt reproduced both telegrams but only the first, dated 29th January 1940, in full:

PERSONAL AND SECRET FOR THE PRESIDENT<br>FROM NAVAL PERSON.

> I gave orders last night that no American ship should in any circumstances be diverted into the combat zone round the British Isles declared by you. I trust this will be satisfactory.

JOHNSON[14]

---

[13] See MI5's 'Cross Reference' re Mrs. Nicholson dated 23 June 1940 in KV2/902.

[14] Herschel V. Johnson was acting Head of the Embassy in lieu of Joseph Kennedy who was holidaying in the United States.

With the second telegram, dated the 28th February 1940, Jowitt reproduced what he described as 'the relevant extract':

### STRICTLY PERSONAL AND CONFIDENTIAL
### FOR THE PRESIDENT
### FROM NAVAL PERSON.

Very many thanks for your most kind letter of February 1. Since on January 29 I gave orders to the Fleet not to bring any American ships into the zone you have drawn around our shores, many of the other Departments have become much concerned about the efficiency of the blockade and the difficulties of discriminating between various countries. The neutrals are all on them and they are all on me. Nevertheless the order still stands and no American ship has been brought by the Navy into the danger zone.

*Asterisks, known in legal jargon as ellipses, indicate that Jowitt had omitted the 'non-relevant' part.*

I do hope that I may be helped to hold the position I have adopted by the American shipping lines availing themselves of the great convenience of Navicerts[15] which was an American invention and thus enable American trade to proceed without hindrance.

It is a great pleasure to me to keep you informed about Naval matters, although alas I cannot have the honour of a talk with you in person.

JOHNSON.

Jowitt added his own observation:

I need hardly point out how important it was that this document should remain secret; for if every neutral were to claim the same concessions as had been made

---

[15] Navicerts were certificates that all neutral ships had to get from a British Consulate before they could put to sea. They were intended to help enforce the blockade on the shipment of goods to Germany.

to the Americans, the conduct of our war at sea would have been gravely prejudiced.

Later, when the full text of the telegram was published, it became evident that Jowitt had omitted the 'non-relevant' part because 'the concessions' were already in the public domain and had even been advertised by the Moore McCormack Line:

> But you can imagine my embarrassment when Moore McCormack Line actually advertises in Norway that they do not have to worry about navicerts or Kirkwall[16], and when all the Scandinavian countries complain of discrimination in American favour. I wonder if there is any way in which the Moore McCormack Line could be persuaded, in addition to accepting navicerts as a general rule, not to carry mails for Scandinavia until the arrangements that we are trying to make at St John, New Brunswick, or elsewhere, are ready. All our experience shows that the examination of mails is essential to efficient control as only in this way can we get the evidence of evasion.

Despite the triviality of the first telegram and the public awareness of the matters described in the second, Captain William Derek Stephens, a Deputy Director of Naval Intelligence, had stepped into the witness box and had solemnly testified that the two documents 'contain information which would be useful to the enemy'. Under cross-examination, Stephens also agreed that 'they would be of considerable interest to anybody taking an interest in American politics'.

Guy Liddell had previously testified that the information contained in his letters 'would certainly' be helpful to an enemy but as far as the Churchill-Roosevelt correspondence was concerned, Kent had evidently been found guilty of disclosing information that was already in the public domain.

Understandably, Jowitt omitted reproducing the headings from

---

[16] A British contraband base in the Orkney Islands.

the telegrams, both of which included the telltale word 'GRAY' that showed that they had been transcribed in the non-confidential code.

It is highly likely that the second telegram (which had arrived in Washington at 3 p.m. on 28 February 1940) was the one referred to by Alexander Cadogan in his diary entry dated 27 February 1940:

> Had to wait at the Foreign Office until about 8.10 to see a draft telegram from Winston to Roosevelt. (I deprecate this procedure.) It contained what I thought a quite poisonous sentence, which I cut out and went home to dinner.

So, contrary to the speculation by Captain Ramsay, among others, Churchill had evidently not been communicating with Roosevelt behind the back of the Foreign Office and Cadogan, the Permanent Under-Secretary at the Foreign Office, had apparently been given editorial control.

Unfortunately for posterity, Cadogan failed to make it clear why he should have 'deprecated' the procedure.


Kent had been charged with seven offences: five under the Official Secrets Act and two under the Larceny Act. Four of the five charges under the Official Secrets Act related to his having obtained each of the four documents that were introduced in evidence; the fifth charge was of having communicated two of these to Wolkoff. Kent had obliged by admitting all these offences in his statement.

The Prosecution then rammed its point home by calling Nicolas Eugenovitch Smirnoff into the witness box. Smirnoff testified that he had been a professional photographer since 'about 1918' and that previously he had worked at the Russian Embassy in London. He had known the Wolkoff family 'for some time' but he had 'rather lost touch with them' until Saturday the 13 April 1940, when Anna had unexpectedly called at his home and asked him to photograph three foolscap documents[17].

He photographed the documents with his Quarter-Plate Camera and produced the three glass negatives. As he didn't have any photographic paper, Wolkoff took the documents away. She returned the following Tuesday when she collected the prints. Smirnoff admitted that he didn't know if the glass negatives produced as exhibits were the ones that he had taken but he did say that because he didn't have an enlarger, he had only been able to produce contact prints.

On cross-examination, Smirnoff confirmed that he had been an Examiner in the Censorship Department. Evidently, he was interned after giving his evidence at the trials but nothing more is known about him[18].

Kent was also charged with two offences under the Larceny Act. Presumably, this was a contingency measure just in case the jury should acquit him of the offences under the Official Secrets Act. This was always a possibility because Kent's offences under the Official Secrets Act were entirely dependent upon Wolkoff also being found guilty when she came to trial. Some smart juror may have picked up on this and influenced the others accordingly.

Similarly, there was always a possibility that Wolkoff might be acquitted because juries don't always follow the Judge's directions as the case of Sjoerd Pons, cited by Jowitt, illustrates. Pons was acquitted although Kieboom, who had evidently told a similar story, was executed. Jowitt commented wryly that it was 'a merciful if not entirely logical view'.

'So', the thinking may have gone, 'Let's throw in a couple of Larceny charges for good measure. At least, we should be able to get these past the Jury'.

As it turned out, the Prosecution decided not to pursue one of the charges and Jowitt cleverly glossed over the reason why Kent had been found 'not guilty' on this charge. This was because Kent

---

[17] The telegram dated 28 February 1940 ran to two pages.
[18] See Brian Simpson, *In the Highest Degree Odious* (1992).

had made his own copy of the telegram dated 29 January 1940, whereas he had taken a carbon copy of the telegram dated 29 February 1940.

The truth of the matter was that under the Larceny Act 1916, the prosecution had to prove that the accused had the intention of permanently depriving the owner of his goods, in this case the information. However, as the owner of the goods still retained possession of his information, the Larceny Act was totally inappropriate for a situation where Kent had made his own copy. It was still largely inappropriate for the second charge but because Kent had taken two sheets of paper that belonged to the Embassy, the charge could be made to stick. Therefore, Kent had been found guilty of stealing two sheets of paper.

But did it really matter whether Kent and Wolkoff were found guilty or not? They were both being held under Defence Regulation 18B so whatever the verdicts, they were both destined to spend some considerable time inside. Well, yes it did because some very significant political consequences had followed in the wake of the Kent-Wolkoff Affair.

Jowitt took great pains to explain the implications of the Official Secrets Act:

> On a prosecution under this section it shall not be necessary to show that the accused person was guilty of any particular act tending to show a purpose prejudicial to the safety or interests of the State, and notwithstanding that no such act is proved against him he may be convicted if from the circumstances of the case or his conduct or his known character as proved it appears that his purpose was a purpose prejudicial to the safety or interests of the State.

There were two important requirements: (a) that the document is one that might be useful to an enemy, and (b) that the purpose of the communication must be a purpose 'prejudicial to the safety or interests of the State'.

Jowitt confidently asserted that 'There could be no possible doubt that the first of these requirements was fulfilled in relation to the two documents from the Naval Person to the President of the United States' but he admitted that the second requirement is always the one which causes difficulty.

He also explained that the Official Secrets Act of 1920 stipulated that if it could be shown that the person accused had 'been in communication with or attempted to communicate with a foreign agent', that fact should be evidence from which a jury might draw the inference that the purpose of any communication which was the subject of a prosecution under the Act of 1911 was 'prejudicial to the safety or interests of the State'.

He added that the term 'Foreign Agent' was defined so as to include any person who was reasonably suspected of having committed such a prejudicial act and that Kent had undoubtedly been in communication with Anna Wolkoff. Therefore, if Wolkoff were a 'Foreign Agent' within the meaning of the Act, the jury would be entitled to take that fact into consideration in the case against Kent in determining whether his purpose in communicating the documents to her was 'prejudicial'.

Jowitt argued that there were grounds upon which the jury might well draw the conclusion that Anna Wolkoff was a 'Foreign Agent' within the special definition, even though she was certainly not a 'Foreign Agent' in the ordinary acceptance of the phrase.

Evidence was therefore called to show that she had attempted to communicate during the war with William Joyce (commonly called Lord Haw-Haw) and that she had been in touch with one of the military attachés at the Italian Embassy during the war against Germany when Italy was still neutral, though there was no evidence that she had passed any secret information to such attaché.

When the Judge decided that the case against Kent should be tried separately from that against Anna Wolkoff, it became necessary to call the same evidence in both cases; because if it could be established that Anna Wolkoff came within this category, the fact that Kent had communicated the documents to her would be evidence that the 'purpose' of his communication was 'prejudicial'.

The jury at Kent's trial evidently had no problem following the Judge's directions and after retiring for twenty-five minutes they returned the required 'Guilty' verdicts for six of the charges and 'Not Guilty' for one of the Larceny charges that had been withdrawn.

Jowitt didn't mention (and there was no reason why he should) that Kent had lodged an appeal that was heard on 5 February 1941 at the Royal Courts of Justice before The Lord Chief Justice of England (Viscount Caldecote of Bristol), Mr. Justice Humphreys and Mr. Justice Singleton. Kent the Appellant appeared in person and the Right Honourable Sir William Jowitt KC and Mr. G.B. McClure appeared as Counsel for the Crown. Kent's Appeal was dismissed but although the MI5 files show that the Appeal was correctly described as 'Rex v Tyler Gatewood Kent'[19], the version in the Law Times Reports appeared as 'Rex v A.B.'. This was rather unusual.

Interestingly, when Kent was nearing the end of his prison sentence, his mother raised the question of his release date. After discussion, it was decided that his entitlement to remission was to be based on the time that he had served following his Appeal. In other words, it was deemed desirable that Kent should be kept inside as long as possible.


Malcolm Muggeridge who had attended both trials as an observer for the Field Security Police would later recount that Wolkoff had passed many of the documents that she had obtained from Kent to Lord Haw-Haw via the Rumanian Embassy, as material for his broadcasts from Berlin and that 'the Italian and German Intelligence Services also got a sight of them'[20].

This was totally untrue and had never been alleged at the trials. What was undoubtedly true was that Anna Wolkoff had been entrapped in a sting operation so that she could be

---

[19] KV 2/544.
[20] Malcolm Muggeridge, *Chronicles of Wasted Time: Volume 2 - The Infernal Grove* (1973).

categorised as a 'Foreign Agent' within the meaning of the Official Secrets Act.

# 8: Anna Wolkoff

Anna Wolkoff[1] was born in St Petersburg on 30 October 1902 to Nicholai Androvitch Wolkoff (1870-1954) and his wife, the former Vera de Scanlon (1879-1942). Anna was their first child and she would have a brother Alexander and two sisters, Alexandra later known as Alice, and Kyra. At one time Anna's father had been personal aide-de-camp to the Emperor Nicholas II and her mother had been a lady-in-waiting to the Empress, so they had been well to the fore in Russian society. During adulthood, Anna always referred to herself as Anna de Wolkoff.

According to Anna, her paternal grandfather Alexander Nikolaevitch Wolkoff-Mouromtzoff (1844-1928) had been one of the most erudite men of his time. He was both a musician and a painter, and three of his works are in the Victoria & Albert Museum. He signed his paintings 'A.N. Roussoff' to avoid confusion with another painter also called Wolkoff. The Mouromtzoff suffix was introduced later in life to satisfy the terms of a large legacy. He had married an Englishwoman, the former Alice Gore, who was related to Sir John Gore. Latterly, he had lived in a palace in Venice where he had rubbed shoulders with Wagner and Liszt. After Wagner's death, he was proud of having made arrangements for a death mask against the initial wishes of the family. His memoirs[2], published in 1928 the year he died, feature a pencil drawing of the author by Queen Victoria's daughter, H.R.H. Princess Louise, Duchess of Argyll. After explaining why, despite their nobility, his family never had any titles bestowed upon them, he ended his memoirs with the assurance that:

> The day that Russia will again become Russia, my descendants may perhaps be glad to know that the documents confirming their appurtenance to the ancient nobility exist.

---

[1] Sometimes her name appears as 'Volkoff', which is phonetically correct.
[2] *Memoirs of Alexander Wolkoff-Mouromtzoff* (1928).

Anna's father had been Chief of Staff to the Commander in Chief of the Baltic Fleet of the Imperial Russian Navy prior to his appointment in 1913 as Naval Attaché at the Russian Imperial Embassy in London. Wolkoff and his family then came to live in London in March 1913 shortly before the outbreak of WWI.

On 13 October 1914, two of Wolkoff's naval colleagues arrived from St Petersburg with a gift for Winston Churchill, the First Lord of the Admiralty. The gift was three codebooks from the Magdeburg, a small German cruiser that had run aground in shallow waters on 26 August 1914. It was Captain Wolkoff's job to escort them to Churchill who turned the books over to the Admiralty's Intelligence Division, where they made an early contribution in helping the code-breakers to read German radio signals.

As a token of appreciation for his services to the British war effort, Wolkoff was awarded a Companion of the Most Honourable Order of the Bath on 25 June 1915, which entitled him to use the initials 'CB' after his name[3]. Thereafter, Wolkoff proudly displayed his honour and between the wars he even used it in the London telephone directories. At some stage, he was promoted to Rear Admiral and became chummy with the legendary Captain (later Admiral) Reginald Hall, the head of Room 40 at the Admiralty, Britain's code-breaking operation in WW1.

After the Bolshevik revolution of 1917 had precluded a return to Russia, Wolkoff settled for exile in Britain and anglicised his forename to Nicholas. In 1932, he opened the Russian Tea Room & Restaurant at 50 Harrington Road, near the South Kensington Underground Station.

In Russia, Anna had been educated at home by a governess. In England, she went to St James' School, West Malvern from 1914 to 1916; Sandycotes School at Parkstone, Dorset until she was 18

---

[3] It does not seem specially significant because six other Military Attachés based in London were also honoured on the same date: another one from the Russian Embassy, two from the Italian, one each from the French and Japanese Embassies, and one from the Belgian Legation.

and to the Architectural Association in London until she was 21. When she realised that she couldn't handle the maths required to become an architect, she became an apprentice dressmaker and studied painting. She was fluent in Russian, English, French and German and had some Italian.

During 1929-1930, Anna went to the United States with a friend Barbara Cavendish-Bentinck[4] where they sold old masters for Spink & Son. On her return she joined the staff of Ducave Ltd as a dress designer.

In June 1935 she established her own business Anna de Wolkoff Ltd with a nominal capital of £100 and a loan of £3,000 from Major Philip Gribble, a director of the Anglo-Rhodesian Tobacco Co Ltd. The business had a shop at 37 Conduit Street off Regent Street in London's fashionable Mayfair. At its peak, it had 30-35 employees with Mrs. Wallis Simpson, later the Duchess of Windsor, and the Duchess of Kent among its clientele. Anna was contracted to receive £520 p.a. plus 10% of the profits.

In 1935, Anna applied for British nationality and a police report advised that 'nothing has been ascertained'… that …'she holds extreme political views or is connected with any subversive organisation'. MI5 also reported that they knew 'nothing to her detriment'. Her application was supported by Admiral Hall who wrote on 28 April 1935 that he had known the family 'for 20 years and they have most gallantly faced their entire loss of fortune and have been a fine example to others'. Her application was granted on 10 September 1935.

In April 1937, Anna had one of her creations featured in *Vogue's* Special Coronation issue, photographed by Cecil Beaton. She must have been riding high.

In 1938, Anna de Wolkoff Ltd took out a £1,000 mortgage from Lady Janet Bailey, the second daughter of the Earl of Inchcape. A Receiver was appointed in January 1939. When the company was wound up, it had unsecured creditors of over

---

[4] Barbara Cavendish-Bentinck (b 1902) was the daughter of Ruth (1867-1953), a Fabian Socialist, a suffragette and an aristocrat, who founded the Cavendish-Bentinck Library in 1909.

£4,500, including Lady Janet Bailey over £2,000 and Admiral Wolkoff over £800.

The rag trade was a tough business that was notorious for its sweatshops and traditionally many operations were Jewish owned. She attributed her failure to 'Jewish influences' but the harsh trading conditions of the thirties were probably the real factor.

After the failure of her own business, Anna joined Busvines in Hanover Square. A big romance then loomed in her life and she could hardly contain herself when she shared the news in a letter to Enid Riddell, her best friend, on 14 February 1939. She was seeing Cotty tomorrow, hurrah, hurrah! He had invited her to dinner ... Oh Lord! Fancy having to get through all today and all tomorrow![5]

Cotty was Mark Pepys, the 6th Earl of Cottenham, who had been or would be divorced that year. Anna not only failed to catch her man but Cotty never even wrote to her while she was in jail. She had written to him soon after her detention but she didn't get a reply and 'that was indeed a bitter disillusion'.

On 10 April 1939, MI5 agent U35 (Klop Ustinov) reported that Anna was a 'staunch Nazi propagandist' adding 'You will remember that Fitz Randolph and Baron Hohenberg used to meet Lia Voss at the Admiral's Restaurant'[6].

After succumbing to illness, Anna went on a European holiday from 7 July to 27 August 1939. A copy of a long report on her six-and-a-half week visit was found in her flat when she was arrested. It is undated and bears no addressee but it was evidently sent to Louis-Ferdinand Céline, the vitriolic French novelist who had written about the International Jewish Conspiracy that would start a world war in *Bagatelles pour un Massacre* (1937).

Anna told Céline about her European tour, which had been a fact-finding mission in which she set out to discover 'the truth' for herself. She had first visited Princess Lichtenstein, who lived

---

[5] KV 2/839.
[6] KV 2/840. Fitz Randolph was evidently connected with the German Embassy but the significance of Klop Ustinov's observation is not now evident

in a castle in the Sudetenland, which had already been ceded to Germany. She had met General Frank on 17 July 1939 and they had talked for two and a half hours. General Frank was apparently deputising for Konrad Henlein the Gauleiter of the Sudetenland, who had been suddenly called to Berchtesgaden, by implication to see Hitler. Wolkoff then learned 'of the forthcoming German-Soviet pact and all that it would imply'. On 15 August 1939, she went on to Hungary where she stayed in another castle, this one belonging to Count Sigray. By her account, the castle owners of Europe were all living in fear of the Communists and were looking to Hitler for salvation.

Copies of other correspondence between Anna and Céline have also survived but all are undated. In one, which may have been her first, Anna expressed her admiration for three of Céline's novels: *L'Ecole des Cadavers*, *Bagatelles pour un Massacre*, and *Voyage au bout de la Nuit*. She advised him that she had always been well instructed on the 'Jewish Peril' because her father had had a copy of *The Protocols* since 1904. 'We have never ceased to disseminate propaganda', she assured him, 'but until the arrival of the brave Hitler, people ridiculed us, saying these poor Wolkoffs have got Jews on the brain.'

Anna confided that she had discovered that the Pope was half-Jewish and that Jewish-American high finance had directed that Cardinal Mundelein (Jew) would be the next Pope (to assure Jewish succession to the throne). Anna's claims followed in the wake of the Cardinal having publicly condemned Hitler. These had resulted in Nazi complaints to the Vatican, which the Vatican had failed to address. This shows that Anna had written her letter some time before 2 October 1939, when the 67-year-old Cardinal of Chicago passed away without ever landing the top job.

It also proved that these poor Wolkoffs really did have Jews on the brain. In fact, the Okhrana, the Tsarist Secret Police, had concocted *The Protocols of the Elders of Zion* in 1895 from a German novel that had borrowed heavily from a French satire. Purporting to be secret Jewish plans for world domination, *The Protocols* were first printed privately in Russia in 1897. An abbreviated version appeared in a Russian newspaper in 1903 and they reappeared in a book *Velikoe v Malom* (The Great in the Little) authored by Sergei Nilus, a religious mystic in 1905. Nilus's version had found a receptive audience: Russia had been defeated in the Russo-Japanese War and scapegoats were required, a role that the Jews had always played to perfection. The Bolshevik Revolution then provided further confirmation for those White Russians, like the Wolkoffs, who had been separated from their inherited estates and required an explanation for the loss of their God-given properties.

In her letter to Céline, Anna had referred to an unnamed Member of Parliament who had asked her to make contact with the Frenchman because they had both been astounded by Céline's knowledge about the British Intelligence Service, presumably from his books. She requested all the information that he had, 'above all on Admiral Sinclair, a most sinister personage'. Admiral Sir Hugh P. Sinclair, who would die on 4 November 1939, had been the head of MI6 but most of the others listed by Céline as members of the British Intelligence network had been invented.

Céline replied to Anna and apologised for the delay. He had been overwhelmed by lawsuits as a consequence of his last book *L'Ecole des Cadavers* (1938), in which he had again written about the Jewish conspiracy. He planned to visit London in early April 1940 and would be pleased to meet her friend, the MP. In another letter, Céline thanked Anna for her hospitality and enquired 'How are the English rebels? Captain Ramsay and the other plotters.'

Their correspondence apparently ceased at this point, possibly because Céline had offended his hosts. He was notorious for showing up in rumpled pants held up by a string, wearing a three-day beard, spewing forth streams of invective and gibes. There is no record of what his British hosts had thought of Céline, but the fact that Anna had kept his correspondence suggests that she had valued his opinions, which paralleled her own. Céline believed that France should form an alliance with Hitler, and like the Wolkoffs, he also hated the English. 'The English our Allies?

Balls! Another great swindle! We'll be maggots by the time the first Oxford queers disembark in Flanders.'

Anna returned to Britain 'a week before war was declared' and went to live with her parents who had a basement flat at 18a Roland Gardens in South Kensington. She joined the Auxiliary Fire Service but resigned three months later after catching septic tonsillitis. Thereafter, she did dressmaking in her rooms. She had joined Captain Ramsay's Right Club 'before the war' and although it had supposedly been wound up when war was declared, both Ramsay and his wife continued to recruit new members including Tyler Kent. They also attended meetings with others who shared their belief that it was a Jews' war and that Britain should opt for a negotiated peace.

Anna was always boasting of having friends in high places and she considered Vernon Kell, the head of MI5, as one of these. She wrote to him on 22 February 1940 on a letterhead bearing her personal logo. It looked like the side of a house constructed from tall pillars, which on close inspection formed the word 'Wolkoff'. A crown was perched pretentiously upon the apex of the roof. As always, she had signed herself 'Anna de Wolkoff'.[7]

Anna reminded Kell of the 'one and only time' that she had had the pleasure of meeting him. It was at a dinner given by Mark Cottenham last winter at which 'a certain subject was under a very lively discussion'. It doesn't take much imagination to figure out what 'certain subject' was under discussion. Mark Cottenham was, of course, Mark Pepys, the 6th Earl of Cottenham, who was running MI5's Transport Section when Joan Miller joined the organisation in September 1939. Miller never claimed that Anna had known 'Cotty', so presumably Miller had been kept in the dark.

Anna then told Kell her sob story about how she had lost her business; had been discharged by Busvines; had joined the Auxiliary Fire Service because 'she had to live'; but then had to

---

[7] See Appendix: Images for a reproduction.

resign after having fallen ill. 'So here I am a paying guest in my parents' home and back again where I was 18 years ago, dressmaking'.

After Kell had acknowledged her letter, she wrote to him again on 18 March 1940. Alexander, her brother who worked for Shell, had warned her that unless she stopped her anti-Government activities, she would be 'put inside'. She solemnly protested to Kell that this was an untrue accusation and she found it difficult to believe that her natural anti-Jewish hatred (sic) and propaganda could be construed as anti-Government. This only supported her contention that there was too much Jewish influence in this country and it was a bitter reward for being truly patriotic. She asked Kell for his advice. Kell responded by asking Maxwell Knight to interview her, which he did by inviting her to visit him at the War Office. He met her on 19 March 1940, in the guise of Captain King.

Knight reported that it had been a real pleasure to cross swords with Anna. Evidently, Prince Schubatow, who worked with Anna's brother at Shell, had tipped him off that she had been attracting 'undesirable attention' from the authorities. Anna dragged in Admiral Sir Reginald Hall's name and claimed that he was a close friend. Knight then had to listen to a very garbled version of the search that had been made at Anne van Lennep's flat, with an amusing description of himself in mufti.

Anna had confessed that she was an ardent 'stickyback performer'[8] and asked if it was an offence to hold anti-Jewish views. Knight had evidently been non-committal because she followed up the interview with a letter to 'Captain King' and warned him that 'if this sort of nonsense goes on, I shall simply write to ….. (you know whom I mean)'.[9]

Anna Wolkoff was arrested at her parent's flat 18a Roland Gardens at 11.30 a.m. on 20th May 1940 by Sergeants Sutling

---

[8] Anna Wolkoff and her associates made a practice of wandering the streets at night sticking up anti-Jewish notices.
[9] KV 2/840. Presumably, she was referring to Vernon Kell.

and Smith and Woman Patrol Urquhart. A Mr. Dickson of MI5 was also in attendance. This would have been J.G. Dickson who was 'on loan' to MI5 from the Ministry of Labour. Wolkoff 'kept her mouth firmly closed' when she was cautioned and the order read. The order specified that she had 'Hostile Associations' under Defence Regulation 18B. It was signed by Captain Guy Liddell and 'approved' by Toby Pilcher[10], one of MI5's legal gurus who later became a Judge.

It had been arranged that Maxwell Knight would deliver the order to Special Branch and that Wolkoff was to be 'conveyed' to Holloway Prison in London but after being formally charged at Rochester Row police station she was actually conveyed to Strangeways Prison in Manchester. This was distinctly unusual because Holloway had been specifically designated as the internment camp for the women who would shortly be rounded up from around the London area.

On 15 May 1940 five days before Anna would be detained, another of Knight's agents known only as M/M reported having met Admiral Wolkoff and his wife 'recently'. The agent noted that they appeared to be cautious but were 100 per cent pro-Hitler and think that he will make 'a wonderful peace'.

On 18 June 1940 nearly a month after Anna's detention, yet another of Knight's agents, M/G, had lunch at the Russian Tea Rooms. The lunch had lasted an hour-and-a-half and the Admiral took the opportunity to share his delight at the collapse of France. He kept saying how splendid it was.

The Admiral also said 'How good it would be if there were a revolution here under General Ironside'. When asked, 'Why Ironside?' the Admiral replied, 'Well, he has got all those men under him now'. M/G assumed that this was a reference to the Local Defence Volunteers, later renamed the 'Home Guard'.

The Admiral and his wife also referred to a pilot in the RAF named Romanoff who had once piloted Winston Churchill. Mme.

---

[10] Gonne St Clair Pilcher (1890-1966) was known to his friends as 'Toby'.

Wolkoff said that it was a pity that he did not drop him out of the aeroplane.

The *Daily Sketch* announced the commencement of the trials of Kent and Wolkoff on 24 October 1940 under the dramatic headline 'Even Police Barred at Old Bailey'. This was untrue as evidenced by a report made by the three officers from Special Branch. Other police officers would also be called to give evidence.

However the article was not entirely without interest because the reporter had caught sight of 'a lonely figure in the great hall outside the closed doors'. It was Admiral Wolkoff who was described as 'black coated, be-spatted and be-spectacled, his beard trimmed in the same style as the late Tsar'. The reporter had little to say about Anna except that she left the dock 'clasping her fur cape to her throat'. Malcolm Muggeridge was more forthcoming and described her as 'short, compact and, though still quite young, already white-haired'. According to a report in her MI5 file, she was 5 foot 4 inches and had green eyes.

Kent would later recall that Anna 'was a smart woman, fun to talk to, but plain as hell. He considered her 'well-filled' and 'not sexually attractive'[11]. The cook and the housemaid at Kent's flat reported that they had seen a woman who was obviously Anna on several occasions but neither knew her name. In a statement, the cook said that Anna had a 'gruff' voice but later in the same statement, she said she had a 'rough' voice. Whichever, her voice evidently lacked musical quality.

The *Daily Sketch* reporter was apparently unaware that when Anna's turn came she would have to face three charges, two under the Official Secrets Act and one under the Defence Regulations.

The charge for the first of her offences against the Official Secrets Act was that 'for a purpose prejudicial to the safety or interests of the State on or about the 9 April 1940, you obtained

---

[11] John Costello *Ten Days to Destiny* (1991).

from Tyler Gatewood Kent two documents that might be useful to the enemy, that is to say two copies of a telegram (sic)[12]'.

The charge for the second of her offences against the Official Secrets Act was that 'for a purpose prejudicial to the safety or interests of the State on the 14 April 1940, you recorded two documents that might be useful to the enemy'.

The charge for her offence against the Defence Regulations was that 'you on the 9 April 1940, with intent to assist an enemy, did an act which was likely to assist an enemy and to prejudice public safety, the defence of the realm, and the efficient prosecution of the war in that you, by secret means, attempted to send a letter in code to one Joyce, known as Lord Haw-Haw, in Berlin'. She pleaded 'Not Guilty' to all charges.

Even though the first and last charges were entirely unrelated, they had been synchronised as having occurred 'on or about' the same date, Tuesday the 9 April 1940. For some of those at the trial, this would have implied that Wolkoff had sent copies of the telegrams that she had obtained from Kent to William Joyce in Berlin. Malcolm Muggeridge had clearly believed this to be the case.

Before the trials, Kent's solicitors had asked to see a copy of the Coded Letter. This was refused but at the start of Kent's trial, and evidently before the Jury had been sworn in, his Counsel produced a letter from the Director of Public Prosecutions in which it was stated that the Prosecution did not allege that Kent had anything to do with or even have knowledge of the sending of the letter by Wolkoff to Joyce.

At the end of their trials and before pronouncing sentence, the Judge had asked 'Have either of you anything you wish to add?' Prisoner Tyler Gatewood Kent made a short statement in which he claimed that his Counsel had been prevented from reading to the Jury a certain letter from the Public Prosecutor in which it was stated that the Prosecution had no intention to claim that he was in any way connected with or had knowledge of Anna's alleged communication with Germany and yet the Jury has

---

[12] It should have read 'copies of two telegrams'.

listened to evidence concerning this matter and that had undoubtedly influenced their minds.

The Judge responded by asking him if he would like him to read the letter now. Prisoner Tyler Gatewood Kent replied, 'I would, my Lord'. Accordingly, the letter was handed to the Judge, who read it and he confirmed this by saying, 'Very well; I have read it.' By that time, the jury had already found Kent guilty and had been dismissed, so it was far too late to help his case. Kent may have hoped that after reading the letter, the Judge would hand down a more lenient sentence but it is unlikely to have influenced the Judge.

However, the Judge's silent reading ensured that the contents of the letter were not placed on the official record. Fortunately, the official observers from Special Branch filled out the details.

No transcript of Wolkoff's Trial has ever come to light even though three copies were made. Therefore more reliance has to be placed on the Earl Jowitt's summary than is the case with Kent. Fortunately, the four-page report by the three members of Special Branch who attended the trials as observers corrects some of Jowitt's spin.

According to Jowitt, to support its case against Kent, the Prosecution had to prove that Kent had shown some Embassy documents to Wolkoff. This was the easy bit because Kent had already made a statement which included this admission. The tricky bit was that the Prosecution also had to prove that Wolkoff was a 'Foreign Agent' within the meaning of the Official Secrets Act.

Beneath a mountain of innuendo, the crux of the issue was that Wolkoff had received a message from a friend of hers, a young naval officer, asking her to go to the Russian Tea Rooms in Harrington Road, Kensington 'because he had a friend whom he wanted her to meet'.

At around 11 a.m. on 9 April 1940, Wolkoff duly met these two men. They had some refreshments and indulged in anti-Jewish talk. The young naval officer then went to pay the bill.

While he was away, Wolkoff stayed at the table with her new acquaintance whom Jowitt called 'X'.

Wolkoff's story was that 'X' had asked her 'Would you be prepared to do something that would really help the cause of anti-Semitism?' On receiving her confirmation, he then asked 'Have you ever sent anything to the Continent through a diplomatic bag?'

Wolkoff replied 'Well, if it's very important I might be able to get it sent'. 'X' then produced a letter addressed to 'Herr W.B. Joyce, Rundfunkhaus, Berlin' and handed it to her. When she asked what it contained, she was told 'Some good anti-Jewish stuff'. Wolkoff also ascertained from 'X' that the writer was a friend of Joyce's.

Jowitt then reported that Wolkoff handed the letter to Miss 'A', an undercover agent, for forwarding to Joyce. The next day, Wolkoff had second thoughts because she asked Miss 'A' if the letter could be recovered because she had something 'more important' to add. As a consequence, Miss 'A' recovered the letter. Wolkoff visited her at her flat on 11 April 1940 and, using Miss 'A's own typewriter, she added a few words of her own in German.

According to Jowitt, Miss 'A' then took the letter to 'our authorities' who decided to photograph both the original letter and Anna's postscript. They then forwarded the envelope to Joyce.

As the letter had been 'intercepted' by MI5, it beggars belief that it would have actually then been forwarded to William Joyce but in a pre-trial statement, Maxwell Knight wrote that, 'As it was desired that Lord Haw-Haw should receive this communication and reply to it, I gave the letter to a Secret Service agent and asked him to see that it was posted in Italy'.

The routing of the letter was not revealed at Kent's trial and in his version, Jowitt immediately jumped to its supposed acknowledgement:

> It is interesting to record that shortly after the letter would have reached Joyce, a broadcasting station calling itself the 'New British Broadcasting Station'

but in fact operating from Germany broadcast a talk containing the following sentences: 'We thank the French for nothing. Where is their Shakespeare? Who is their Carlyle?' This, no doubt, was the acknowledgement 'by Carlyle reference' for which the letter to Joyce had asked.

Jowitt's explanation of 'the acknowledgment' clearly lacks precision, perhaps intentionally, and he then distanced himself from the story of how the Coded Letter had been passed to Wolkoff by saying that this was Wolkoff's version of events. He reported that 'as 'X' was never identified, he could not be called as a witness at the trial'.

Jowitt also reported that Wolkoff had made enquiries about 'X' from Captain Ramsay who advised her to have nothing to do with him because he was believed to have several aliases. Despite Ramsay's advice, Wolkoff had handed the letter to Miss 'A'.

Possibly without realising, the Earl Jowitt provided a valuable clue that pointed to the identity of 'X' by revealing that Captain Ramsay had 'believed [him] to have several aliases'.

The man who fitted this profile was James Hughes. He had been listed as a member of Ramsay's Right Club as Hughes, his real name. He had also been a senior member of the BUF[13] under the alias of P.G. Taylor. The Special Branch Report confirmed this assumption and also identified 'the young naval officer' who had introduced him to Wolkoff as Lord Ronald Graham (1912-1978), the second son of the 6th Duke of Montrose.

MI5 had previously identified Graham as one of the leading members of the Right Club in a report dated 2 October 1939 and Tyler Kent had mentioned him at his trial as his having been among the 'four or five' other members of the Right Club that he had met[14].

---

[13] The 'British Union of Fascists' changed its name first to the 'British Union of Fascists and National Socialists' and finally to the 'British Union'. The 'British Union of Fascists' (or BUF) is used throughout, for simplicity.

[14] Apart from the Ramsays, the others were: Anna Wolkoff, Anne de Lennep, Enid Riddell and Christabel Nicholson.

A further MI5 report dated 14 April 1940, based on information collected by its undercover agents stated that 'Lord Ronald Graham claims to have a friend at the CID[15] who gives him information. It is known, of course, that the Right Club regard P.G. Taylor as a CID man but it is almost certain that this reference is not to Taylor, as P.G. Taylor was present when the conversation took place'[16].

In a further report, dated 3 May 1940, one of the undercover agents revealed that 'Captain Ramsay stated that he had heard from P.G. Taylor that he himself, Anna Wolkoff and Lord Ronald Graham were all being specially investigated by MI5 at the moment and that there was a great deal of information on record about their current activities'.

If this piece of intelligence was dropped to persuade those who were being 'specially investigated' to take their incriminating material round to Tyler Kent for 'diplomatic protection', it obviously worked.

In his version of the Wolkoff case, Jowitt had claimed that 'I need not set out her evidence in detail, for I have tried to summarise it fairly. After certain witnesses as to character had been called and Anna herself had given evidence, her father and Captain Ramsay were called.'

Fairly? Well, hardly. There were indeed 'certain witnesses as to character' including Admiral Reginald Hall, Britain's legendary spymaster in WWI. However, Lord Ronald Graham who was also called went beyond testifying as to her character by confirming that he had introduced Hughes to Wolkoff. He had also said that she had not told him anything about the letter. Of course, if Graham did not know about the letter then he would not have known that it was in code.

Sir Oswald Mosley also appeared. According to Malcolm Muggeridge, he was 'bearded at this time, his suit crumpled, speaking in the vibrant voice of a wronged man who asked only to be allowed to join his regiment in the battle-line to fight for

[15] Criminal Investigation Department.
[16] KV2/677.

King and Country'[17].

The Special Branch report corroborated Muggeridge's claim that Mosley had testified but it went further because Mosley had also said that he knew Hughes as P.G. Taylor and that he had been the Industrial Adviser to the BUF. Mosley had added that 'he believed that Taylor was a spy for some Government Department but notwithstanding that belief, he had continued to have him in his movement because of his undoubted ability and aptitude for the work'.

Anna Wolkoff would subsequently claim that Hughes was 'a character with three aliases, one of which I believe was Cunningham who was an MI2 man' and that the woman to whom she had passed the letter was employed by MI5 and that she was 'a drug fiend'[18].

Captain Ramsay had also appeared as a character witness for Wolkoff but Malcolm Muggeridge reported that a letter of his had been read out in court in which he had referred to 'those two lovely ships (*Scharnhorst* and *Gneisenau*) and how sad it would be if anything happened to them'. This provided Jowitt with the opportunity to ask Ramsay 'Was this the way to speak about two enemy warships?' Ramsay had explained that when he wrote the letter it still seemed that the war, though declared, would 'never get going'.

Jowitt carefully refrained from denouncing Ramsay in his book because with Ramsay still alive, he could have exposed himself to an action for defamation. What Jowitt had said in Court was 'privileged' but what he said outside of Court was not. The problem that Jowitt faced was that although Ramsay had been interned, he had never been convicted or even tried so, unlike Kent and Wolkoff, he had survived his spell in jail with his reputation sufficiently intact to support a libel action, whereas Kent and Wolkoff had lost their reputations in the eyes of the law as a result of their having been convicted of serious criminal

---

[17] Malcolm Muggeridge *Chronicles of Wasted Time: Volume 2 - The Infernal Grove* (1973)

[18] Joan Miller corroborated the claim that Hélène de Munck (whom she called 'Helen') had an addiction.

offences.

Clearly, Jowitt had no wish to rouse any sleeping dogs, so he went to the other extreme and gave Ramsay a reasonably glowing testimonial. This delighted Ramsay who interpreted it as a complete vindication for his views, which he then committed to print in *The Nameless War* (1952)[19] published three years before his death in 1955.

The Special Branch listed Admiral and Mme. Wolkoff, Admiral Reginald Hall, Dorothy Newenham, Joyce Tregear and Enid Riddell as having been called as witnesses for her defence. While Admiral Hall had been a force to be reckoned with in WWI, he obviously lacked the pull to help his old friends in their time of need.

Joyce Tregear was the secretary of Norman Hay who with Lancelot Lawton ran the Information and Policy Group. She was a former movie actress who had used the stage name of Lilian Bell. She was interned on 8 August 1940 but her file has not surfaced in the National Archives. All that is known is that she died in hospital in Aberdeen in 1961 at the age of 59. She was described as single and a smallholder at an address in Smithton, Inverness. Her father had been a Lieutenant Colonel in the Indian Army. Dorothy Newenham and Enid Riddell were also interned.

The last witness called by Wolkoff's Defence was a Process Server who testified that he had endeavoured to trace Hughes and serve a subpoena upon him, but without success. This was bizarre because Hughes who lived at 144 Sloane Street SW1 was listed in the London telephone directory where his number was shown as SLOane 5911.

The Gestapo even listed Hughes/Taylor/Howard twice in their *Informationsheft GB* - Special Wanted List GB - prepared in anticipation of the planned German invasion in 1940. Walter Schellenberg[20] has claimed responsibility for the *Informationsheft GB* but it is believed that two German students

---

[19] Jowitt's account of the Kent and Wolkoff trials had been published previously in a London newspaper.
[20] Schellenberg rose through the ranks to become Brigadefuehrer (Brigadier General) and General of Police and Waffen SS.

resident in pre-war Britain did the legwork. Although both entries contained glaring inaccuracies, Schellenberg's sources were evidently better than the Process Server's:

189   **Howard**, brit, Cpt, London S.W.1, Sloane Street 144, Deckname: Hughes, auch S C **Tavlor**[21], RSHA IV E 4.

199   **Hughes**, James Mogurk[22], richtig: **Howard**, brit, Cpt, London S.W.1, Sloane Street 144, RSHA E 4.

Nothing at all is known about what Hughes had got up to when posing as Cunningham or Captain Howard but there are many references to him under his alias of P.G. Taylor.

Knight gave a progress report on Wolkoff's trial on 3 November 1940[23]. He was pleased that his two witnesses had done 'very well' with one of them having to submit to a 'very ruthless and personal cross-examination'. He had briefed Sir William Jowitt, the Solicitor-General, about the various character witnesses that she intended to call and he claimed that Jowitt seemed 'very satisfied'. Jowitt was only worried about Hughes and wondered whether or not it was incumbent upon him to assist the defence in locating Hughes. He had asked the Director of Public Prosecutions for guidance and was waiting for an opinion. Whatever guidance he was given, he certainly did not assist the defence.

So, contrary to Jowitt's later claim in *Some Were Spies*, he clearly had known more about Hughes than he had admitted.

On the Third Day of Kent's trial, the Prosecution introduced a witness who had not originally been listed to appear. He was Malcolm Argles Frost who described himself as 'the Director of Intelligence at the British Broadcasting Corporation'. Frost had been brought in to substantiate the claim that William Joyce had

---

[21] A corruption of 'P.G. Taylor'.
[22] The name on his Birth Certificate is 'James McGuirk Hughes'. Sometimes, he called himself 'Hughes' but at other times he was 'McGuirk Hughes', with or without a hyphen.
[23] KV 2/872.

broadcast the word 'Carlyle', the acknowledgment signal specified in the Coded Letter.

According to the transcript of Kent's trial, Frost was asked: 'Was it your duty to supervise the broadcasts from what I will call the New British Broadcasting Station?' Frost agreed that it was. He was then asked:

> Was the following broadcast in the programme of the New British Broadcasting Station: 'We thank the French for nothing: where is their Shakespeare? Who is their Carlyle? But we have certainly been told that they excel in mathematics. Certainly, at a glance, they excel in this respect. But Isaac Newton can probably hold his own about Coué. (Reference to French music). The world looks to Handel, Wagner and Verdi but, in this respect, we need not at least hide our heads from the French. These comparisons might go on forever in the world of art and science.' Was that broadcast in English?

Frost answered 'Yes' but Kent's defence counsel failed to challenge what was clearly hearsay evidence and significantly no evidence was introduced that Joyce had actually used any of the material that Wolkoff had supposedly sent him other than the word 'Carlyle'.

It is now known that Malcolm Frost was yet another MI5 officer. He had been seconded from the British Broadcasting Corporation to head up the new Section 'W' (for Wireless). He also became a member of its powerful Security Executive that was better known as the 'Swinton Committee' that actually ran MI5. At the time he was a very big fish.

The quote was typical Joyce. It is highly likely that he had made the broadcast that Frost had attributed to him on the afternoon of Saturday 27 April 1940. So it all fitted together nicely except that earlier Hélène de Munck had testified that Wolkoff had 'heard from one of the members who listened to the wireless … when Lord Haw-Haw speaks; and she knew he had got it'. According to de Munck, Anna had informed her of Lord Haw-Haw's supposed acknowledgment on 8 May 1940.

De Munck's testimony was not only hearsay but it was also weak and unconvincing. Presumably this was why Frost had been drafted in even though his testimony actually conflicted with de Munck's because, although Joyce did broadcast on NBBS, he never spoke in the persona of Lord Haw-Haw.

The New British Broadcasting Station (NBBS) was a clandestine station that had started broadcasting 'black propaganda'[24] on 25 February 1940. It purported to be a station set up in Britain by dissidents, although it was actually being beamed in by short wave from Berlin and elsewhere.

Joyce is said to have been responsible for much of its material, possibly 90%. In the early days, he had made a few broadcasts himself as 'The Professor', an allusion to a nickname that he had been given on first joining the BUF. Joyce never appeared on that station as Lord Haw-Haw because this would have destroyed the illusion that it was being broadcast from somewhere within Britain.

There was even speculation that Captain Ramsay might have been a speaker. Joyce was an excellent mimic but some of his friends may have recognised him from his material, much of which he was recycling from his pre-war speeches. Otherwise it is unlikely that many listeners would have been able to identify him with any certainty.

The MI5 files released into the National Archives in 2001 reveal precisely how Wolkoff had 'attempted to communicate with William Joyce'.

Lord Ronald Graham had set up the meeting between Hughes and Wolkoff on 9 April 1940; Hughes had propositioned Anna and she had accepted the Coded Letter that he had said he wished to send to William Joyce. Later that same day, Anna had consulted Captain Ramsay but notwithstanding his advice, she had fallen for the ploy of an MI5 undercover agent that same evening.

---

[24] 'White propaganda' was broadcast from recognisably German stations.

Hélène de Munck, the Belgian-born mystic who had already gained Anna Wolkoff's confidence, visited the Russian Tea Rooms and 'casually' mentioned to Admiral Wolkoff that she had a friend at the Rumanian Legation who was leaving for the Continent within a few days. The old Admiral swallowed the bait and bustled off to give Anna the news.

Anna rushed over to de Munck, asked for confirmation and demanded, 'Why didn't you tell me this before?' Anna then handed de Munck the letter.

So Anna's crime was to take the Coded Letter from one Government undercover agent and to pass it to another. Given the circumstances, it is not difficult to figure out that the letter had actually been written within MI5. The content of the Coded Letter also provides further corroboration.

# 9: The Coded Letter

The Coded Letter that Anna Wolkoff 'attempted' to send to William Joyce on 9 April 1940 was introduced into evidence at Kent's Trial and at her own trial. According to Jowitt, she had testified that she did not know what it contained other than 'some good anti-Jewish stuff'. The Judge observed that 'if that be true, it makes your offence more serious'.

If this were true, how could she have determined that her Postscript was 'more important'? Or how could she have known that it contained an acknowledgement signal and that the word 'Carlyle' was the one to listen out for? Possibly she had been given a plain text version that she had chosen to destroy or, more likely, she may have been told that Joyce had received the letter.

The envelope itself was strange because it was addressed to 'Herr W.B. Joyce, Rundfunkhaus, Berlin' although William Joyce did not have a middle name. This puzzled Margaret, Joyce's widow, while she was collaborating with J.A. Cole on his biography[1]. She thought that Wolkoff 'was unlikely to know that he had a second Christian name'. Of course, it was never alleged that Wolkoff had written either the envelope or the letter and according to Jowitt, Wolkoff had simply ascertained from 'X' that the writer was a friend of Joyce's.

Notwithstanding Margaret Joyce's comment, her late husband only had one forename. His English-born Protestant mother, the former Gertrude Emily Brooke, had wanted to name him 'William Brooke Joyce': 'William' after her father and 'Brooke' to perpetuate her own maiden name. This was an English tradition but Michael Francis Joyce, her Irish-born Catholic husband, didn't go along with the idea. The Catholic tradition was for the second name to have some religious significance, such as a Saint's name. Gertrude had already accepted that their children should be brought up as Catholics.

Perhaps as a sop, Michael had conceded that their son could be christened in church in accordance with his wife's wishes, a

---

[1] J.A. Cole *Lord Haw-Haw and William Joyce: The Full Story* (1964).

meaningless gesture. As far as can be established, William Joyce never used a middle name or even the initial 'B'.

There was no such mistake on any of the documents produced at Joyce's own trial for High Treason in 1945 or on his death certificate.

Detective-Inspector Thompson was called upon to identify the Coded Letter when it was introduced into evidence at Kent's Trial. This he did from the three German words along the top: Schlüsselwort - Weissreich - Spitzname. However, some copies of the letter in the MI5 files show that 'Alphabetische System' preceded the three other German words but this was only one of several slightly different versions

When asked if 'Weissreich' meant anything to him, Thompson replied that 'The Fascists had their headquarters, when they started, in a school called Whitelands in Chelsea'[2]. No questions were raised about 'Schlüsselwort' or 'Spitzname' but all three words had presumably been introduced to indicate that the message had been enciphered using a method that involved the use of a Keyword (Schlüsselwort) that would be required for decoding. The nickname of Whitelands was 'The Black House', so the Keyword may have been THEBLACKHOUSE or possibly BLACKHOUSE.

As Mosley had sacked Joyce in 1937, Joyce would not have found this amusing and it is unlikely that any of his friends would have made such a barbed reference.

But notwithstanding the clue, the Keyword turned out to be HACKENSCHMIDT[3], which has no evident relationship with 'Weissreich'. The authors may have been deliberately obscure to allow for the possibility that Anna Wolkoff could have handed the Coded Letter to Tyler Kent, for example, and – being a code and cipher clerk – Kent may have been able to arrange for its decryption. The authors may not have wanted to make it too easy.

---

[2] Mosley's British Union of Fascists had used Whitelands in King's Road Chelsea as their HQ from 1933 to 1935.
[3] This may have been an allusion to George Hackenschmidt, a famous strong man and wrestler, who was known as 'The Russian Bear'.

Hugh Rose Foss, a code breaker from GC&CS (Government Code and Cipher School), then testified that he had been able 'to work out' Exhibit 6 - The Coded Letter. He had found out 'the real meaning' and had produced 'a translation' which was introduced as Exhibit 17.

The Prosecuting Counsel then asked 'If Mr. Healy (Kent's Defence Counsel) wants to know how you worked it out, you can tell him?' Foss answered 'Yes'. Healy then cross-examined Foss with what might be the most inane question in the annals of British criminal justice. 'Were you able to make use of telepathy when you worked it out?' Foss replied 'No, Sir' and then withdrew. That brought an end to proceedings on the Second Day of the Kent's trial.

Had the Prosecution produced the same witness at Wolkoff's trial, surely her own Counsel would not have been so facetious? Wouldn't any Defence Counsel worth his salt have challenged the code breaker to prove that his interpretation was correct?

Although unchallenged, Foss actually consolidated the reputation of the GC&CS by being perfectly correct.

Mr. Justice Tucker quoted from the translation of the Coded Letter in his Summing Up and Jowitt published some carefully selected extracts from the 'translation' but the paragraphs that he chose not to publish (which have been under-lined[4]) clearly point to the writer having had access to some very privileged information. Several commentators have provided interpretations of the more cryptic comments.

The following is this author's effort:

> Talks effect splendid news bulletins less so. Palestine good but IRA etc. defeats object. Stick to plutocracy. Avoid King.

---

[4] Several slightly different versions are now available. The text shown here has been taken from the MI5 File on Captain Ramsay KV 2/678 (579), punctuated in accordance with the trial transcripts.

These 'instructions' corresponded with the material that was already being broadcast by Joyce in his persona of Lord Haw-Haw, so the advice was redundant.

> Reception on mediums fair but BBC 376 tends to swamp, while BBC 391 and Toulouse try squeeze Bremen and Hamburg off air at times. Why not try Bremen at 500? Bremen 2 on longs very weak, needs powerful set to get.

> On shorts Podiebrad difficult. DXQ easier but always distorted even on big set. DJI not bad. DXB very hard as 31 band overcrowded. 49 to Africa, but all round reception on shorts much inferior to Rome stations

The reception information appears authentic and it may have been introduced to lend credibility to the remainder of the message.

> Here Kriegshetze only among Blimps. Workers fed up, wives more so. Troops not keen. Anti-Semitism spreading like flame everywhere, all classes.

> Note refujews in so-called Pioneer Corps guaranteed in writing to be sent into firing line.

> Churchill not popular. Keep on at him as Baruch tool and war-theatre-extender, sacrificer Gallipoli, etc. Stress his conceit and repeated failures with ex-proselytes and prestige.

'Kriegshetze' means haste for war; 'Blimps' were diehard military types who were characterised in cartoons drawn by 'Blimp', the pen name of David Low. The claim that 'anti-Semitism was spreading like flame everywhere' was false and was probably introduced to appeal to Wolkoff who would have wished it to be true.

'Refujews' means Refugee Jews, a term of abuse apparently coined by the BUF. It is unlikely that any Jews had been 'guaranteed in writing' that they would be sent to the firing line. On the contrary, many Jewish immigrants were interned and others who were recruited were consigned to the Pioneer Corps, where they would have no need for any weapons. Certainly many Jewish volunteers had a burning wish to fight Hitler because of his persecution of the Jews.

Winston Churchill was First Lord of the Admiralty at the time, the same position that he had held during the First War until he was forced to resign on 25 May 1915. It was generally believed that he had been unseated by the disastrous Gallipoli campaign that he had championed. Churchill was later exonerated.

Bernard Baruch was an American-Jewish financier and a 'Wall Street Legend'. He was very friendly with Churchill and gave him investment advice but, as with any investment adviser, it was not always good advice. In 1931, Baruch contributed £100 to a fund that was being raised to present Churchill with 'the best Rolls-Royce that money could buy'. Churchill would step up as Prime Minister on 10 May 1940.

> Altmark atrocities debunked by Truth. This is only free paper, circulation bounding. Editor fearless anti-warmonger and lie exposer. Big man behind paper, no fear ruin.

The 'Altmark' was a German supply ship from which some 300 British Merchant Navy prisoners had been rescued in February 1940 while it was sheltering in a Norwegian fjord. This incident, initiated by Churchill, had preceded the Norwegian campaign. It had also created many claims and counter-claims: that the British had infringed neutral territory, which was true; that the British had used 'dum-dum' bullets[5], which was considered very ungentlemanly and contrary to the agreed rules of war and that the Altmark was actually armed.

The British propaganda machine had also shouted 'atrocity' by claiming that one of the prisoners had leprosy and that by forcing him to live among the other prisoners, the Germans had risked their catching the disease. Apparently it wasn't leprosy, just some non-contagious skin condition. By April 1940, the

---

[5] Dum-dum bullets were designed to fragment on impact, rather than make a (theoretical) nice clean hole.

Altmark story was stale particularly as William Joyce had already used it in a broadcast that he had made in February.

*Truth* was an anti-Jewish paper that made regular attacks on Churchill, even after he became Prime Minister. Later, it also agitated for the release of political detainees. Its editor was Henry Newnham, a friend of Prime Minister Neville Chamberlain. It is now known that Sir Joseph Ball, the Director of Research for the Conservative Party, had secretly controlled *Truth* since 1936.

A former MI5 officer, Ball was also a close friend of Neville Chamberlain and his personal adviser on intelligence matters. Later, Ball became the deputy chairman of the Home Defence (Security) Executive, better known as the 'Swinton Committee', which had been put together 'to clean up MI5'. It also had a say on the fates of the political detainees. Curiously, this coincided with *Truth*'s campaign for their release.

It is evident that the 'big man' was either Ball or possibly even Prime Minister Chamberlain himself. It is highly unlikely that anyone other than a very privileged insider would have been aware of Ball's involvement with *Truth* at that time.

Collin Brooks who had been Lord Rothermere's personal assistant for many years, took over as Editor of *Truth* in November 1940. Later, Brooks revealed in his journals that Lord Luke of Pavenham ('the Bovril King') had funded the operation.

> Nearly all your friends still sound, e.g. pay gay 00 hundred percent ...

With a rating of '00 hundred percent', pay gay was evidently considered totally unsound which was fair comment because pay gay was probably a teasing reference to P.G. Taylor who, under his real name of Hughes, had handed the Coded Letter to Wolkoff.

This was an in-joke because Taylor was actually a freelance Intelligence Agent who did subcontract work for Special Branch. As P.G. Taylor, he had served Mosley as his Industrial Adviser. Mosley and others in the BUF offices knew about Taylor's intelligence activities and they all considered it amusing.

Joyce had once been a leading member of the BUF and he would certainly have known Taylor because they had both served on its 'Research Directory', a sort of management committee.

### ... though Lewis wants murder you.

It has been suggested that Lewis may have been a reference to Ted 'Kid' Lewis, a former world champion boxer. Originally known as Gershon Mendeloff, he was a Jew of Russian extraction who had fought his way to the top from a life of poverty in London's East End. Mosley had taken him onto the payroll of his New Party for his publicity value.

The Kid had taught boxing in the New Party's Youth Clubs, acted as Mosley's bodyguard and had even stood as a Parliamentary candidate in the October 1931 elections. The party performed abysmally and collapsed soon after. At that time, Mosley did not have an anti-Jewish stance. This came later after the New Party had metamorphosed into the BUF.

Joyce had never been a member of the New Party and The Kid had never been a member of the BUF so the two men may not have known each other except by reputation. Joyce's hatred of the Jews was common knowledge and doubtless his feelings were reciprocated.

However, there is another Lewis: Captain Charles Cecil Courtney Lewis, whom the writer may have had in mind. Charles Lewis was a solicitor who had joined the BUF in its early days. He had known Joyce previously and it is likely that he persuaded him to join. Lewis had been the first Editor of *Blackshirt* and a director of several BUF companies. He had also been in overall charge of their accounts and this could be relevant because, according to Joyce, the 'real' reason that Mosley had dismissed him was because of an allegation of some financial irregularity.

Joyce had denied the allegation and he had insisted that it had been based on a forgery designed 'to blacken his name'. Joyce's friend John Angus Macnab, who had survived Mosley's cutback, had investigated the allegation and had found evidence that it was, indeed, a forgery. However, instead of Mosley showing any appreciation, Macnab was also 'evicted'.

John Beckett, another former Blackshirt, had also been kicked off the payroll in March 1937 but unlike Joyce, he had been invited to stay on as a voluntary worker. Joyce had never been given that option, presumably because of the alleged financial irregularity. However, Beckett's finances did not permit him to make such a gesture and he demanded a termination settlement. This did not endear him to the Leader and Beckett left as well.

Beckett was later detained under DR 18B (1A) and when interviewed on 10 July 1940 by the Advisory Committee Beckett revealed that:

> There was a deliberate and to my mind most discreditable case manufactured against him [Joyce] that would not bear examination. When I went to Mosley and protested about Joyce being expelled on such evidence, he produced some documents that seemed to prove that Joyce was something of a dishonest liar, but I happened to know the man, a man called Alexander Scrimgeour ... who had financed the British Union. I went to see him and saw the original documents of which Mosley had shown me copies and they bore out what Joyce said and not what Mosley said. I gave an ultimatum to Mosley that unless Joyce was given a fair hearing I should resign.

Beckett did resign and a further consequence was that Alec Scrimgeour, a wealthy stockbroker and previously one of the BUF's main sponsors, also transferred his support to the National Socialist League. This would have seriously hurt the BUF's finances and would have made Mosley hopping mad. Consequently, those in the know about the source of the movement's funding presumably including Lewis, would certainly have wished to 'murder' Joyce, at least metaphorically.

However, with Joyce in Germany beyond the reach of either Lewis the comment seems pointless. It may therefore have been introduced to impress Wolkoff with the writer's familiarity with the circumstances of Joyce's dismissal from the BUF.

All league sound.

The 'league' was the National Socialist League that Joyce and Beckett had started in April 1937 shortly after Oswald Mosley had dismissed them from the BUF. It never really got off the ground and when Alex Scrimgeour, its chief sponsor, died in August 1937, it effectively collapsed.

Joyce reorganised it in October 1938 when it became largely a family affair. Joyce was then the only director. Margaret his wife, Quentin his brother and Joan his sister were listed among the 'H.Q. Officers'. It had degenerated into holding street-corner meetings four times a week. Joyce officially closed it down shortly before he left for Germany. By any test, it could hardly have been described as 'sound'.

Family not persecuted by public but only by Anderson who keeps Q. imprisoned without trial and got F. and R. sacked BBC. Still family not in distress, master teaching school again.

Sir John Anderson was the Home Secretary; Q, F and R were Joyce's brothers: Quentin, Frank and Robert. Quentin, who was suspected of espionage, was arrested on 6 September 1939 and detained for nearly four years. Frank and Robert had worked for the BBC but the BBC had been leaned on to dismiss them. This wasn't generally known in April 1940 and this also shows that the writer had access to some very privileged information.

Frank would later be arrested 'during a weekend round-up' reported on 3 June 1940. He was detained for about eleven months and then joined the Royal Air Force. Robert joined the Army as a regular soldier and served with the Royal Electrical and Mechanical Engineers. He was 'very technical' and took part in the Italian campaign with the 8th Army.

William Joyce also had a sister, Joan, who had worked in the Ministry of Food until December 1939 when she was dismissed, presumably also following pressure from MI5. Joan then went to Ireland and worked in Dublin as a typist for the Irish Broadcasting Service. She returned to London after the war and was once spotted working as a clippie on the London buses. She was then married to a London policeman. Her married name helped to distance her from her late brother who had brought her unwanted infamy by association.

'Master' was the nickname given to John Angus Macnab, a former member of Mosley's BUF and Joyce's National Socialist League. He had been Joyce's erstwhile partner in a coaching school, hence schoolmaster. He was among those detained in May 1940. He remained a good friend to Joyce and helped J.A. Cole, Joyce's biographer. After the war, he emigrated to Spain and wrote a book on bullfighting.

Baphomet (or B.A.P. Home T.) very friendly, wife also.

This is the most cryptic and the most interesting phrase in the Coded Letter because the original typewritten version in the MI5 files simply reads 'Baphomet very friendly, wife also'. The bracketed part '(or B.A.P. Home T.)' had been superimposed in ink, as though someone had decided to improve on the code breaker's initial offering.

'Baphomet' has several meanings but in this context it suggests an allusion to the mediaeval name for Mohammed, the prophet who came to power reputedly through a bloodless coup. However, it is rather meaningless without the amplification in brackets. Emphasis on the word 'Home' suggests a cryptic reference to Oswald Mosley the leader of the BUF who was known as 'OM' within the movement. Like Mohammed, Mosley also saw himself as a prophet and since 1932, he had cherished the hope of making a 'march to power' or, in other words, staging a 'bloodless coup'.

Following his dismissal by Mosley in 1937, Joyce had grown to detest his former leader and if the phrase were to be interpreted as assumed, it could only have caused offence. In his book *Dämmerung über England (Twilight Over England)*, Joyce referred to 'the sons of Baphomet' as 'agents of International Darkness' so the writer may have been familiar with his fondness for the word, although not from that book that was first published in Germany in 1940.

Mosley's second wife, Diana, was also a prominent personality although she never actively participated in the movement until after her husband had been interned on 23 May 1940. She had then stepped into the breach by paying wages until she was herself interned on 29 June 1940.

> Ironside believed very anti-Jewish, not so anti-German, possible British Franco if things reach that stage here.

This is a very illuminating phrase because General Edmund Ironside was the Chief of the Imperial General Staff and he was, indeed, anti-Jewish. He was also believed to be sympathetic to Oswald Mosley's BUF and may even have been a secret member. He had wanted to promote Major-General J.F.C. Fuller, a leading expert on tank warfare and a prominent member of the BUF.

Fuller was never promoted but he was never interned either. Sonia[6], his wife, explained this by claiming that 'he knew too much'. Certainly, according to Ironside's Diary, Britain was totally ill-prepared to wage a war against Germany and he was scathing about the designs of the two tanks that were in the pipeline.

At his own request, Ironside gave up as Chief of the Imperial General Staff on 25 May 1940 to become Commander-in-Chief Home Forces, a job that he found 'much more to his liking'. On 12 July 1940, he was tipped off that there was a 'whispering campaign' going on about him. A week later on the 19th July, he was dismissed but 'in order that the matter should be placed on a good footing' he was later promoted Field Marshal and elevated to the Lords.

Malcolm Muggeridge, who was investigating the loyalty of the military on behalf of the Field Security Police, would later reveal in his autobiography[7] that he received a report that Ironside's car was often seen standing outside a house in Holland Park, some of whose occupants were known to have 'dubious

---

[6] Fuller married Margarethe Auguste Karnatz, who was always known as Sonia, in 1906.
[7] *Chronicles of Wasted Time - Part 2 The Infernal Grove* (1973).

political associations'. Ironside was sacked the day after Muggeridge had submitted his report. However, Muggeridge never discovered whether or not this was sheer coincidence.

Muggeridge may have only corroborated earlier concerns because Knight's undercover agent M/Y (Marjorie Mackie) had reported on 17 January 1940 that 'Ramsay was being urged by the leading members of the Right Club to get in touch with General Ironside'[8]. Another MI5 undercover agent M/G had also reported Admiral Wolkoff's hope for a revolution under Ironside. None of these reports would have been helpful to Ironside's career prospects.

Certainly, if there were to have been a military coup, then Ironside would have been regarded by MI5 as the most likely leader and hence the allusion to General Franco, the leader of the Spanish Fascists. With help from Hitler and Mussolini, Franco had established a totalitarian state in Spain.

At that time, the political leanings of Ironside would have been very privileged information. After the war, Ironside was a prominent member of the League of Empire Loyalists another extreme right-wing group formed by A.K. Chesterton, once a leading member of the BUF.

> Butter ration doubled because poor can't buy, admitted by Telegraph, bacon same. Cost living steeply mounting. Shopkeepers suffering. Suits PEP.

> Regret must state Meg's Tuesday talks unpopular with women. Advise alter radically or drop. God bless and salute to all leaguers and CB.

'Telegraph' clearly refers to the *Daily Telegraph* newspaper; 'PEP' stood for Political and Economic Planning, which had been founded in 1931 to plan for a British recovery from the Great Depression. It carried out investigations into the British economy, education and health. The inclusion of Jewish businessmen made it a particular target for abuse because it provided 'proof' that it was a Jews' war.

---

[8] KV 2/677 (141a).

Meg was a reference to Joyce's second wife, Margaret, who had gone with him to Germany. She also worked on the Nazi propaganda service and made occasional broadcasts. Later, when Margaret Joyce was collaborating with J.A. Cole on his biography, she observed that it was unlikely that Wolkoff 'not being an intimate of the family' would have referred to her in the letter as 'Meg'. Although Margaret Joyce had completely missed the point that it had never been alleged that Wolkoff had written any part of the letter except the Postscript, the cosy familiarity was clearly out of place.

'CB' probably stood for Christian Baur, Joyce's pre-war German contact in London, whom both Joyce and MI5 had assumed to be a German spy. Perhaps, like other journalists, he may have been passing information to the German authorities. However, he apparently had no influence and was unable to help Joyce on his arrival in Germany.

> Acknowledge this by Carlyle reference radio not
> Thurs or Sun. Reply same channel, same Cipher.

'Carlyle' was either a very good or a very bad choice for an acknowledgement signal. It was good from the point of view of MI5 who were looking for confirmation that Joyce had received the Coded Letter but it was bad from any other point of view because Joyce was always referring to Thomas Carlyle who was one of his idols.

In Joyce's opinion, Carlyle had been the 'first Fascist' and when Joyce had founded the National Socialist League in 1937 after having been dismissed by Mosley, he also established a drinking club called 'the Carlyle Club'. Carlyle also had a homonym, 'Carlisle', so it was altogether inappropriate as an authentic acknowledgement signal.

> P.S. If possible, please give again sometime in the week, the broadcast which the German radio gave in German about three days ago, namely: The Freemasons Meeting - The Grand Orient in Paris, 1931 where Lord Ampthill was also present. It is now

141

very important that we hear more about the Jews and Freemasons. P.J.

Wolkoff had contributed the Postscript, which she had written in German; Lord Ampthill was a senior British Freemason; and 'P.J.' stood for 'Perish Judah', the slogan of several anti-Jewish groups.

It is significant that the author of the Coded Letter was never identified. Moreover, he was never even sought! This suggests that someone in MI5 had crafted the letter, possibly Maxwell Knight himself.

Similarly, the inclusion of the very privileged information regarding the 'Big Man' behind *Truth*, General Ironside, and the fate of Joyce's three brothers makes it extremely unlikely that the Coded Letter would have been forwarded to William Joyce, as had been claimed.

# 10: The Joyce Cipher

Any possible doubts about the authorship of the Coded Letter were attenuated when an MI5 file on William Joyce was released into the National Archives on 10 November 2000. Described as 'William Joyce artefacts: The Joyce Cipher'[1], its contents appear to give the game away.

It contains a plastic insert holding two pieces of graph paper both marked SECRET: one piece, headed 'Model for Vigenère Cipher', carries the letters of the alphabet across its centre and was described as 'Fixed Alphabet'. The other piece described as 'Moving Alphabet' carries two copies of the alphabet side-by-side across its bottom edge.

A two-page document[2] headed 'The Joyce Cipher' also marked SECRET provides 'Instructions for Enciphering' using 'the Vigenère system with straight alphabets'. The document shows the methodology, using the Keyword HACKENSCHMIDT. It involved finding the first letter of the Keyword ('H') on the Moving Alphabet and positioning it above the letter 'A' on the Fixed Alphabet. The first letter of the word to be encoded (say 'T') is then located on the Fixed Alphabet and its cipher-equivalent is found on the Moving Alphabet.

The second letter of the Keyword ('A') is then used for the next letter and so on until all thirteen letters of the Keyword have been exhausted, at which stage the cycle is started again and again, as often as necessary.

The document also provides an example, by demonstrating how to encipher the clear text "TALKS EFFECT SPLENDID BUT ..." Apart from the added 'BUT' this is essentially how the decrypt of the Coded Letter starts.

The Code is also reproduced over two pages, the first headed:

---

[1] KV 2/345.
[2] See Appendix: Images for a reproduction of Page 1.

# THE KENT-WOLKOFF AFFAIR

2.IV.40

AANUWRXHLOBVISEPNMPTWAZMZLIUNVIGAPZUMVLZORKPRKVPZMJHVDDEX
VJCLFKGXMECDWBTLLOBVMFCMDSCAWAAKUTJYCFSVVMPZOVMVPZOGRHVPA
RGZEFSYZKHHUZENABDMXUJGLEMYXUSKHXRFFZFWVPHMRGLVDGINKWAYEG

And so on for a further 27 lines.

At the bottom of the second page, a geometric figure captioned 'Schnitt von Schnitten' had been drawn but its significance is not known.

Subject to typos, this decrypts into essentially the same message as the one described by Hugh Rose Foss as the 'real meaning' of the Coded Letter at Tyler Kent's trial. The only difference is the reference to Baphomet. This decrypts into 'Baphomet very friendly, wife also'. In other words, the bracketed phrase '(or B.A.P. Home T.)' is not included but, as previously noted, this had been superimposed in ink, as though someone had decided to improve on the code breaker's initial offering

Most likely, Hugh Rose Foss of GC&CS had supplied the encryption methodology for MI5 but, whoever the provider, the choice of the Vigenère system cannot be faulted.

It was a highly serviceable, easily understood system that had been developed by a Frenchman, Blaise de Vigenère, in the 16th Century. For over 300 years it was considered unbreakable until Major Kasiski of the Prussian Army evolved a method for finding the length of the Keyword by measuring the distance between repeated bigrams in the ciphertext.

Kasiski then divided the message into Keyword lengths and used frequency analysis to suggest a solution. So, even though it was an ancient system it was robust enough for most purposes and yet it would not defeat an expert. Nor was it too obscure, having been described in a 1939 book on cryptography[3].

These days, a computer program can be used to decrypt the ciphertext at lightning speed but in 1940, cracking the code would still have required considerable manual effort unless, as in

---

[3] Fletcher Pratt *Secret and Urgent: The Story of Codes and Ciphers* (1939).

this case, the code breaker knew the system used and its Keyword 'HACKENSCHMIDT'.

Therefore, it would not have presented a challenge to Hugh Rose Foss and he certainly would not have had to resort to telepathy, as Kent's Defence Counsel had facetiously enquired.

It is also significant that the encrypted message was dated 2.IV.40, seven days before James Hughes passed the Coded Letter to Anna Wolkoff on 9 April 1940.

All things considered: the privileged content of the Coded Letter, the explicit instructions for enciphering the message, the code itself dated 2.IV.40, the revelation that the Keyword was 'HACKENSCHMIDT', the later introduction of the bracketed phrase '(or B.A.P. Home T.)' and the facts that the Coded Letter was handed to Anna Wolkoff by James Hughes (a Government undercover agent) and then collected by Hélène de Munck (another Government undercover agent) make a compelling argument for the hypothesis that MI5 created the Coded Letter, specifically for the purpose of its sting operation.

# 11: Kent Speaks

As documents relating to WWII events trickled out of Government archives, new assessments of the Kent-Wolkoff Affair started to appear. Peter and Leni Gillman examined the general topic of internments in wartime Britain in *Collar The Lot!* (1980), taking their title from the order given by Churchill when asked for guidance on the treatment of the Italian residents in Britain when Italy entered the war.

The Gillmans contrasted the different environments leading up to the two world wars and the new problems that had arisen during the Thirties. These included the large numbers of Jewish refugees who had fled from Germany and the Nazi charm offensive designed to foster the belief that they had no designs on Britain or her Empire. The Nazi offers of friendship and co-operation made good sense to many and particularly veterans of WWI who had witnessed the horrors of trench warfare.

With Britain in the depths of an economic depression, Hitler became an inspirational figure and he captured the imagination of those who despaired at the ineffectiveness of the British politicians. Many yearned for a charismatic leader who could take the country forward to emulate the apparent success of the Nazis. Few recognised that Hitler's economic miracle was a sham and that his strategy of building a military machine could only be paid for by an escalating series of conquests.

Hitler cleverly capitalised on a general wish for peace and a perception that Germany had had a raw deal at the end of WWI. A number of organisations took Hitler at his word and echoed his sentiments. The most prominent of these was Sir Oswald Mosley's BUF. In MI5's view, the BUF was pro-German until the declaration of war and pacifist thereafter.

There was also The Link founded by Admiral Sir Barry Domvile, a former director of Naval Intelligence. The Link arranged cultural visits to Germany and Austria to encourage mutual understanding. There were also the supposedly secret societies, specifically the Nordic League and the Right Club, that were vehemently anti-Jewish and various Pacifist outfits spearheaded by the Peace Pledge Union that wasn't a political party and The British People's Party that was. Some, such as Captain Ramsay and Admiral Domvile, were associated with several organisations.

The Gillmans traced the political struggles to toughen the internment regulations. They noted that it was 'stunningly convenient' that Tyler Kent and Anna Wolkoff should have been arrested while there was dissension within the Cabinet about whether or not to crush Britain's putative Fifth Column. The main target was Sir Oswald Mosley's BUF and suspicions centred on various secret meetings that he had held with the leaders of other dissident groups, including Captain Ramsay and Admiral Domvile. Maybe they were planning a coup?

The Cabinet debate on internment started on 11 May 1940, the day following Churchill's appointment as Prime Minister and it was resolved on 22 May 1940, two days after the arrests of Kent and Wolkoff.

Having taken a hard look at the Kent-Wolkoff Affair, the Gillmans noted the gap of six weeks between the date when Wolkoff had 'attempted' to communicate with William Joyce on 9 April 1940 and the date of their arrests on the 20 May. Perceptively, they expressed their opinion that Wolkoff had been set up by MI5. Their opinion was not shared by one naïve reviewer who derided them for having dared to suggest there might have been some kind of conspiracy. 'As if the Security Service would behave in that way', the reviewer had protested.

The Gillmans would not have been aware that the Churchill-Roosevelt exchanges had continued being routed through the American Embassy in the non-confidential Gray Code, as if nothing had happened. Nor that Marjorie Mackie, an MI5 undercover agent, had been stalking Wolkoff since December 1939. Nor that Hélène de Munck, the Belgian-born mystic, had joined her on 1 February 1940. Nor that Joan Miller had been introduced to Wolkoff on 9 April 1940, to fulfil her wish to make contact with one of the young secretaries in MI5. Nor that yet a fourth undercover agent known only as 'Special Source' had joined the investigations on 16 April 1940, just one week after Miller.

It is highly significant that MI5 mounted its sting operation against Wolkoff on the day that Britain and France started their Norwegian campaign. This was effectively the start of the shooting war and it gave due notice to Hitler that the peace talks had failed. Indeed, Chamberlain had told the Conservative Conference on 4 April 1940 that 'Hitler has missed the bus'. Although the Norwegian campaign was a military setback for the Allies, it probably triggered the German invasion of France, Belgium and the Netherlands on 10 May 1940.

It was therefore even more 'stunningly convenient' than the Gillmans had supposed that the Kent-Wolkoff Affair had run in parallel with the Cabinet wrangle over whether or not to crush Britain's putative Fifth Column.

The Tyler Kent Affair attracted the attention of two American academics, Warren F. Kimball and Bruce Bartlett, who published their study *Roosevelt and Pre-war Commitments to Churchill: The Tyler Kent Affair* in *Diplomatic History*[1] (7 September 1981).

Kimball and Bartlett decided that there were actually two stories; one based on the rumours that had circulated about the contents of the Churchill-Roosevelt exchanges before these had been unveiled to the public; the other on their actual contents that became public in 1972. Kimball would become the accepted authority on this material after he published a monumental 3-volume opus *Churchill & Roosevelt: The Complete Correspondence* (1984).

After reviewing the previously published material, the academics dismissed much of the earlier reports, particularly those generated by the 'Roosevelt lied us into war' revisionists like Harry Elmer Barnes and Charles A. Beard. They observed that none of the documents found in Kent's apartment contained anything to substantiate Kent's allegations. 'There was nothing

---

[1] Volume 5, pages 291-311.

about Churchill planning to replace Chamberlain as prime minister, nothing to suggest firm promises to aid England in any secret, illegal way and nothing that even remotely resembled the Lend-Lease concept, which the Roosevelt administration did not put forth until some seven months after Kent's arrest. There was no promise of American intervention by William Bullitt, the US Ambassador in France, and no word of any plan by Roosevelt to circumvent Congress and provide aid to Britain. In fact, the president told Churchill that any transfer of destroyers would have to be approved by Congress.'

Nevertheless, Kimball and Bartlett acknowledged that 'though it is always possible to dismiss official files as selective, in this case it would have taken a vast conspiracy stretching from London to Washington and lasting for over thirty-five years, an unlikely possibility'.

Because the academics considered it 'unlikely' did not mean that it was impossible. In fact, it would have been a relatively simple matter to destroy most, if not all, 'sensitive' documents if the exchanges between Churchill and Roosevelt had covered the topics that Kent claimed to have seen. But in the absence of any documentary evidence what other conclusion could they have reached? Unlike journalists such as Singer, Spiro, Farago and Firmin who readily switch into imaginative fiction, academics are required to base their research on verifiable facts.

They also reviewed Richard Whalen's biography of Joseph Kennedy. They took a highly charitable view of Kennedy and claimed that Whalen 'simply accuses the ambassador of invariably choosing personal interests over professed beliefs'. They also claimed that Kennedy 'had remained personally loyal to Roosevelt but he vehemently condemned the excesses of Hitler's Germany'. However, Roosevelt didn't see it that way, nor did the British. Evidently, the academics didn't realise the extent to which Roosevelt had been helping behind the scenes.

Kimball and Bartlett readily accepted the official line that the 'prime concern of the State Department and the Embassy remained that of communications security, both of specific messages and codes in general'. They regurgitated the story that

'Kent had photographic plates of two highly confidential messages', apparently without realising that the contents were already in the public domain and in the possession of a German Intelligence Agency months before the photographs were taken. They also noted that a further Churchill-Roosevelt telegram had been transmitted in the Gray Code on 12 June 1940. They explained this to their own satisfaction by assuming that 'fear of compromise had obviously subsided by then'. The significance of the Gray Code completely eluded them.

Kimball and Bartlett reported that 'the official British decision to prosecute Tyler Kent was not made until 30 July 1940' and that 'the primary reason for the delay ... was to permit counter-intelligence investigators to complete their checks on the activities of others in the case, particularly Captain Ramsay'. Unfortunately, their source was a report from Joseph Kennedy who had fallen out of favour with Roosevelt and was not in a position to know.

In all probability, the reason for the delay was more likely to see whether or not Roosevelt would win the democratic nomination, which he did on 17 July 1940. Also, as MI5 had been monitoring Captain Ramsay and the Right Club since August 1939, the only 'checks to complete' were the legal and political considerations as to whether or not Ramsay should stand trial.

Kimball and Bartlett took note of Richard Whalen's remark that 'Tyler Kent still has not had his day in an American court. When that day comes, the American people may at last learn what this strange witness can tell of the route they took to war[2]' and concluded that 'in one sense it is clear that Kent never really wanted his day in court and we now know what this strange witness had to tell us - nothing!'

The two academics had taken a lofty view of events without either explaining or, in some cases, even considering the skulduggery that had taken place on both sides of the Atlantic in 1940. In other words, theirs was a conventional restatement of history as officially recorded without realising that if Tyler Kent

---

[2] Richard Whalen, *The Strange Case of Tyler Kent*, p. 64.

had no secrets to disclose, this only added to the mystery, without providing an explanation.

Evidently riled by Kimball and Bartlett's remarks, Tyler Kent finally spoke his piece in September 1982 at the Fourth International Revisionists Convention. Having turned seventy and totally devoid of any public speaking skills, he harangued his audience with his own extreme right wing views and insisted that 'much of the warmongering engaged in by Roosevelt's diplomatic agents in the late 1930s, particularly in France and Poland, was in the form of verbal exhortations and promises of aid and support of all kinds, including direct military intervention'. As he could not have been privy to any 'verbal exhortations', this was not convincing. However, according to Home Office files, it appeared that Kent had revealed details that he had gathered from documents that had been exchanged between the American representatives in Warsaw and the US Government prior to the war[3].

Kent criticised Kimball and Bartlett's account of Roosevelt's pre-war commitments to Churchill and argued that 'these two academicians have poked around in the National Archives and looked at the Roosevelt-Churchill exchange of cables which have so far been published and have come to the conclusion that there is nothing much there worth making a fuss over'.

He claimed that 'much of the American activity was never committed to paper in the exact manner in which it transpired. Thus, to the chagrin of historians, it will never appear in the National Archives as hard facts. Bullitt[4] in France and Biddle[5] in Poland did not commit to paper blunt promises of almost immediate military aid in the event of war but such was the gist of their private conversations.'

This was also nonsensical because if Bullitt and Biddle had not committed their promises to paper then Kent could not

---

[3] HO 45/25696.
[4] Anthony J. Drexel Biddle - The American Ambassador in France.
[5] The American Ambassador in Poland.

possibly have discovered what verbal promises had been made 'in their private conversations'.

Kent addressed the State Department's press release of 2 September 1944 as 'a hodge-podge of innuendo, smears and lies'. He referred to Anna Wolkoff who, according to the police, had a channel of communication with Germany of which she was making use and the clear implication that he was supposed to be transmitting information to Germany through her.

However, he correctly pointed out that his solicitors had requested a copy of the Coded Letter that Wolkoff had attempted to communicate to Joyce. This had brought an admission from the Director of Public Prosecutions that it was not alleged that he had had anything to do with or even knowledge of the sending of the Coded Letter by Wolkoff to Joyce 'nor does the prosecution contend that he acted in concert with his co-defendant, Anna Wolkoff, in this matter'.

Notwithstanding the admission from the Director of Public Prosecutions, Kent complained that the State Department had still disseminated the innuendo that he had some 'vaguely defined' confederates who were attempting to communicate with Germany. He also pointed out that this had not prevented the American press from featuring him in banner headlines such as 'He Helped The Nazis'.

Kent argued that if Kimball and Bartlett had been correct to dismiss his allegations, why all the secrecy? Why was the consent of Prime Minister Winston Churchill required before the proceedings could be initiated? He also noted Ambassador Joseph Kennedy's report to the State Department dated 6 July 1940:

> The British prosecutors further inform me that the proposed defendants take the view that they are safe from trial and punishment because neither of the Governments concerned dare have these matters discussed in public ... The documents in question would certainly be produced only behind locked doors in a cleared court. Not only would the press be

ordered not to publish their contents. No pressman would be present.

Kent asked his audience 'What was it that dared not be discussed in public? That is really the crux of the case'.

Kent reiterated his claim that the Lend-Lease program had been the subject of discussion between Roosevelt and Churchill in their private correspondence for many months. He alleged that Roosevelt had kept stressing that he needed time to overcome the objections of Congress, while Churchill had kept insisting that unless something were done soon, Britain would be forced to her knees.

The grand strategy, he declared, was to preserve the precarious balance of power in Europe and the dominance of the British Navy in the Atlantic, a navy that was also protecting America, so 'Nazi Germany could not under any circumstances be allowed to win in Europe'.

He continued 'Why, if my motive was to keep the United States out of the war, did I show the documents to British subjects? The answer is simple and straightforward. Ramsay and the members of his Right Club all knew that the principal warmongers in Britain were the Churchill, Eden, Duff Cooper, Vansittart gang and it was our joint intention in our amateurish way to undermine Churchill's position in Parliament by making use of some of the American documents I had in my possession. This, it was hoped, could be done through the assistance of Captain Ramsay who was, after all, a Member of Parliament. We all understood that the Western democracies could not emerge from this war as genuine winners. The only real winner would be Bolshevik Russia'.

He ended with a long rant about how much better and safer the world would have been if he had been allowed to expose the conniving politicians. He made no reference to Joan Miller who had surfaced the previous year with her fanciful claims.

Tyler Kent failed to recognise that the Nazis had perfected much more effective ways of silencing dissident voices. Had he been in Germany and if he'd had a run-in with the Gestapo, then it was unlikely that he would have still been around to tell his tale.

# 12: A Vintage Year

Nineteen ninety-one was a vintage year for anyone interested in the Kent-Wolkoff Affair because three very different accounts appeared. Dead men cannot sue for libel, so they may have been inspired by Kent's death in 1988.

John Costello, a British historian with a flair for sensational disclosures, entered the fray with *Ten Days That Saved the West*, published in the US as *Ten Days to Destiny*. Any reader who imagined that these were ten consecutive days would soon be disabused because they weren't 'days'; they were actually 'events'. However, beneath the snappy titles, Costello had unearthed a mass of new material including an interview with Tyler Kent on 10 April 1982 at Phoenix Airport, Arizona.

According to Costello, Kent 'might have passed at a distance for Colonel Saunders with his white goatee and bolo tie … but his sneering high pitched voice, yellowing panama hat and rumpled seersucker suit would not have made him a popular pitch-man for Kentucky Fried Chicken'. Costello discovered that Kent had fallen on hard times and that he and his once wealthy wife had been reduced to living in a mobile home in a Texas trailer park.

The report of their historic meeting was interlarded with a mishmash of background including quotes from Joan Miller, whom Costello would later interview in August 1982. Kent insisted that he had never been a spy and that he had shown his horde of Embassy documents to Ramsay and Wolkoff 'in confidence'. Apparently, Costello accepted Kent's assurances because he then identified the man whom he reckoned was MI5's real target in the American Embassy in London.

In Costello's view, MI5 had used Kent in some way as part of an undercover sting operation to damage the credibility of Joseph Kennedy, the defeatist American Ambassador, so that they could somehow blackmail him into giving his support to Roosevelt. It was, he decided, a case of 'catch a monkey to scare a tiger', as in an old Indian saying.

Costello spotted that Kennedy had cabled Washington on 23 May 1940 to request approval for Eddie Moore[1], his faithful secretary and confidant, to resign and return to the United States. Coming just three days after Kent's arrest, Costello concluded that Kennedy's action 'could only have been a direct response' to this. Five days later, Moore, his wife and Kennedy's daughter Rosemary were on their way. Costello reckoned that 'Kennedy simply did not dare risk Moore being arrested and interrogated under the Official Secrets Act'.

Costello's hypothesis fails because Moore was protected by diplomatic immunity and it is unlikely that Kennedy would have withdrawn the privilege from his trusted lieutenant, particularly if it risked exposing himself to some dreadful consequences. Kennedy had been progressively withdrawing his family from Britain because of the war situation. Rosemary was the last to go because she had 'learning difficulties' and, having found a school that was catering for her needs, Kennedy left her there as long as possible. So, after the shooting war had started in earnest, the Moores were given the task of escorting Rosemary back to the US.

Costello's hypothesis also fails because it was predicated on the assumption that there really was a spy in the American Embassy, as suggested by Guy Liddell's letter to Herschel Johnson on 7 February 1940. An MI6 man calling himself 'Gill of the Foreign Office' had made a follow-up visit on 14 February[2].

Johnson had wanted to learn more about the leakage that, according to Liddell's letter, was being routed through the American Embassy in Berlin. Gill told him that the informant was a German who knew another German named Jahnke who was running an intelligence bureau known as Abteilung Pfeffer in

---

[1] Edward Moore served Joseph P Kennedy 'devotedly' for 40 years and Teddy Kennedy, the youngest of the three brothers, was named 'Edward Moore Kennedy', after him.

[2] 'Gill' evidently worked for Felix Cowgill in MI6 but his real name cannot be determined from his signature. In some versions, it looks like 'H. Irwain'. See KV 2/755. There was apparently a code breaker called Gill in GC&CS, which also came under the Foreign Office

the office of Hess. Gill also confided that the report formed 'part of a long report about chinks in our own armour which thorough investigation had unfortunately shown to be accurate'. The only clue to the source of the leakages that the informant could offer was that he had heard Jahnke say to his translator, in reply to a question as to whether there was any American material on a particular day, 'No, the Doctor has not dictated this morning'.

The Jahnke in question was Kurt Jahnke who during WWI had worked in America as a saboteur based in San Francisco. After America had declared war on Germany in 1917, he moved to Mexico with his colleague Lothar Witzke. Subsequently, they were described as 'the most deadly sabotage team in history'[3]. During the Thirties and beyond, Jahnke had run a semi-private Intelligence Service popularly known as the Jahnke Büro. The informant was later revealed to have been Carl Marcus[4], Jahnke's secretary, who 'crossed over' to the Allies in 1944. Later, he was given the codename 'Dictionary' after being hauled back to the UK to help with investigations into the Burgess and Maclean Affair.

Johnson told Gill that he thought it almost impossible for anyone in the American Embassy in Berlin to have given away 'practically everything from Ambassador Kennedy's despatches to President Roosevelt … [because] … these were only sent to the State Department in Washington, usually by direct cable'. He concluded that the leakage could only have occurred either at the American Embassy in London or in Washington.

Gill added a note in which he suggested that 'another possibility which neither of us mentioned is, of course, leakage from our own Foreign Office'. As Gill had already admitted to there being 'chinks in our own armour' then the British Foreign Office would have been the more likely source of leakage, a view taken by those in the know within the British Establishment.

Gill's note clearly implied that British Intelligence was intercepting the American Embassy's communications but this

---

[3] Captain Henry Landau *The Enemy Within* (1937)
[4] His name appears in various spellings in the MI5 files. See KV 2/755 for examples. He also had an alias Marienhofer.

was no surprise because all foreign Embassies and Legations based in London were targeted, both friend and foe. In those days, it was easy enough to intercept telegraphic and radio traffic. These together with the required decryption were handled by GC&CS (Government Code and Cipher School) later known as GCHQ (Government Communications Headquarters) that operated under the Foreign Office. It was accepted that the leaks could have occurred either in the Foreign Office itself or in GC&CS, where it was suspected that Jahnke may have had an agent.

There is a further flaw in Costello's hypothesis. He had assumed that MI5 had helped Roosevelt in some way by dishing up some dirt on Kennedy but this was unlikely to be the case. The information on Kennedy had been gathered by the Foreign Office and if Kennedy had been compromised in some way, then the chances are that this operation would have been handled by MI6. There is no evidence whatsoever in MI5's files that Kent had ever been used for this purpose.

Costello also claimed that Churchill had sent 'a sheaf of tapped conversations of Kennedy's in which he expressed critical opinions of Roosevelt'. This may have been the case but there is no supporting evidence. If true, there would have been no point in catching Kent 'to scare a tiger'.

Richard Whalen had addressed Kennedy's mercurial behaviour in his on-off support for Roosevelt in his biography *The Founding Father* (1964). Evidently, Kennedy had intermittently worked on his Memoirs and he had 'intended to set the record straight'. He had even hinted that he would demonstrate Roosevelt's large degree of responsibility for America's involvement in the war. However, when his two sons, Jack and Bobby, entered politics, Kennedy's interest in publishing an exposé waned.

Similarly, when Kennedy had shown signs of favouring Roosevelt's rival in the 1944 Presidential Election, he had made a surprise visit to the White House and came away in a different frame of mind. Whalen reports that 'there were many versions of what had occurred' ranging from a threatened investigation into his income taxes to unspecified favours.

The relationship between the two men was quite bizarre but evidently Kent had never been used as a pawn in their game. On the contrary, it had clearly been MI5's intention that Kent should be deported and a deportation order was made out on 23 May 1940. Knight visited the American Embassy on 25 May 1940 where 'it was decided that it would be advisable to hold Kent on his deportation order and eventually deport him back to his own country to be dealt with. In the interval Kent would be subjected to intense interrogation with a view to getting something out of him to incriminate Ramsay or Anna Wolkoff'[5].

Kent's arrest was only incidental to the real thrust of the exercise which as the Gillmans had correctly perceived was to justify a crackdown on Britain's Fifth Column.

Kent had drifted into the plot only on or around 21 February 1940 when he was introduced to Wolkoff. Contrary to the claims that MI5 had been continually monitoring him since his arrival in Britain on or around 5 October 1939, he had actually attracted very little interest. Even after Wolkoff had started boasting about her new contact at the American Embassy, Marjorie Mackie was not able to identify him positively until 29 March 1940. And even then it was 22 April 1940 before MI5 discovered that 'Kent lived at 47 Gloucester Place (this agrees with the Foreign Office List)'[6] so evidently Kent's address was already known in the Foreign Office.

If Kent had really been considered such a serious threat to National Security, then MI5 would surely have checked him out earlier. And had it been necessary, Wolkoff would have been placed under close surveillance until her contact had been exposed. In fact, Knight did not request that 'some observation' be placed on Anna until 16 April 1940, by which time Kent had already been identified.

---

[5] KV 2/543 (23).
[6] KV 2/543 (3a).

The four earliest entries on the 'Minute Sheet' at the front of Kent's MI5 file[7], say it all:

| 8.10.39 | Photostat copy of report on MATTHIAS. |
| 8.10.39 | Cross ref; to B6 report re; KENT, Tyler. |
| 14.4.40 | Extract from B5b re KENT, Tyler |
| 29.3.40 | Copy of note re KENT and WOLKOFF. |

Section B6 provided 'The Watchers' who had reported Kent's arrival. Evidently, The Watchers were seriously under strength at that time and lacked the resources to carry out sustained surveillance on low priority targets. Maxwell Knight ran Section B5b and he included references to The Watchers' observations in his later reports to strengthen their impact. The American Embassy officials took Knight's exaggeration on board and they wrongly assumed that Kent had been continually under suspicion from the time he had arrived. Similarly, John Costello had assumed that Knight's report was factually accurate.

By contrast, the MI5 files[8] contain a wealth of documents generated after Kent's arrest. Although heavily 'weeded', there are still more than enough to get the general drift that he had never been a spy, despite later efforts to get some dirt on him.

In a report dated 12 March 1945, Maxwell Knight admitted that he had been 'brooding' about the Tyler Kent case and 'various loose ends which are still untied'. He had written to a colleague to ask if the Italian Government could be approached to enquire about Anna's friend, the Duke del Monte, and what had happened to the information that he had received from Anna Wolkoff[9].

Enquiries were made, possibly as a result of Knight's urging, and in 1951 MI6 reported that the Italians had 'strenuously denied' that del Monte had been involved in intelligence activities. Del Monte was described as 'having no ideas in his

---

[7] KV 2/543.
[8] KV 2/543, KV 2/544 & KV 2/545.
[9] KV 2/545.

head beyond horses and high society' and they remarked that 'a person such as del Monte could not possibly have been entrusted with any intelligence mission'. Although it was evident that he had met Kent and Wolkoff, there was no evidence that any information had actually been handed over to him[10].

A few weeks after having initiated the enquiry, Knight visited Kent on Friday 11 May 1945.

Kent was still at Camp Hill Prison on the Isle of Wight and he had requested the meeting. As Knight had correctly anticipated, Kent wanted to air grievances rather than to volunteer information. His first grievance was that, in calculating his release date, the Authorities had refused to take into account the time that he had spent in prison between the day of his arrest and the day of his conviction. Kent was also concerned about the deportation order and he apparently dreaded being deported to the United States. Finally, Kent said that he had heard rumours that if he were sent back to the United States then 'certain parties' wished to put him on trial again and he asked Knight if he considered it likely. Knight told Kent that he had nothing to do with any of the issues but each could be taken up through channels that were well known to him.

They then had a long discussion about the Duke del Monte and Kent admitted that when Anna had introduced them, he knew that the pseudonym of Mr. Macaroni was an alias 'and a rather silly one at that'. Kent maintained that he had no idea that Anna was going to transmit information that she had obtained from him out of this country via del Monte or anyone else.

It is significant that Knight then reported that he felt 'forced to record that I am now prepared to believe Kent'.[11] So there it was, even before his enquiries into del Monte had drawn a blank, Maxwell Knight had come to believe Kent. Coming from the man who had investigated the Kent-Wolkoff Affair exhaustively, this was highly significant.

The original plan had been to deport Kent and to send Ramsay and Wolkoff for trial. Detective Inspector Pearson had served the

---

[10] KV 2/1698.
[11] This extract is reproduced in Appendix: Images.

Deportation Order on Kent on 24 May 1940. Later, it was considered 'too complicated' to try Ramsay, possibly because of the lack of hard evidence. Kent was sent for trial because the Americans wanted Kent muzzled and with emergency measures already in place in wartime Britain, a secret trial provided the mechanism.

If Kent had been deported he may or may not have faced charges under the Yardley Act; probably not. The priority was to ensure his silence at least until after the Presidential elections in November 1940. Britain certainly wanted Roosevelt to be re-elected because although he was approaching the end of his second term as President, he was already doing everything within his power to help the Allies.

Roosevelt's re-election for an unprecedented third term was the top priority in 1940.

Ray Bearse and Anthony Read were the next to enter the arena and although they were essentially accessing the same material as John Costello, the title of their book *Conspirator: The Untold Story of Churchill, Roosevelt, Tyler Kent, Spy* (1991) left no room for doubt that they had reached a vastly different conclusion.

Bearse and Read produced the most exhaustive offering on the subject, largely by collecting titbits that supported their conclusions from a variety of sources including Joan Miller and Ladislas Farago, both of whom were less than reliable.

They had apparently never met Miller who had probably died before they embarked on their investigations but they recycled her fanciful claims. They asserted that Miller's daughter, Jonquil, had been born out of wedlock to a certain Norman Richards. However Jonquil's birth certificate shows this allegation to be false[12].

They dug deep into Kent's background and uncovered some of his smuggling activities while stationed at the Moscow Embassy.

---

[12] Jonquil Francesca Kinloch Jones was born on 22 May 1948. Her father was Thomas Parker Kinloch Jones and her mother was Joan Priscilla Kinloch Jones, formerly Miller. She died age 49 on 3 September 1997.

They were suitably shocked to discover that he had a mistress who was probably an NKVD agent and that he had owned some photographs of nude women. They decided that he had 'lived in a style far above his income' but without having the slightest idea of what he had been making from his smuggling racket.

Bearse and Read overlooked the fact that the American Diplomatic Codes of that era were puny and that Soviet Intelligence would not have required assistance from Kent or anyone else to intercept or decrypt American Embassy messages. Possibly, the NKVD was cultivating Kent among others 'just in case' they might require some future assistance. Who knows? Soviet Intelligence had the reputation for being very far sighted and quite prepared to take a long view.

The authors focused on Kent's arrival in England in October 1939 when he was spotted in the company of Ludwig Matthias, a suspected German spy, whom Kent had apparently met while en route to take up his London posting.

As we now know, MI5 had noted their meeting but without ever following it up. MI5 did not consider it significant at the time. It was only after Kent 'came to their notice' again on 29 March 1940, several weeks after having been introduced to Anna Wolkoff on or around 21 February 1940 that the connection was made. In the interim, Anna had boasted to Marjorie Mackie and others about her contact at the American Embassy. However Mackie was unable to discover his correct name any earlier. On 24 February 1940, it had been 'wrongly given' as 'William Tolley' but even on 29 March 1940 she could still only get it half right as 'John Kent', although this was apparently sufficient for the correct name to be deduced from the Foreign Office lists.

The authors were wide of the mark when they claimed that 'it was through Anna Wolkoff that Kent met Irene Danischewsky … in late December 1939 or early January 1940'. When interviewed by Detective Inspector Pearson on 21 May 1940, Irene said that she had met Kent at a Russian New Year Ball on 20 January 1940, a month before Kent had been introduced to Wolkoff.

Bearse and Read reported that 'Kent claimed at his trial that he had not met Ramsay until March 1940 but this is difficult to believe (this author's emphasis) because he had been close friends with Anna since at least the end of 1939 and had attended Right Club meetings'.

The date when Kent first met Ramsay is not known but it could not have pre-dated Kent's first meeting with Anna on or around 21 February 1940 and it must have been before 25 March 1940 because there is a letter on file from Ramsay who wrote to Kent thanking him for the cigarettes that he had sent 'for Bob' (Ramsay's son).[13]

Also, Kent never attended any Right Club meetings as he didn't join until 2 May 1940 and no meetings were held after this date. Having already made it clear that he knew Ramsay, Kent testified at his trial that he knew only 'four or five' members of the Right Club. He named Anna Wolkoff, Lord Ronald Graham, Anne van Lennep[14], Enid Riddell and Christabel Nicholson[15].

Despite any supporting evidence, the authors insisted that Kent was 'an enthusiastic member' of the Right Club and that 'Anna went often to Kent's flat [and] had her own key'. Having her 'own key' or anybody else's key was totally inappropriate because there was no lock on the door. It was a 'serviced' flat and the door could be bolted only from the inside.

As incredible as this might seem, particularly in these days, Charlotte Durbridge the 53-year-old cook signed a Witness Statement to this effect on 25 May 1940. Charlotte also stated that Kent 'was frequently visited by two women [Anna and Irene] and a man'. The two women never gave their names but 'she could pick them out again'. The man gave his name as Captain Ramsay and he sometimes arrived in a small red racing car in the company of 'the woman with the rough voice' [Anna]. Emily King the 43-year-old housemaid also signed a Witness Statement on the same date in which she corroborated her colleague's recollections. Detective Inspector J.W. Pearson, the police officer

---

[13] KV 2/841 Ex 4.

[14] Also known as Anne de Lennep.

[15] Lord Ronald Graham, the second son of the Duke of Montrose, joined the RNVR but the four women were interned.

who may or may not have been on the search party five days earlier, had witnessed both statements.

Again without any evidence, Bearse and Read claimed that Anna had passed the photographic prints of the two telegrams to 'her friend the Duke del Monte of the Italian Embassy who relayed them to Germany via Rome'. The authors also claimed that there was 'convincing circumstantial evidence' to this effect. Anna's explanation was that she had destroyed the photographic prints because they were unreadable. This was only what could have been expected with contact prints made from images of foolscap documents taken by a quarter-plate camera[16]; so there was also convincing circumstantial evidence that supported Anna's claim. There is also the intriguing possibility that MI5 may have removed the prints if and when they effected an illegal entry into Kent's flat.

The authors made two common mistakes when they summarised Maxwell Knight's personal history: they got his date of birth wrong and the year that he joined MI5. They also claimed that Knight's 'big chance' within MI5 came when 'he was put in charge of placing agents in the Communist Party'. Obviously, they had missed out on the fact that Knight had been running agents for the privately funded Industrial Intelligence Board since 1924 and in a report dated 31 January 1925, he had stated that he had received information of value from 52 sources. Knight was actually recruited by MI5 in 1931 when responsibility for monitoring political parties was transferred from Special Branch. Knight had been recruited precisely because he already had a network of agents in place in various Communist organisations and he had a good record for providing useful information to Special Branch.

---

[16] The photographic images were of high quality and MI5 produced some excellent enlargements that were shown to Nicolas Smirnoff, the photographer, at Kent's trial. Smirnoff agreed that the documents on the enlargements were 'the sort' that he had photographed, but he was unable to identify the documents positively beyond 'they might have been'.

The authors mistakenly referred to Marjorie Mackie as 'Miss Amon' when her maiden name, which she used in her undercover role, was Marjorie Amor[17].

Bearse and Read also contended that Anna lived in a flat above the Russian Tea Rooms but there is absolutely no doubt that latterly she had lived with her parents in a basement flat at 18a Roland Gardens, where she was arrested. There is no evidence that she had ever lived in a flat above the café. This mistake may have arisen from Joan Miller's unreliable recollection of events.

The authors claimed that the jury at Wolkoff's trial 'took only a few minutes to find her guilty', when they reportedly took two hours. Afterwards, Anna was 'moved to prison on the Isle of Man where she remained until she was released in 1947'. She was actually incarcerated in Aylesbury Prison.

So their tale continued until they reported that Anna had been killed in a car accident in 1969, but the Home Office files show her to have been still alive in 1973. There is no record of her death in the English Family Records, so she may have died overseas.

And what did Bearse and Read have to say about the politically sensitive information, supposedly exchanged between Churchill and Roosevelt including their discussions on the Lend-Lease formula, that Kent claimed to have seen? The authors took their cue from Warren Kimball and Bruce Bartlett and confidently proclaimed that 'the wild charges made against Roosevelt were finally exploded'.

They totally ignored the caveat introduced by the academics that 'though it is always possible to dismiss official files as selective, in this case it would have taken a vast conspiracy stretching from London to Washington and lasting for over thirty-five years, an unlikely possibility.'

The authors were necessarily handicapped by not having access to the MI5 records but their book is not without interest and, in particular, they provided an Appendix in which they

---

[17] This was revealed in the transcript of Tyler Kent's trial and it is corroborated in the MI5 files.

reproduced in full the fifteen messages exchanged between Churchill and Roosevelt or more correctly, between Naval Person or Former Naval Person and President, prior to Kent's arrest.

They also identified the six signals that had supposedly been found in Kent's possession at the time of his arrest, although apparently one of these hadn't. It was the only one from Roosevelt to Churchill dated 16 May 1940. Maxwell Knight had been particularly interested in this because Christabel Nicholson had obtained a pencil copy from somewhere but Kent's copy, which he remembered typing out for his collection, had somehow mysteriously disappeared.

These tallied with those reproduced in Warren Kimball's three volume opus *Churchill and Roosevelt: The Complete Correspondence 1939-1945* but, unlike Kimball, they also included the 'headers' that showed the dates and times received or generated in Washington or London and the coding methodology. All the telegrams had been fully or partly encoded in GRAY.

By far, Andrew Lownie produced the best analysis in an excellent article *Tyler Kent: Isolationist or Spy?* It appeared in *North American Spies*, a compendium of ten articles that took 'a fresh look at the history of espionage in the United States since 1898'. Lownie, who was the co-editor, had used the Freedom of Information Act to obtain FBI documents that were pertinent to the case. He was limited by not having access to the MI5 files that appeared later but his analysis was brilliant and devoid of sensationalism.

Lownie noted that after his posting to London, Kent was at the nerve centre of American foreign policy because all 'important' European diplomatic traffic passed through the London Embassy. And as one of the code clerks, 'he saw everything'.

He made the further point that 'if Kent had been successful in publicising the contents of their correspondence, the political careers of both Roosevelt and Churchill might well have been curtailed'.

There were, and are, strong opinions on both sides of the Atlantic that still believe that the 'real enemy' was Soviet Russia, and that the Western democracies should have supported Hitler in his plans to obtain lebensraum in the East; a metaphor for grabbing Ukrainian grain and Caucasian oil. Unfortunately, Hitler had a long history of failing to honour his promises. It was not too difficult to see that his so-called economic miracle was a sham and that the payoff from his investments in military capability could only come through economic conquests. One year Czechoslovakia, the next year Poland, then Russia ...it could easily have become a never-ending pursuit for economic power.

So Kent had to be stopped from making any public disclosures. Similarly, the various dissident groups in Britain who advocated a peace deal with Hitler had to be silenced. In a way it was probably fortunate that Kent was introduced to Wolkoff so that the two cases could be run in parallel. There was no knowing what mischief he might have got up to if he hadn't been arrested and detained on 20 May 1940.

The fact of Kent and Wolkoff having been introduced to each other was not as a result of some deep conspiracy. It may have been inevitable after Kent started socialising in American expatriate and White Russian émigré circles. Mrs. Barbara Allen reportedly made the introduction although later when MI5 questioned Sam, her husband, he claimed that Anna had introduced his wife to Kent. On another occasion, Geoffrey Allen had entertained Kent and Wolkoff at The Ritz.

There were three Allen brothers, Bill, Geoffrey and Sam, the husband of Barbara née Dixon, an American. Bill (W.E.D. Allen) was the eldest and the best known, having been the Conservative MP for West Belfast from 1929 to 1931. He defected to the New Party founded by Sir Oswald Mosley in 1931. Mosley had been a minister in the Labour Government[18] but he had grown disillusioned with the British Parliamentary system.

---

[18] Sir Oswald Mosley was the Chancellor of the Duchy of Lancaster in Ramsay MacDonald's Labour Government that had come to power on 5 June 1929. Mosley was not in the Cabinet.

The New Party was a disaster and it metamorphosed into the BUF thanks partly to Bill Allen's contributions both financial and literary. However, he was a canny operator who realised that sporting a Fascist label would not be good for the family business, David Allens, a big name in the field of bill poster advertising. Bill therefore kept well in the background. He wrote one book using the pseudonym of James Drennan and he was the anonymous contributor of 'The Letters of Lucifer', a regular column in Mosley's publications[19].

Both Mosley and the Allen brothers were keen to get into commercial radio and they constructed a deal with Peter Eckersley, a pioneer of broadcasting in Britain, and eventually with Hitler who agreed to provide the transmission facilities. It was intended as a commercial venture on the lines of Radio Luxemburg and Radio Normandie that used long wave transmissions that could be received in Britain at a time when the BBC held a monopoly for inland transmissions and a well-deserved reputation for boringly dull programmes. The commercial stations based in Luxemburg and France attracted 70% of the audience at peak times. MI5 knew all about 'Radio Mosley' but it never reached the airwaves, having been overtaken by the war.

Lownie investigated Kent's earlier career at the American Embassy in Moscow and discovered that after arriving on 2 March 1934, he had 'made a bad start in which he was almost fired for laziness'. However, in June 1934 Ambassador William Bullitt reported that 'young Kent seems to have turned over a new leaf'.

After Kent had refused to register under the provisions of the new Internal Security Act in 1950, the FBI questioned some of his former colleagues. Bill Bullitt was among those interviewed. On 2 June 1950, he told the FBI that he regarded Kent as 'brilliant but neurotic'. The FBI interviewed Kent on 7 September 1951 and considered him 'quite cooperative and appeared to be sincere and straightforward in his answers'. Six

[19] Bill Allen's MI5 file shows that he was the writer of 'The Letters of Lucifer'.

weeks later, Kent was told that 'registration was not required' and the case was formally closed in March 1952.

In between times, Bullitt had told British Intelligence a very different story. Shortly after Kent's arrest, Bullitt was quoted in a report dated 8 June 1940 as having said 'he had known him for a long time; that he came from a very good family but was a complete rotter and always had been. He had been foisted on him (Bullitt) against his wishes … [and] … at the end of three months he was discovered to be in the pay of the Soviets'. Bullitt went on to say 'the sooner you shoot him the better'. He kept repeating 'I hope you will shoot him and shoot him soon. I mean it'. Bullitt also expressed the view that 'he was sure there was a lot of it going on' and that shooting Kent 'would put a stop to the same sort of thing elsewhere'[20].

It is hard to believe that Bullitt would have given Kent a good report in June 1934 or a good enough report in June 1950 or that he would have continued to employ him if the comments that he made in 1940 were true. But who knows? Maybe in 1950, Bullitt had been told to let sleeping dogs lie.

Lownie reported that 'progress was slow' in the search to find the identity of 'The Doctor'. In fact, there would be no progress whatsoever. This prompted Lownie to the intriguing thought that 'perhaps The Doctor never existed'. Lownie would have been even more intrigued had he been aware of the post-war efforts that British Intelligence had made to resolve this same issue, mainly through a series of interviews with Carl Marcus, their 'informant whose statements have in other respects proved to be accurate'.

If Kent were a spy was he working for the Nazis or the Soviets? Lownie had unearthed 'a fragment' of an FBI memorandum dated 4 March 1944 that included a sentence that started 'At the present time it would appear that Kent was actively engaged in espionage for the Russian Government'. Unfortunately, the remainder of the sentence had been deleted.

---

[20] KV 2/543.

This was decidedly in conflict with all the assumptions made on or around the time of his arrest when Maxwell Knight had reported that Anna Wolkoff had 'means of communicating with persons in Germany'.

This information was included in a Secret Memorandum[21] that had been put before the War Cabinet on 22 May 1940[22], the meeting at which it was decided to strengthen the Emergency Regulations in order to intern members of the potential Fifth Column; in particular Sir Oswald Mosley and members of his BUF.

It was the critical step that transformed Britain from a democracy where 'free speech' was largely acceptable to what was effectively a totalitarian state. In a wartime emergency and with a Nazi invasion in prospect, what else? It was no time to be fooling around debating human rights issues. This was the time for action, no pun intended: *Action* was one of the newspaper-style periodicals published by Mosley's Fascists. William Joyce had been among the contributors when he had been associated with the movement.

Joyce heard about the internment of his former colleagues during his sojourn in Berlin and he made the most of it on his black propaganda channel, NBBS, a broadcasting station that was supposedly being run by a group of dissidents within Britain. It was actually being beamed in by short wave. This didn't fool the British authorities for a moment because they could pinpoint the source, but it did fool many 'men in the street'.

Consequent upon the wave of arrests, the NBBS spokesmen reported on how they had almost been arrested, although some of their collaborators had not been so lucky. The British authorities were not amused and the Monitors noted that 'NBBS on its new wavelength of 25.08 m was jammed tonight but 50.63 m was audible'[23].

At the time, things were going all Germany's way and William Joyce probably figured that he had done the right thing

---

[21] CAB 65/13.
[22] CAB 65/7
[23] W.J. West *Truth Betrayed* (1987).

by fleeing to Germany on 26 August 1939, after having been tipped off that he had been listed for internment under the first wave of emergency regulations that had been enacted on 24 August 1939.

The information had been perfectly correct and, according to J.A. Cole (Joyce's first biographer), 'the call came from the Intelligence Officer to whom he had reported on Communist activities and who had sounded him out on his willingness to go to Germany as an agent'.[24]

There had been speculation that the Intelligence Officer in question was Maxwell Knight and when the MI5 files on Joyce were released into the National Archives there was a report dated 25th September 1939 confirming that the writer had had a telephone conversation with Joyce but that 'there was no question of Joyce having been warned or given any improper information'.[25]

The writer was responding to a report that Joan Joyce (William's sister) had told a Special Branch officer that her brother had 'slipped away because he had been told unofficially that he would be arrested on the outbreak of war if he were then in England'. She also stated that an officer of the Secret Service had visited her brother Quentin Joyce in prison on 19 September 1939 and had told Quentin that 'there was nothing to worry about as far as he was concerned'.

Although the document was unsigned, the source of the response from MI5 was given as 'B.5b.' - Maxwell Knight's Section. Therefore, there is now absolutely no room for doubt that Maxwell Knight had tipped off William Joyce. They had known each other since 1924, when they were both members of Britain's first Fascist Party, the British Fascisti. The British Fascisti had been founded in 1923, over nine years before Sir Oswald Mosley started to sport his own Fascist credentials on 1 October 1932.

---

[24] J. A. Cole *Lord Haw-Haw and William Joyce – The Full Story* (1964).
[25] KV 2/245 – 179x

# 13: The Right Club

Britain started preparing for war in a half-hearted fashion during the latter half of the Thirties. The military strategists had correctly perceived that air and sea power would be more important than in WWI. They worked slowly on the development of what was then known as ASDIC (Anti Submarine Defence & Identification Committee) and is now known as Sonar, an electronic detection aid. At the time, it was wrongly believed that this would provide an effective answer to the threat of the submarine, which the Germans had used to such devastating effect in WWI.

Efforts were also made to develop a similar system to detect the approach of enemy aircraft. This would become known as Radar. Until then, it had been an article of faith that 'the bomber will always get through'. Even if this were to be proved true, Britain was unable to deliver effective bombing attacks because it lacked a suitable bombsight. By contrast, the Germans had developed a radio navigation system that worked far too well for comfort, until British scientists figured out how to 'meacon'[1] or 'bend the beams'. Unbeknown to most people, the wavebands used by Lord Haw-Haw for his propaganda broadcasts formed part of that navigation system. One consequence was that the Lord Haw-Haw channels were being re-broadcast from within Britain on other frequencies. This not only confused the German aircraft but it also improved reception and explains why efforts were never made to jam Lord Haw-Haw's 'white propaganda' broadcasts.

Britain's lack of a bombsight worried military planners who coveted the Norden bombsight, an American development. After demonstrations, the observers became convinced that this bombsight was the way forward. However, the Americans were unwilling to share their technology, correctly figuring that once an enemy had downed a plane so equipped, their technology

---

[1] Meacon 'to give false signals to (electronic navigational equipment) as by means of a radio transmitter'.

would be secret no longer. Worse, despite the bombsight's impressive performance in daylight, it was soon discovered that bombing was best carried out at night where the Norden's visual system was absolutely no use whatsoever. So it was back to the drawing board.

Britain and its Allies also had a touching faith in their numerical advantage over Germany without fully appreciating that WWII would be a mechanised war. The horse and the Maginot Line, a string of fortresses that might have held back the German cavalry or infantry, were obsolete. Although comfort was drawn from the Treaty of Versailles that supposedly limited Germany's military potential, successive German Governments had been secretly building up the country's military capability.

The Wall Street Crash and the subsequent Depression brought economic chaos that quickly led to political chaos. Clearly, the politicians of that era were not delivering the answers required. Perhaps Fascism, National Socialism, Communism or some other -ism would be better?

Hitler became one of the icons of the Thirties and many in Germany and elsewhere came to believe in his magic. Surprisingly, there was even a man sitting in the British Parliament who truly admired Hitler. He was Captain Archibald Henry Maule Ramsay who was known to his friends as 'Jock'. He was the 45-year-old Conservative MP for Peebles.

Ramsay had inherited well and after being educated at Eton, he went to Sandhurst and thence into the Coldstream Guards, seeing action in WWI. He was severely wounded in 1916 and had been invalided out in 1919. In 1917, he had married Ismay, the widow of Lord Ninian Crichton-Stuart MP who had died on active service in 1915. Known to her friends as 'Mosh', she was the eldest daughter of the 14th Viscount Gormanston. Twelve years older than Jock, she had three surviving children from her first marriage, her first child having died in infancy, and she gave Jock four sons of his own. They lived in some style, commuting between Kellie Castle near Arbroath in Scotland, and a London house in fashionable Kensington.

The Ramsays were devout Catholics and were horrified by events in Russia where the Communists were persecuting those with the Christian faith. In 1931, they participated in the 'Christian Protest Movement' but Stalin and his cohorts evidently took no notice. In 1937, Ramsay became chairman of the United Christian Front Committee and in 1938 the Ramsays discovered the Jewish plot for world domination, as set out in *The Protocols of the Learned Elders of Zion*.

Although soon discredited as a forgery, many people in Britain's so-called 'Ruling Class' believed in the veracity of *The Protocols*. The necessary 'proof' for the Ramsays had arrived in 1938 with the publication of *The Rulers of Russia* by the Reverend Denis Fahey, a Professor of Philosophy and a Church Historian. The Ramsays then became fervently anti-Jewish and anti-Masonic. Captain Ramsay was later reported as being 'prominently associated' with the Nordic League, a secret anti-Jewish organisation that met behind closed doors. William Joyce had also been a leading member.

Ramsay was also associated with The Link, an organisation founded by a retired admiral Sir Barry Domvile (1878-1971) who had been Director of Naval Intelligence from 1927 until 1930. Although supposedly intelligent, Domvile also swallowed the concept of the Jewish plot as set out in *The Protocols* as well as another conspiracy theory that said that the Illuminati had penetrated the Masonic movement. This was even more worrying; one secret society hiding inside another. Domvile coined the word 'Judmas' that recognised that both sets of conspirators were collaborating in a quest for world domination.

On the surface, The Link purported simply to encourage cultural exchanges between Britain and Germany whose peoples have always got on well together despite having fought on opposite sides in two World Wars. Below the surface, Domvile was working to overthrow the British Government; and happily for posterity, he kept detailed diaries extending from 1892 almost until his death[2].

---

[2] Admiral Sir Barry Domvile left 'his papers' to the National Maritime Museum. They consist mainly of his diaries.

Domvile had taken the precaution of hiding his most recent diary 'under the hen house' in case he should get interned during the war. Although bitten by rats, the diary was rescued by his 'faithful housemaid and taken indoors'.

The knock on Domvile's door came on 8 July 1940 and he was interned until 29 July 1943 under the provisions of Defence Regulation 18B. His German born wife Alexandrina, whom he referred to as 'Pudd' in his diaries if not to her face, and one of his sons were also interned. During his time inside, Domvile came to believe that the suspension of habeas corpus imposed by DR 18B, had been 'clearly outlined' in *The Protocols*[3].

Inevitably Jock Ramsay's activities came to the attention of British Intelligence who had been monitoring various pro-German organisations. In a report dated 10 March 1939 Ramsay was described as 'a very unbalanced individual'. The description was almost certainly accurate. He was next reported at a meeting of the Nordic League in which he outlined his ideas for the Right Club. It was to provide a common link between Right Wing organisations such as the Nordic League, The Link, the Militant Christian Patriots, the British Union of Fascists, the National Socialist League, the Imperial Fascist League and the Liberty Restoration League among others.

Strangely, considering his objective, Ramsay apparently didn't invite Mosley or Domvile to join the Right Club. On 5 December 1955, a few months after Ramsay's death on 11 March 1955, Domvile wrote to Charles Parsons, Tyler Kent's wealthy American supporter, and revealed that he 'had never heard of this Club until I met Jock in Brixton'[4].

Ramsay's ideas had crystallised in May 1939 and he announced the launch of the Right Club at a meeting of The Link held at the Crofton Hotel on 16 June 1939[5]. According to Maxwell Knight's Agent M/T, Ramsay told the meeting that, 'Hitler is a splendid fellow with whom we should be proud to be

---

[3] Brian Simpson *In the Highest Degree Odious* (1992)
[4] The Tyler Kent Collection, collected by Charles Parsons -Yale University Library.
[5] KV 2/677 (23a).

friends'. He described the new organisation that he had founded some three weeks previously. He visualised that it would have fleets of small vans with loudspeakers and 'men who could speak well' going all over England to reveal that their troubles were entirely due to the Jews. M/T considered Ramsay 'a real fine speaker' and reported that at the end of his speech, Ramsay was overwhelmed with applications to join.

Also in June 1939, Ramsay approached Prime Minister Neville Chamberlain and warned him of the Jewish plot. When Chamberlain paid little attention, Ramsay decided that he must act himself and he arranged to hire Wigmore Hall for a public meeting. However, Domvile's diary entry for 10 July 1939 reports that it was 'cancelled at last moment - a very dirty trick - we are thinking up a plan to amalgamate'.

William Joyce applied for membership on 1 July 1939 and sent 5/- 'to effect my admission'. He was sorry that he could not spare any more. Joyce's application for membership was promptly accepted.

During the summer of 1939, Maxwell Knight decided to plant a mole in the Right Club and he called upon Agent M/Y who had worked for him previously. It has never been revealed where she had worked previously but an MI5 report on Enid Riddell suggests that she had infiltrated some Communist organisation.

Agent M/Y, now known to have been Marjorie Norah Mackie, was 39 at the time. She was separated from her husband, Thomas, whom she had married in 1921 when he was a sergeant in the Royal Army Service Corps. She had reverted to using her maiden name of Amor. Knight considered her 'ideal' because she had had 'some training' and was already known to the Ramsays, whom she had met in 1931 when they were on their crusade to rescue Christendom in Soviet Russia. The Ramsays knew her as the Assistant Secretary of the Christian Defence Movement. This gave her the right credentials because Mosh's brother-in-law from her first marriage was one of its leading lights.

Joan Miller would later claim that Mackie had reminded her of Agatha Christie's 'Miss Marple' but without saying which actress's portrayal she had in mind. When Mackie died in

Cambridge in 1975, obesity and over-eating were cited among the causes. James Amor Mackie, her 52-year-old son, gave his mother's occupation as 'Domestic Manciple (Retired)'.

Mackie accepted the assignment and re-established contact with Mrs. Ramsay, who invited her to tea. After a 'long talk on political topics', Mackie reported that she found her 'violently anti-semitic and violently opposed to Freemasonry'. Mosh assumed that Mackie already knew about the Right Club, and gave her a copy of *The Protocols* and 'a book' by Father Fahey. Mackie didn't mention the title but it was almost certainly *The Rulers of Russia*[6] because for those who wanted to believe, this provided proof positive that the Bolshevik Revolution was a part fulfilment of the Jewish plot for world domination, as set out in *The Protocols*.

Mackie then remained 'in fairly close touch' with Mosh, and in August 1939 she joined the Right Club by sending a one guinea Postal Order as her Entrance Fee and Subscription. The membership categories were:

|  | Entrance Fee | Annual Subscription |
| --- | --- | --- |
| Warden | £25 | 10 guineas |
| Steward | £5 | £5 |
| Yeoman | 1 guinea | 1 guinea |
| Keeper | ½ guinea | ½ guinea |
| Freeman | 2s 6d | 2s 6d |

Mackie reported that the club operated on two levels; ostensibly it was to disseminate propaganda against the Jews, but its real purpose was to disorganise the Home Front by subversive propaganda.

---

[6] The pamphlet originally appeared in 1938 over the name of the Rev. Denis Fahey, C.S.Sp., and it bore the Imprimatur of the Roman Catholic Bishop of Dublin.

Special Branch had also been keeping an eye on the Right Club. Albert Canning, its chief, reported on 22 September 1939 that information had been received that it was 'centred principally upon the contacting of sympathisers especially among officers in the Armed Forces' and that 'the talk has now reached the stage that a military coup d'état is feasible ... it was felt that if a leader should step forward the movement would make rapid headway. Naturally, the name of the Duke of Windsor is mooted by some as favourable to the ideology behind the movement but little hope is felt that he would lend himself to such an intrigue.'

Perhaps as a consequence of Canning's report, Mackie asked Ramsay if in the event of a Right Wing revolution breaking out, should she follow Sir Oswald Mosley? Ramsay replied, 'Certainly not. Before such a situation arises I shall be in touch with all the members and you will then be told who is to be your leader'.

When Mackie enquired what she could do to help, Ramsay suggested that she should try to get a job in Censorship because he wanted to have a contact there. Knight quickly found her a job in Censorship.

Mrs. Ramsay was evidently the driving force behind her husband and it is believed that she had first alerted him to the threat of the Jewish conspiracy. Mackie would see much more of her than Jock and when the two women met on 25 October 1939 Mackie told her that she had got a job in Censorship. Mosh was delighted, and she showed her appreciation by telling Mackie that she would now be invited to a meeting of the Inner Circle.

Mackie and Mosh met twice again during November and Mackie gleaned the names of some other members including Lord Ronald Graham, the second son of the 6th Duke of Montrose. Mosh told her that 'Captain Ramsay thinks you will be most useful when the time comes' and confided that Mosley 'tried hard and often to get Jock to join in with him' and 'he had promised him Scotland'.

On 6 December 1939, Mackie went for tea with Mrs. Ramsay and was introduced to Anna Wolkoff and Claudia Crichton-Stuart, Mosh's daughter from her first marriage. Claudia was an

# THE KENT-WOLKOFF AFFAIR

ambulance driver at Newhaven. Mosh told them that she and Jock had been to Mosley's house and among the others present were Lord Tavistock[7], General Blakeney[8] and Lord Lymington[9]. However, Mackie reported that 'nothing much was said about the meeting'. At this point, Maxwell Knight had inserted the comment that 'There is a Special Branch Report which I think refers to this meeting'. Although MI5's informant was not named, he was described as 'having been in the inner councils of the B.U.[10] since its inception'[11]. James Hughes aka P.G. Taylor was undoubtedly the man in question.

This was one of a series of 'secret meetings' that Domvile had mentioned in his diary. The Ramsays had gone to a meeting on 26 July 1939 but they were evidently not present at the one held on 19 September 1939 when Domvile noted 'a new council formed' and that this 'may become an important meeting'. Domvile went to see Mosley on 3 October 1939 but there was no Ramsay 'which was a pity'. The Ramsays attended the meetings held on 22 November 1939 and also on 6 December 1939 when Domvile wrote that he 'thought that a description of OS MOS [Mosley] as the greatest political leader in the world was going a bit far'. The date given by Domvile is one different to that of Mackie's, but it was undoubtedly the same meeting.

According to Mackie, Mosh told Anna that Mackie was 'making herself very useful for when the crisis came'. Anna told Mackie that she had an aunt working in Censorship. Knight had confirmed this by adding 'True'.[12]

---

[7] Lord Tavistock was the President of the British People's Party that had been founded in April 1939. He would become better known as the 12th Duke of Bedford, a title that he inherited on 12 August 1940.

[8] General Robert Blakeney was prominently associated with many anti-Jewish movements and he had been the President of the British Fascisti from September 1924 to April 1926.

[9] Viscount Lymington later the 9th Earl of Portsmouth founded The British Council Against European Commitments, an anti-war body, in 1938.

[10] British Union (of Fascists and National Socialists).

[11] KV 2/834 (22a).

[12] This was Vera Wolkoff-Mouromtzoff. Reports that Anna's parents had also worked in Censorship are false.

Mackie had evidently made all the right noises because Anna invited her to dine at the Russian Tea Rooms and started visiting Mackie at her flat at 71 Linden Gardens. Their relationship developed and Mackie was introduced to other members of the Right Club.

Mackie also overheard a conversation between Anna and Molly Stanford from which she gathered that Molly was in communication with Margaret Bothamley, who was said to be 'at liberty' in Germany. This information would certainly have piqued Anna's interest, because she had often boasted about her own contacts at various Embassies and her ability to send correspondence abroad without troubling the Censor.

Molly Stanford and Margaret Bothamley used a code in their correspondence:[13]

| | |
|---|---|
| Father | Germany |
| Mother | England |
| Philip's Family | Poland |
| Germs | Jews |
| Skin Infection | Jewish Influence |
| Divorce Proceedings | War |
| Yellow Powder | Gold |

Margaret Bothamley was one of Britain's most fanatical Jew haters and she supported several movements that promoted her beliefs. The daughter of a solicitor, she had gone on The Link's last cultural visit to the Salzburg Music Festival that had left Britain on 31 July 1939. After the Festival, she had opted to stay in Germany. She then went on to work alongside William Joyce, broadcasting Nazi propaganda. After the war, she was sent for trial at the Old Bailey in March 1946 and was handed down a year's imprisonment 'in the first division'[14].

One barrister who summarised her case considered this 'a very unusual concession'[15]. It was certainly very different from the death sentence that had sent William Joyce to the scaffold a few

---

[13] KV 2/840 (196).

[14] This was a soft option that was available for political prisoners.

[15] Carl Bechhofer Roberts, *The Trial of William Joyce* (1946)

weeks earlier for essentially the same offence. Joyce had been charged with High Treason and after being found guilty he was sentenced to the so-called 'mandatory' death sentence. Mandatory or not, this would not have prevented The King from stepping in to save 'a deserving soul' from punishment handed down by his minions. Even though William Joyce was an American by birth and therefore owed no allegiance to the Crown, no one who mattered beseeched His Majesty to prevent a blatant miscarriage of justice. Evidently Joyce had failed to give the Court convincing evidence of his ongoing loyalty to the Crown.

By contrast, the 67-year-old Margaret Bothamley had satisfied the Court of her enduring loyalty by claiming that she had hung pictures of the King and Queen in her German apartment. The Court was probably unaware that before the war she had a picture of Hitler in her London flat; or perhaps her father having been a solicitor was a mitigating factor.

Early in 1940, it was also ascertained that Molly Stanford was looking after 'some of Bothamley's papers'.

On the evening of 29 January 1940, Mackie visited 10 Courtfield Gardens, the home of Lord Ronald Graham, where she also met Mrs. Dorothy Newenham who was known to her friends as 'Dolly'. Both were enthusiastic members of the Right Club.

Stimulated by Mackie's description of Anna's superstitious nature, Knight introduced a second agent into the investigation on 1 February 1940. His new agent was Hélène Louise de Munck a 25-year-old Belgian-born mystic. She had been brought to Britain at the age of three months, possibly because her parents had wished to get her away from the battlefields. She was educated in England until she was 16 and had then travelled widely.

De Munck said that she had met the Wolkoffs and one of their daughters around 1935 through a Russian friend, but she couldn't remember whether it was Anna or her younger sister Alexandra, who preferred to be known as Alice.

This didn't say a lot for de Munck's mystical abilities because, apparently, Anna was as plain as Alice was attractive. Alice had tried to become an actress without success. In the process, she had become friendly with the actor Michael Wilding and his wife, long before Wilding found international fame by marrying Elizabeth Taylor. Wilding probably never realised that he had been investigated by MI5 because of his association with Alice, who was then in a lesbian relationship.

As instructed, de Munck started going to the Russian Tea Rooms. After having made Anna's acquaintance and having expressed sympathy with her anti-Jewish beliefs, Anna gave her some 'sticky-backs' to post. De Munck duly made Anna aware of her mystical abilities. Wolkoff fell for the yarn and asked for tuition that would enable her to see into the future. De Munck obliged and later reported that she had persuaded Anna to stare at a piece of silver in a glass of water. This prop probably substituted for a crystal ball or a pendulum that are more commonly used in fortune telling.

There is no record to show how de Munck interpreted Anna's fortune but, some time later, Anna was heard to express the belief that the Right Club would come to power in the aftermath of a successful German invasion. She was also looking forward to the triumphal procession through London and promised Mackie a seat of honour, sitting alongside Himmler. Was this Anna's own fantasy or had de Munck produced the idea when she was telling her fortune?

It is possible that Maxwell Knight may have provided fuel for her imagination after Marjorie Mackie had discovered that Anna 'like most Russians had a superstitious nature and an interest in spiritualism, clairvoyance, astrology and anything to do with the occult'[16]. This was evidently his cue to introduce a fortune-teller into his investigation. Anna was obviously impressed because she later used de Munck's skills as a graphologist to check out her associates.

On 4 February 1940, Mackie met Ramsay at his home at 24 Onslow Square and was given 'practically three hours of third degree' mainly on how many Jews were working in Censorship, and did she know their names? She evidently came through the third degree with honours because Ramsay then showed her his

---

[16] KV 4/227 page 49.

list of supporters, which Mackie considered 'very surprising'. He also asked her if she knew any people in MI5? Did she think that she could 'influence' the younger girls who worked in Wormwood Scrubs? Knight had added the observation that 'This is very important in connection with the visit of Miss Miller'.

Mackie 'first mentioned' that Anna had a new contact at the American Embassy in a report dated 24 February 1940 but at the time his name was incorrectly given. On 23 March 1940, Mackie reported that Anna was spending 'a great deal of time with this man from the American Embassy and was concentrating upon him'. Anna told her that 'he was definitely pro-German' and from what Mackie had been able to glean, 'it was clear that he was engaging in disseminating defeatist and anti-Allied propaganda'.

On 25 February 1940, Anna told Mackie that she had a contact at the Belgian Embassy who would send letters to William Joyce through the diplomatic bag. She said that she had sent a letter that had merely described the activities of the Right Club. But, in a report dated 26 February 1940, Mackie had claimed that she herself was arranging a test letter to be sent!

On 28 February 1940, yet another of Knight's agents M/W surfaced with a report that he had had tea with H.T. 'Bertie' Mills, A.J. Miller[17] and P.G. Taylor at a café adjoining the BUF headquarters. Mills who had been a prominent member of the Nordic League was also listed in the Right Club's Membership Book. Mills advised that 'the meetings at the Rembrandt (Right Club) had been stopped and would in future be held at St. Ermin's Restaurant, Caxton Street, Westminster at 6 p.m.' Mills also said that he had 'no definite knowledge but feels that all is not right with the Right Club'[18].

Curiously, Mackie never reported on these meetings, so possibly Captain Ramsay was not sharing all his activities with Anna, despite supposedly being his aide-de-camp. Maybe Ramsay knew that Anna was a gossip or maybe Anna was only telling Mackie what she wanted her to hear. At some stage, Anna

---

[17] A.J. Miller was not connected with Joan Miller.
[18] KV 2/1212 (24b).

became aware that Mackie had been formerly associated with some Communist organisation and she then suspected that she might have been a Communist spy. Evidently, Anna never considered that Mackie might have been an MI5 agent but, despite her suspicions, Anna never challenged Mackie, although she then treated her to some outrageous tales.

On 26 March 1940, Mackie reported that the Right Club hoped to secure a flat at 24 Manson Mews as a meeting place.

On 29 March 1940, Anna's contact was identified as Tyler Kent. It was also discovered that Anna was making use of his car.

On 9 April 1940, Knight mounted his sting operation against Anna. On the evening of the same day, Mackie introduced Joan Miller to Anna Wolkoff. Anna later told Mackie that she had sent a letter to William Joyce through the Rumanian Legation courier who was leaving the following day. According to Mackie, Anna 'seemed extremely pleased'.

In the light of this supposedly damning evidence, it is remarkable that Knight had failed to strike. The legislation was already on the Statute Books and Anna could have been interned under the existing provisions. In fact, she and Kent were interned under the existing provisions when the time was right.

On Wednesday 10 April 1940, Anna told Mackie that Kent was 'to our way of thinking' and that he was to be introduced to Ramsay 'that week'. This was evidently disinformation because Ramsay had written to Kent on 25 March 1940[19]. Later, Anna told Mackie that Ramsay was 'delighted' at her new contact. She apparently didn't tell Mackie that Ramsay had asked for copies of two of the telegrams that he had spotted in Kent's collection. Anna went to the photographer on Saturday the 13 April 1940, to carry out his request.

The 13 April 1940 was an eventful date because it also marked the establishment of the Right Club's own meeting place, known as 'The Parlour'. It was a flat built above a garage at 24 Manson Mews and conveniently it was just around the corner from the Russian Tea Rooms. There was a suggestion that the Duke of

---

[19] KV 2/841 Ex 4.

Westminster had provided the funding but there is also the possibility that MI5 had been the benefactor.

In the *Sunday Times Magazine* article[20] in which she had made her first public appearance, Joan Miller claimed to have 'other remarkable and so far unreported stories ...[that] ... range from an MI5 rented flat'. Miller never revealed anything further about the rented flat, but Marjorie Mackie was the occupier of 24 Manson Mews and Anna would be her guest on more than one occasion.

On 16 April 1940, another of Knight's agents referred to as 'Special Source' reported that Anna was obtaining 'a great deal of information through Tyler Kent'. According to Special Source, she had dined with Kent at the Russian Tea Rooms on 12 April 1940 and claimed that he had given her confidential information regarding the North Sea battles[21].

'Special Source' was not named in any of the files released into the National Archives and speculation will probably prove false. From his reports, we know that he was a married man because he and his wife visited Mrs. Ramsay while her husband was in jail. He also visited Mme. Wolkoff while her husband and daughter were 'inside'. Evidently, he was well known to Mrs. Ramsay and Mme. Wolkoff and both women sought and respected his opinion. Mrs. Ramsay had even asked him, 'Was Joan Miller working for MI5?'

Although 'Special Source' was known and respected within this little community, his continuing reports show that he had not been interned. This follows the general rule that MI5 agents were only interned when it suited MI5 to allow them to pursue their investigations inside. This points to someone very special, and the only person who springs readily to mind is Major-General J.F.C. Fuller, known to his friends as 'Boney', supposedly because he looked like Napoleon. The Ramsays certainly knew Fuller because, like Captain Ramsay, he had been prominently associated with the Nordic League and he had also attended some of Mosley's secret meetings.

---

[20] 18 October 1981.
[21] Arising out of the Norwegian campaign.

Boney Fuller (1878-1966) has been characterised as 'Soldier, Strategist and Writer' by one of his biographers[22] but there was more to him than that. The son of an Anglican clergyman, he had a 'predilection for the occult'. He had once been a disciple of Aleister Crowley, the notorious black magician and Fuller's first book *Star in the West* (1907) was dedicated to 'Crowleyanity'. Although it sounds like a disease, it was actually a glorification of Crowley that had started off as an entry in a prize competition. Crowley had offered a prize of £100 for the best tribute essay. Fuller, who was then a Captain in the 1st Oxfordshire Light Infantry based in Lucknow, was declared the winner. Unfortunately, despite his magical gifts, Crowley was unable to conjure up the promised prize money. Fuller found some consolation by getting his work published. Although the two men soon fell out, they both retained ongoing interests in the occult.

After the development of the tank in WWI, Fuller became recognised as a strategist on mechanised warfare. He took a view that was revolutionary at the time that tanks should be used *en masse* as an attack force, rather than just playing a supporting role to the Infantry. He took up the pen to propagate his opinions and became known as the 'Intellectual General'. He is credited with having conceived the Blitzkreig that Hitler used to such devastating effect in WWII.

Fuller was a guest at Hitler's 50th Birthday Parade held in Berlin on 20 April 1939 where for some three hours a completely mechanised and motorised army roared past the Führer and an admiring multitude. In the afternoon, the foreign guests were lined up to meet Hitler. According to Fuller, the Führer shook his hand and said 'I hope you are pleased with your children?' Fuller replied, 'Your Excellency, they have grown up so quickly that I no longer recognise them'.

Fuller had established his own Fascist credentials by joining Mosley's BUF and he had been pencilled in as Minister of Defence in the prospective Mosley Government. He had also established his anti-Jewish credentials through the Nordic League alongside Captain Ramsay and William Joyce.

---

[22] Anthony John Trythall *'Boney' Fuller* (1977).

However, there may have been another side to Fuller. It is possible that he might have been gathering military intelligence under the guise of his other enthusiasms. According to one of his biographers, Geyr Von Schweppenburg suspected his motives. Von Schweppenburg had been the military attaché at the German Embassy in London and he was a future Panzer General. He may have been correct because Fuller is now believed to have acted as a military adviser to Churchill during his 'wilderness years'.

What is for sure is that Fuller was never interned, unlike Mosley and most of his other senior management. The most notable of the other exceptions were W.E.D. Allen who had previously joined the Army[23] and P.G. Taylor, Britain's most active *agent provocateur*. According to Fuller's wife, this was 'because he knew too much'. But maybe it was because the internment of any well-known General was perceived as 'not being a very good idea'? Or, perhaps the very reason that he knew too much was because he had been MI5's 'Special Source'?

MI5 had also intercepted a letter (dated 11 May 1940) from Christabel Nicholson to Anna Wolkoff. Nicholson, who was holidaying in Wales, had expressed the wish that she 'could see our friend Fuller who is usually right about strategy'.

Whether or not Boney Fuller was 'Special Source', Knight had four agents working on the case by 16th April 1940 but, strangely, he still didn't know where Tyler Kent lived. This was resolved on 22 April 1940 when it was discovered that Kent lived at 47 Gloucester Place.

The discovery came almost two months after Kent's introduction to Wolkoff, so evidently Knight had seen no urgency in investigating Kent. In the meantime, Kent was continually adding to his private collection of Embassy documents, including copies of the supposedly top-secret communications between Roosevelt and Churchill. He kept these in a suitcase in his London flat, despite it not having a lock on the door.

---

[23] Contrary to several earlier reports, there is absolutely no evidence that W.E.D. Allen had ever acted as an undercover agent for MI5.

190

On 21 April 1940, Wolkoff told Mackie that she had found a man named Smirnoff who was working in Censorship and who was 'ready to undertake some photographing work for her'[24]. So when the time came to track him down, the rest was easy. This is very different from the imaginative fiction generated shortly after the end of the war. There was neither microfilm nor microdots to challenge the wits of the vigilant investigators.

On the evening of 22 April 1940, Wolkoff dined at the Ritz where she had been joined by Kent and 'another rich young man referred to as Geoffrey'. Knight noted that 'this is possibly Geoffrey Allen, brother of W.E.D. Allen'. Geoffrey was also the brother of Sam, whose American-born wife Barbara had taken Kent to the Russian Tea Rooms in February 1940, and had introduced him to Wolkoff. Apparently, Kent had met Anna's parents some time previously.

On one of her visits, Anna told Mackie that Joan Miller might be 'a most useful asset' and that she was going to invite her to dinner. The dinner took place at the Russian Tea Rooms on 23 April 1940 and after dinner Anna took Joan to her flat at Roland Gardens where she showed her some dresses that she was making. Joan admired everything that Anna showed her. Later that evening, Anna visited Mackie in very high spirits and told her that 'the child' (Miller) was quite unsuspecting and that she was going to make her a present of a dress she had admired. She said that she had 'a very good reason for doing so'. Her object was to get Miller to write a letter of thanks.

The next day, Joan received a dress from Anna and she responded with a letter of thanks. Presumably, Miller's letter was passed to Hélène de Munck so that she could analyse the handwriting. If so, then Joan Miller's handwriting evidently passed this less than rigorous test because a few days later Anna asked Mackie to invite Miller for dinner at The Parlour.

On 30 April 1940, Wolkoff told Mackie that 'all her incriminating papers were in a safe at the American Embassy'. She also claimed that Ambassador Joseph Kennedy had written

---

[24] Smirnoff stated that Wolkoff had also asked him to photograph copies of some propaganda pamphlets that had been dropped on Germany.

to President Roosevelt saying that 'things were so bad in Great Britain that trouble might be expected in less than a month' according to one version or 'at any time' in another dated 2 May 1940. Perhaps 'less than a month' was rather less compelling but the 2 May version also cited some alleged discussions of the War Cabinet. The discussion was said to have been 'most serious, that Mr. Winston Churchill was drunk and that Mr. Winston Churchill had entirely lost his following due to the appalling losses in Norway'[25].

Drunk or not, Churchill had evidently not 'lost his following' because he stepped up as Prime Minister the following week.

On 1 May 1940, Ramsay was reported as saying that he would 'welcome a Civil War with shots in the streets'. There was also considerable discussion and approval of the New British Broadcasting Station at 50.63 metres. This was the Nazi 'black propaganda' service with which William Joyce was associated.

On 12 May 1940, Mackie ascertained that Kent, Wolkoff, Enid Riddell and an Italian Duke had all dined together but Mackie had been unable to get his name. Mackie described Enid as 'about 35, height 5'6 or 7", slight build, fair hair worn in a long bob, blue or grey eyes, rather snub nose, usually wears a black costume, very good quality stockings and not much make-up'.

The name of the Italian Duke was resolved ten days later when Knight had Enid Riddell brought in for questioning. He reported that 'After some difficulty he had managed to break her down'. The Italian Duke was the Duke del Monte[26] and they had dined at L'Escargot, a fashionable Soho restaurant. Afterwards, they had visited the Embassy nightclub as guests of the Duke who was travelling incognito. Wolkoff, who was considered to be witty, had introduced him to Kent as 'Mr. Macaroni'.

Knight was ecstatic at this breakthrough and concluded that 'it is therefore reasonably certain that the known confidential information extracted from the Embassy records by Kent is now in the hands of the Italians'. But this breakthrough only came on

---

[25] KV 2/677 (94a).
[26] A photograph of del Monte is reproduced in Appendix: Images.

22 May 1940 two days after Kent and Wolkoff had been arrested. But only 'reasonably certain'? Surely under English Criminal Law a person can only be found guilty if it can be proved 'beyond reasonable doubt'. Was it possible that Maxwell Knight had acted rather hastily?

Mackie, Miller and Wolkoff dined at The Parlour on 13 May 1940, feasting on omelettes made to a recipe that Anna had brought back from her summer visit to the Sudetanland. Over dinner, they talked disparagingly about the Jews, the Freemasons and Winston Churchill. After Miller had left, Anna 'executed a dance of triumph' and declared 'I am sure that she suspects nothing. She will be a convert and prove most useful.'

On the evening of the 15 May 1940, Anna told Mackie that she wanted her help with a 'missing letter'. Apparently, she had put a letter in a letterbox in Cadogan Square but the intended recipient had never got it. 'I now want you to tell me a thoroughly dirty story and we will type it out and put it in the letterbox.' Anna addressed the envelope by hand but Mackie was unable to see what she had written. They then went together to Cadogan Square where Anna handed Mackie the envelope and asked her to put it through the letterbox at Number 67.

On their way home, Anna again showed her wit by saying 'It is something to have a name like a tin of fruit'. She was, of course, referring to the Duke del Monte, the assistant military attaché at the Italian Embassy.

On 16 May 1940, Mackie reported that Anna had told her that she had some documents photographed and that she had arranged for the photographs to be passed on to the Duke.

Kent and Wolkoff were arrested on 20 May 1940 and Captain Ramsay was picked up three days later. After holidaying in Scotland, he had stepped out of his London home at 8.30 a.m. to find two men waiting. He asked, 'Are you police officers?' and Detective Inspector Pearson replied, 'Yes, sir.'

After enquiring if they had come to arrest him, Ramsey admitted Pearson and Police Sergeant Bushell into his house, where he was served with a Detention Order under Defence Regulation 18B.

Ramsay said that it was ridiculous to accuse him of acts prejudicial to public safety and went into a tirade against the Government and the Press, alleging that they were Jew-ridden and Jew-controlled. He said that he had risen on seventy-three occasions from his place in the House of Commons to speak about Jews and Communists but that he failed to catch the Speaker's eye.

Pearson asked him if he was acquainted with Anna Wolkoff and he admitted that he met her about 18 months ago 'through people who had visited her father's Tea Rooms'. He said that Anna was keenly anti-Jew and had taken an interest in his work. He considered her to be loyal to this country and anti-Semitism was her only fault, if it was a fault.

Asked if he knew Tyler Kent, Ramsay said that he had met him through Anna, who had introduced him about a month or so ago. He insisted that he had never been to Kent's flat. A week later, Knight would have been able to expose Ramsay's lie by producing statements from the cook and the housemaid who recalled having seen Ramsay there on more than one occasion, both by himself and in the company of a woman with a gruff voice, presumably Anna.

The two Police Officers searched the premises and discovered Kent's Membership Card for the Right Club in a box on a table in Ramsay's study. It was dated 2 May 1940. They took possession of a quantity of correspondence and publications, as well as another Membership Card made out for Mrs. Christabel Sybil Nicholson.

On 25 May 1940, Marjorie Mackie was also 'arrested' and she was 'conveyed' to Holloway Prison where she could continue her investigations. Enid Riddell and Christabel Nicholson would join her there. They had both come under grave suspicion because they had actually met Tyler Kent.

In Enid's case, it was apparently only on purely social occasions but Christabel was an altogether more serious threat to National Security because she had actually obtained a pencilled copy of a document dated 15 May 1940 that Kent had taken from the Embassy. This was sufficiently serious for the British authorities to request permission from its American counterparts to allow the document to be produced in evidence at her forthcoming trial.

Herschel Johnson telephoned on 23 June 1940 and advised that the 'State Department much regret that they must refuse permission for this to be produced in evidence as its production might have a very serious effect on Anglo-American relations.'[27]

---

[27] KV 2/902 (32a).

# 14: The Fifth Column

So what had happened between 9 April 1940 when Knight had persuaded Anna to 'attempt to communicate' with William Joyce in Berlin and 20 May 1940 when Kent and Wolkoff were arrested? And why did Knight change his mind so radically about the threat they posed?

The first factor was the resignation of Neville Chamberlain as Prime Minister on 10 May 1940 and his replacement by Winston Churchill. The second factor was a genuine fear of invasion following the unexpected collapse of Allied resistance in face of the German juggernaut. A further fear was that a Fifth Column may have existed in Britain and that it was lying in readiness, awaiting the opportunity to assist an invading force. But as the country was never invaded, nobody knows what might have happened.

There were no surprises when Chamberlain opted to stand down. It was evident that he was not up to the job of leading a War Cabinet. He had only being going through the motions of being at war in the belief that he would eventually be able to deliver a negotiated peace and everyone would live happily ever after. There had been a plethora of peace feelers and Hitler had also been living in hope that a deal could be put together, but it was not to be. In fact, Hitler never gave up hope despite an escalating exchange of shots, bombs, torpedoes and propaganda.

Churchill was not everyone's choice as the man to replace Chamberlain but he did have the support of the Labour Party and that was crucial. The senior members of the Labour Party had refused to serve in Chamberlain's War Cabinet with the consequence that their supporters were not delivering the productivity demanded from the factories. This was an urgent requirement because while it's always the men in the front line who grab the glory, they are ultimately dependent upon the folks back home to deliver the arms and munitions.

Things changed when Churchill stepped up as Prime Minister on 10 May 1940 because he had the support of the Labour Party.

This was reflected in his War Cabinet with the two party leaders coming on board the following day. Clement Attlee[1], the Labour Party Leader, became Lord Privy Seal and Arthur Greenwood[2], the Deputy Leader, became a Minister without Portfolio. Robert Bruce Lockhart, the personal assistant of Lord Beaverbrook[3], told the story in his Diary entry for 15 May 1940[4].

A few days after joining Churchill's War Cabinet, Attlee and Greenwood had popped round to Beaverbrook's place for dinner. With Attlee slightly 'lit up' and Greenwood drunk, they boasted that they 'had turned Chamberlain out'. They had seen him after a recent debate and told him he must go but Chamberlain had wanted to stick on and had talked of reconstructing the government.

Attlee and Greenwood were scheduled to go to Bournemouth for the Labour Party Conference and they said that they would consult the rest of the Party. After consultation, a call was put through to Chamberlain, who was then in a Cabinet Meeting. He was told that 'he had to go and the sooner the better'. Chamberlain resigned within ten minutes. With Winston installed, Greenwood said that opposition to Government would not come from Labour but from Chamberlain Conservatives and that the Government would now deal ruthlessly with the Fifth Column.

On 16 May 1940, Guy Liddell had written in his diary that the Joint Intelligence Committee had made some very strong recommendations about the internment of all the Fascists and Communists and the case against the BUF was being 'worked up' or, in the terminology of the recent Weapons of Mass Destruction report, 'sexed-up'. Mosley's safe had been rifled and a document

---

[1] Clement Attlee (1883-1967) was Prime Minister from 1945 to 1951.
[2] Arthur Greenwood (1880-1954).
[3] Lord Beaverbrook, the Canadian newspaper magnate formerly known as Max Aitken, became Minister of Aircraft Production. A man of enormous energy, he transformed the productivity of Britain's aircraft factories at a critical time.
[4] *The Diaries of Sir Robert Bruce Lockhart 1939-1965*, edited by Kenneth Young (1980)

has been obtained showing the whole scheme for setting up wireless masts in Germany. The masts were for a proposed commercial radio station that Mosley was working on with Hitler. Liddell added that 'we heard about this scheme more than a year ago'.

On 17 May 1940, Liddell 'gathered that Roosevelt was proposing to give us 100 destroyers, somewhat out of date but nevertheless useful. He also proposed to give us a portion of his first-line aircraft ... There is little room for doubt that Roosevelt would bring the whole country [the United States] into the war now, if he possibly could'.

That same day, Sir Ernest Holderness, the Assistant Secretary at the Home Office, phoned Liddell to say that he had been asked to prepare a memo on the BUF. Liddell responded by telling him that 'we had prepared a memo for the Home Office a week ago recommending the internment of 500 selected individuals but that our suggestion had been turned down'. It was then arranged that 'certain representatives from this office should go to help Holderness in his task'. Evidently, Holderness was not in sympathy with the official line within the Home Office.

At 3 p.m. on 18 May 1940, Maxwell Knight visited Herschel Johnson the Counsel at the American Embassy and gave him a 'sexed-up' version of events. He told Johnson that 'Information of a very serious nature has come to the attention of Scotland Yard' and that Tyler Kent had become mixed up in a circle with connections to both the Germans and the Russians. Knight said that Kent had been under observation since his arrival in England in October 1939, following his meeting Ludwig Matthias, a suspected German spy.

Knight assured Johnson that surveillance of both Kent and the American Embassy had been 'very extensive', and that it had been discovered that Kent had been leaking information to a Fifth Column organisation. Knight quoted details from some of the Embassy correspondence that Kent had shown to Anna. He also described the activities of the Right Club and Captain Ramsay, and listed their various meetings.

Naturally, Knight didn't mention that his real objective was 'to work up a case against the BUF'. Or that despite having had four agents on the case for up to nine months, the only evidence that he had obtained about the putative Fifth Column had been contrived by persuading Anna 'to attempt to communicate' with William Joyce. Or that Ramsay's main objective had been to put in place an organisation to counter the Communist uprising that he believed to be imminent. Knight had exaggerated for effect.

After telling Johnson that he was planning to arrest Wolkoff on Monday, he requested permission to search Kent's rooms. Having accepted Knight's fanciful tale, Johnson could hardly refuse and he promised that he would endeavour to get the required authority from Ambassador Kennedy. When this was forthcoming, Knight obtained a search warrant.

Knight's problem all along had been that he had obtained a wealth of Intelligence, but absolutely nothing in the way of hard evidence, only the Coded Letter with the dubious provenance that Anna had supposedly tried to communicate with William Joyce. It was a desperately thin case and it may not have stood up in an open court against a smart Defence team. Knight obviously had 'right on his side' and perhaps he hoped the Gods would be sympathetic.

The following day, Liddell noted in his diary that Johnson 'was very perturbed since Kent had access to the Embassy ciphers'. This was clearly a genuine concern based on Knight's false assertions and it provided the basis for the later cover stories.

Kent and Wolkoff were arrested on 20 May 1940 and the following day Liddell noted that Attlee and Greenwood were 'pressing for some action to be taken against the BUF'. However, John Anderson, the Home Secretary, was 'arguing on judicial lines, saying that he had no evidence that would lead him to suppose that members of the BUF would actively assist the enemy if they landed in this country'.

Later that evening, Liddell and Knight attended a meeting with Anderson among others. 'M [Knight] was extremely good and made all his points very quietly and forcibly and he described something of the underground activities of the BUF and also the present case against Tyler Kent involving Maule Ramsay.'

Anderson agreed that the case against Ramsay was 'rather serious' but he did not seem to think that it involved the BUF. Knight then explained that Mosley and Maule Ramsay were 'in constant touch' with one another and that many members of the Right Club were also members of the BUF.

'In constant touch'? Well hardly, although they did meet up occasionally. Mosley's office was in The Sanctuary, close by the Palace of Westminster and Ramsay may have dropped round for an occasional chat. On the other hand, Mackie had previously reported that Mosh had told her of Jock's hatred of Fascism. Also, apart from some notable exceptions, very few BUF members were also members of the Right Club. Certainly, the elusive James Hughes, who 'couldn't be found' when required to testify at Anna Wolkoff's trial, was a member of the Right Club under his real name and he was also a prominent member of the BUF under the alias of P.G. Taylor. Another of this rare breed was Fay Taylour, a famous biker and racing motorist. Fay later acknowledged that she had joined the Right Club but as far as she could see, it had no political agenda whatsoever.

By 1940, the Right Club was a lame duck except for a few middle-aged women, some of whom frequented the Russian Tea Rooms. Marjorie Mackie often dined there so she could meet Anna and catch up on her gossip. As Mackie had met very few of the listed members and some of these only occasionally, her main source of 'intelligence' was the tittle-tattle that she picked up from Anna.

Marjorie Mackie did her best to liven things up for the Right Club. After taking up residence in The Parlour, she held a flat-warming party and some twenty or so 'sympathisers' turned up. Captain Ramsay made a brief appearance, and Mackie had introduced him by greeting him as 'The Leader'.

Despite Knight having dug deep into his imagination to describe the links between the BUF and the Right Club, Anderson was clearly not impressed. He said that he needed to be 'reasonably convinced' that the BUF might assist the enemy. Unless he could get such evidence he thought that it would be a mistake to imprison Mosley and his supporters, who would be extremely bitter after the war, when democracy was going through its severest trials.

On 22 May 1940, Liddell discussed 'last night's meeting' with Vernon Kell, the Director-General of MI5, and also the question of whether the Prime Minister should be informed through Desmond Morton, Churchill's Intelligence guru. Liddell noted 'Kell thinks that we should not do this but he is going to have a talk with Vansittart'. Presumably, Kell expected that Vansittart would speak to Churchill.

Robert Vansittart had been the Permanent Under-Secretary of Foreign Office Affairs until 1 January 1938 when he was switched to a newly created position of Chief Diplomatic Adviser. Nobody quite knew why or what he was supposed to be doing in his new job except that he ran his own Intelligence Service focused on Germany. Several of his agents have since been identified and although their activities are of interest, they are outside the scope of the Kent-Wolkoff Affair except to the extent that Vansittart had been feeding intelligence to Churchill and obviously had his ear.

Notwithstanding his comment to Liddell, Kell evidently did write to Desmond Morton because Morton's acknowledgment (dated 23 May 1940) is on file. Writing from 10 Downing Street, Morton confirmed that he had shown Kell's letter and attachment regarding the 'deplorable case concerning the American Embassy' to the Prime Minister. Churchill was said to have been very grateful and he had shown the story to members of the War Cabinet[5].

Later in the day on 22 May 1940, Liddell was able to record that 'we appear to have been to some degree successful in our mission to the Home Office yesterday. A selection of leading BUF members are to be interned, including Mosley, also other representatives of the parties of the Right including Maule Ramsay MP.'

---

[5] KV 2/840.

The Minutes of the War Cabinet[6] reflect the sudden change. At a Meeting on 18 May 1940, the War Cabinet had before them a Memorandum by John Anderson, the Home Secretary, on 'Invasion of Great Britain: possible co-operation of a Fifth Column'. In regard to the British Fascists, the Home Secretary explained at length the difficulty of taking any effective action in the absence of evidence that indicated that the organisation, as such, was engaged in disloyal activities.

At a Meeting on 22 May 1940, the Home Secretary gave particulars of evidence that had been discovered, which showed that the leader of a certain organisation had been concerned in subversive activity. The Home Secretary said that he'd had a long talk with two officers of MI5[7] who had devoted special attention over many years to the Fascist Organisation but they had been unable to produce any evidence on which action could be based.

There was indeed some evidence in the other direction but they had given it as their opinion that, say 25-30 per cent of members would be willing, if so ordered, to go to any lengths. The Home Secretary said that his own view was that Sir Oswald Mosley, although a mischievous person, was too clever to put himself in the wrong by giving treasonable orders.

As regards the number of people in the Fascist Organisation, action would be taken in the first instance against 25 or 30 people. It would be seen whether this was sufficient to cripple the Organisation or whether it would be necessary to proceed further.

Neville Chamberlain, the Lord President of the Council, said that 'the view, which the Prime Minister had expressed, was that if any doubt existed the persons in question should be detained without delay'. This view met with general approval.

A Confidential Annex[8] of the same date described the 'Subversive Activities in London'. Chamberlain had presented the Annex at Churchill's request and it disclosed that Captain

---

[6] CAB 65/7.
[7] The two MI5 Officers, who were not named in the Minutes, were Liddell and Knight.
[8] CAB 65/13.

Ramsay, who was the principal organiser of the Right Club, had been in treasonable practices in conjunction with an employee (a United States citizen by name Tyler Kent) at the United States Embassy.

John Anderson, the Secretary of State for the Home Department, said he was in possession of a full report dealing with this matter. The report showed that a woman named Anna Wolkoff, who had been interned some two or three days previously, had been in relations with an employee at the United States Embassy where he held the position of code and cipher clerk.

The report went on to reveal that Captain Ramsay was in relations with this woman and also with Sir Oswald Mosley. A search had been made of the rooms occupied by the employee referred to and a large number of incriminating documents had been discovered, including the membership book of the Right Club.

Chamberlain said that this was obviously a most serious matter. The information disclosed that 'this body' [the Right Club] had been carrying on pro-German activities and secret subversive work with the object of disorganising the Home Front and hindering the prosecution of the war. Chamberlain also said that the report disclosed that Anna Wolkoff had means of communicating with persons in Germany.

Of course, Anna Wolkoff's only 'means of communicating with persons in Germany' was through Hélène de Munck, Knight's undercover agent. No wonder that Jowitt would later report that X could not be found; or that the process server was unable to locate James Hughes, the agent provocateur; or that so many colourful cover stories had been generated after the war.

With some background support from Vansittart, Knight's 'sexed-up' report had now done the trick and the crack-down on Britain's putative Fifth Column got underway the following day. However, it was not confined to the 25 or 30 people that Anderson had considered sufficient to cripple the organisation.

No official list of internees has ever been published but the Home Office reported that 747 members of the BUF had been interned and that by April 1943 all but 30 of these had been released[9]. Information provided by former internees suggests that this number is significantly understated, even ignoring the non-BUF internees like Nicholas Smirnoff (Anna Wolkoff's photographer), Erland Echlin and Jimmy Green (the Canadian journalists) and their secretary Miss W. Hooton, etc.

Guy Liddell noted on 25 May 1940 that 'Vernon Kell had told him that he had met Desmond Morton who advised that Churchill was taking a strong view about the internment of all Fifth Columnists. What seems to have moved him more than anything was the Tyler Kent case'.

The internment of all Fifth Columnists? Well, not quite all because for one the Hon. Mrs. Ismay Ramsay was never interned. Maybe Mosh's status as Viscount Gormanston's eldest daughter gave her immunity, despite her having been regarded as the real brains behind her husband's activities. Certainly, there was a distinct shortage of Landed Gentry among the internees. No Lords, almost no Ladies and no Princes nor Princesses. Viscountess Downe, a friend of Queen Mary and a prominent Fascist, escaped internment. Similarly, the Marquess of Tavistock (later the 12th Duke of Bedford), Viscount Lymington (later the 9th Earl of Portsmouth) and the 35th Earl of Mar were never interned even though they had also attended some of the 'Secret Meetings'.

Lady Pearson seems to have been the exception. She had been a prominent Fascist and was interned until her brother intervened. He was Sir Henry Page Croft MP, the Parliamentary Under-Secretary for War. Reportedly, he stormed in to see John Anderson the Home Secretary and secured her release.

Despite the supposedly sinister influences of the Right Club, it is remarkable that very few of those who had been listed as members were interned. Accordingly, the Duke of Wellington, the Earl of Galloway, Lord Carnegie, Lord Colum Stuart, Lord Sempill, Lord and Lady Ronald Graham, Lord Redesdale (father of the Mitford girls), Sir Alexander Walker (one of its main

---

[9] HO 45/25696.

sponsors) and John Bailey (Churchill's former son-in-law) never had to suffer the indignities of a spell behind bars.

Further proof if it were needed that there is 'One Law for the Rich and Another for the Poor'.

# 15: Internment

Being neither a Hon. nor a Lady, Heather Donovan was arrested at 6 p.m. on 1 June 1940. Her husband, Bryan Donovan, an Assistant Director General of the BUF, had been among the first to be picked up on the 23rd May. Like her husband, Heather had been an active member of the BUF, serving as a Women's District Leader and as a Drum Major. During the Fifties, she wrote a 25-page letter to her cousin Monica describing her experiences.

Heather was 23 at the time of her arrest. She considered herself 'hard working, ambitious, energetic, adventurous and rather crazy'. She had been married for only four months but by the beginning of May, she suspected that she was pregnant. On the day of her arrest, she had returned home to her flat in Notting Hill Gate, London, to find two men and a woman outside waiting for her. After introducing themselves, they searched her flat and seized her wireless set. The technical expert who examined the wireless set later reported that it was a receiver that could not be used as a transmitter. The arresting officer, Detective Inspector Albert Hunt of Special Branch, accompanied by WPC Sanderson then conveyed her to Holloway where they obtained a 'body receipt'.

She wrote that, en route to Holloway, her escort had 'already got me shaken to the core by telling me that my husband would be shot'. She felt 'completely helpless ... [and] ... had exactly $\frac{1}{2}^d$ in the world'. She kept remembering the threat that her husband would be shot. Inside Holloway, she went through Reception and was eventually 'pushed, not very gently' into a box four foot by three. Nearby was 'a tart who told her salacious tales' and a thief. She also got to know another detainee, Fay Taylour the racing motorist. After spending several hours in 'her hole', she was strip-searched and the $\frac{1}{2}^d$ coin that represented her worldly wealth was discovered.

Heather was not impressed by the prison cuisine or by the maggots and cockroaches that were frequently discovered in their food. Soon the 'whole Wing' was full; 'sixty-eight of us and all but five or six were BUF members. And what a wonderful bunch of women they were, with a few exceptions'. She met Lady Domvile, Mrs. Elam who had been there before as a suffragette, Lady Diana Mosley and Mrs. Whinfield who had a grand manner and all the airs and graces of a Duchess.

She also met two members of the Right Club: Christabel Nicholson who was known as Nicky 'what a character ... one of the star comics' and Enid Riddell 'a grand scout'. At his trial, Tyler Kent had named both Christabel Nicholson and Enid Riddell as among the other members of the Right Club that he had met.

Heather also met Rita Shelmerdine whose husband Bill had come under the deepest suspicion because of entries in his diary. On one occasion, he had written 'Remove British Queen' and two days later, 'Install Italian Queen'. According to Heather, it took MI5 six months to discover that he kept bees.

'We had high jinks with an MI5 agent. She was among those already there when I arrived and they'd spotted her for what she was. Heavens, what fun we had leading her up the garden path. We would pretend to some secret, fantastic-sounding plot, discussing it in dark corners in loud penetrating whispers, making quite certain that she could hear us'. Heather Donovan didn't disclose the name of the MI5 agent because 'the poor nut was only doing her duty'.

One day the MI5 agent was called to the Governor's Office and on her return she told the other inmates that she was being transferred to Strangeways[1]. She cried because she was being parted from such good friends. Her good friends responded gleefully with comments such as 'I'll bet you'll be glad when you get home'.

---

[1] The prison in Manchester where Anna Wolkoff was incarcerated whilst awaiting trial.

208

The internees also had to endure the blitz, including one bomb that fell just beyond the prison wall and another that landed 'slap in the middle' of B Wing, which held 200 women prisoners, but no one was seriously hurt.

Later, Heather and several other women received a letter from a husband who had been interned elsewhere that contained the dreaded news 'Just being moved to Ham Common' and then no further news for weeks. Word had got around about MI5's Interrogation Centre and from his cell in Brixton, Captain Ramsay raised his voice in protest. He wrote to Sir Donald Somervell, the Attorney General, on 9 September 1940:

> Dear Somervell
>
> At a place on Ham Common called Latchmere House, MI5 appear to have instituted a system of 3$^{rd}$ degree including 22½ hours of solitary confinement in sound proof cells … In one case, the examiner (one Captain Knight of MI5 who lives at Dolphin Court[2]) tried to wring out some 'evidence' that I knew all about the so-called New BBC (which puts out German propaganda) …

Christabel Nicholson's husband, a former admiral, was never interned, but she became ill and lost weight alarmingly. She was transferred to the Prison Hospital, but the treatment was so bad she pleaded to be returned to her cell where her friends could care for her. Two other women went mad and were placed in padded cells.

Shortly after her imprisonment, Heather had discovered that she was pregnant. She haemorrhaged and lost the baby. This left her debilitated and in need of milk but none was provided and she had no money to buy any herself. Then every morning, a ½ pint of milk appeared outside her cell door. It was months before she discovered the identity of her benefactress. It was Enid Riddell 'whom she hardly knew'. Enid had been a member of the Right Club. According to Heather 'they held her for years for no better

[2] It was actually Dolphin Square.

reason than that she had once spoken to Anna Wolkoff in a Club'.

Heather ended the letter to her cousin with a typical British understatement 'There is such a thing as getting more than you bargained for. You wanted to know about Holloway. Well, you now know.'

The outcome was not as bad as Heather had feared. She was released in November 1940, on condition that she resided with her parents, reported to the police and did not engage in any BUF activities[3]. Her husband also escaped the firing squad but he was sent to Latchmere House on Ham Common. Maxwell Knight interviewed him there on 25 August 1940.

Fay Taylour (1908-1983) also left a memoir of her experiences in Holloway Prison. Born in Ireland, she had been a star of the motorcycle racing circuit before becoming even better known behind the wheel of a racing car. She can be seen on video winning the Ladies' Race at Brooklands in 1931, after clocking up 98 mph[4].

Fay had joined the BUF as a protest against the declaration of war. This resulted in her arrest and she was conveyed to Holloway on 1 June 1940, the same day as Heather Donovan. She remained at Holloway until the autumn of 1942 when she was transferred to the Women's Internment Camp in Port Erin, Isle of Man, where she spent another year. She found the conditions there much better and the internees were housed in seaside hotels. She entitled her memoir 'Holloway Jail by One of the Graces of 18B' and introduced it with several lines of verse. Like Heather, she commented on the MI5 spy who had been amongst their midst.

> The kindly soul who said 'What rot!
> There are no spies amongst our lot'.
> She gave us fruit and sweets and jam,

---

[3] Brian Simpson *In the Highest Degree Odious* (1992)
[4] British Pathé News, *1931 A Year to Remember.*

And heard our story from the pram;
One voice insisted SHE'S A SPY
Which made poor Mata Hari cry,
But it was true! She took her toll,
Agent Provocateur was her role.

Fay had been charged with being a member of the BUF. Under the new regulations, mere membership was sufficient to justify internment and even those who had previously quit the movement could also be interned. A new catch-all clause allowed for internment of members of any organisation where the Secretary of State was satisfied that either:

(a)   The organisation is subject to foreign influence or control or

(b)   The persons in control of the organisation have or have had associations with persons concerned in the government of, or sympathies with the system of government of, any power with which His Majesty is at war.

The new regulation known as Defence Regulation 18B (1A) had been cleverly worded to suggest that it was a general provision but, in fact, it had been aimed squarely at the BUF because at the time Germany was the only country with which His Majesty was then at war. It could easily be argued that the BUF fitted the new criteria, exactly as intended.

Did Mosley have or had he had 'associations' with Germany? Undoubtedly. His second wife Diana and her sister Unity Mitford were famously chummy with Hitler. Unity had been so distressed by the declaration of war that she had attempted suicide shortly after hearing the news. She had been in Berlin when she tried to put a bullet in her brain. She failed to achieve the required result but she was left seriously impaired and from the kindness of his heart Adolf then arranged for her to be shipped home.

For many years, Mosley had cherished the hope of getting into commercial radio, and he and his pal Bill Allen had searched high and low for a suitable offshore transmission facility. Eventually, they started negotiations with the German government but without any success. Then Diana stepped in and after working her charm on Hitler a deal was done. The story goes that Mosley had then double-crossed Allen by excluding him from the deal even though he had been providing some of the initial funding. Whatever the truth, Allen certainly fell out with Mosley. After the war it was reported that there were smiles all round when they re-discovered each other in the same restaurant.

Mosley and Diana had also been wed in secret at the home of Josef Goebbels, the chief of Nazi Propaganda. Hitler had been a guest and Bill Allen was one of Mosley's witnesses.

Was Mosley subject to 'foreign influence and control'? Probably not. Despite having similar political outlooks, Mosley and Hitler never seemed to hit it off and they apparently only ever met twice and one of these occasions was at Mosley's wedding.

There is compelling evidence that Mussolini contributed to the funding of Mosley's Fascist party during the first three years of its existence. Mosley reciprocated by promoting Mussolini's policies in his journals. However, Mussolini eventually realised that Mosley had nothing to offer and pulled the plug. As a consequence, Mosley went cap in hand to Hitler and was given a handout in 1936, with others later. But that's politics: all parties get their funding wherever they can and whether or not they deliver the implied rewards is entirely another matter. Investigations into the sources of funding of any political party are likely to be embarrassing, which is why it's rarely done.

The Secretary of State had no problem in deciding that the BUF satisfied the qualifying conditions of the new legislation and that was it. The big round-up got under way.


Having given of her best in verse, Fay Taylour resorted to prose to provide further details of the woman she called Mata Hari and asked the question, 'Was she real?' She then answered the question herself. 'Yes', she proclaimed, 'Mata Hari was despicably real'.

The moment that Fay had entered 'F' Wing another detainee had pointed her out and said out loud, 'That woman is a spy'. The next morning the woman accused of being a spy entered Fay's cell and protested, 'Ridiculous isn't it, calling me a spy?' Fay recalled her as a member of the Right Club and the woman claimed that she was also the Secretary, Founder and Organiser. She insisted that it was only reasonable that she should have been one of the first to be interned. She claimed that no one could join the club without her sanction and that she had personally sanctioned Fay's membership.

Fay had understood that the club was anti-Communist and against the war. The members went to lectures given by historians, economists and scientists. Fay had joined after going to one such lecture; there were no entry forms or regulations. One afternoon, she had visited Mrs. Ramsay for tea and all the time 'this woman', whom she named as Marjorie Amor, had been present.

After having made herself known to Fay, Marjorie Amor lowered her voice and told her of the 'top secret' plans which the club intended to carry out when the war was over. They included taking over radio stations, newspapers and the government. Fay had a 'barely controllable' desire to laugh at the thought of fat, well-heeled, coffee-drinking women marching on government positions.

Fay knew that the Right Club was not militant, far from it. She decided that this woman must be a little loopy. She recalled her odd introduction of Captain Ramsay at the one and only club gathering that she had heard of or attended. It was just an afternoon bun fight in a long room over a garage[5]. In the middle or towards the end of the tea party, the door opened and Marjorie Amor sprang up and announced 'The Leader'. It was Captain Ramsay but no one else had ever referred to him as such. It had sounded most odd.

The following morning, two men from MI5 interviewed Fay. They wanted to ask her a few questions. What did she know

---

[5] Evidently 'The Parlour'.

about the Right Club? She told them and then they asked if she had ever heard Captain Ramsay having been called 'The Leader'. Having discounted Marjorie Amor's pronouncement at the tea party, she said 'No'.

During the following weeks, 'F' wing was divided on whether or not Amor was a spy. One young woman considered it a shame to call her a spy because she was so friendly and nice and they had decided to open a business together after the war.

But the truth was finally revealed when one of the prisoners attended court and saw Miss Amor on the Government bench testifying against the Right Club. Fay Taylour completed her story by saying, 'And no one has heard of her since'.

MI5's Special Source reported on 6 December 1940 that Anna's mother had informed him that 'the spy' (M/Y alias Marjorie Mackie) was first discovered by Mrs. Nicholson who found out that she was in the service of the Government through an influential friend of her husband, Admiral Nicholson[6].


Maxwell Knight interrogated Bryan Donovan, Heather's husband, at Latchmere House on 25 August 1940. Although described as 'an interrogation', it was more of a friendly chat. The two men had much in common. They were of a similar age and both were ex-teachers. Donovan had a small claim to fame because he had once employed Eric Blair as a teacher, long before he adopted his penname of 'George Orwell'.

Knight prefaced his chat by observing that he had noticed that all the BUF members that he had met were '100% patriotic'. It could have been soft soap, but it was probably true. Knight also revealed that he had spent fifteen years studying political movements of all kinds, Communism as well.

Knight then tried to pump Donovan on what he knew about the funding of the BUF from the two nations Germany and Italy with whom Britain was then at war. Donovan denied all knowledge. Knight then asked him about Mosley's radio venture

---

[6] KV 2/842 piece 421a.

with Hitler and a perceived change in BUF policy as the radio deal approached fruition.

Donovan gave as good as he got. Knight then enquired about 'the much vaunted Intelligence Department'. The infamous P.G. Taylor had headed up this department but his name did not appear in Knight's report. Apparently, without waiting for a reply, Knight then asked an entirely different question. The discontinuity in the interrogation indicates that Donovan's response and any of their other dialogue on this topic had been edited out.

Knight then asked Donovan's opinions on other BUF members ranging from the management down to the lower echelons.

Knight also raised the 'vexed question' of the New British Broadcasting Station, Joyce's black propaganda radio channel, and said, 'I expect you've heard a hell of a lot of hot talk about that, if anybody's discussed it with you. That exercises the attention of the authorities quite a lot'. Donovan admitted hearing it once, but said that he had not been sufficiently interested to listen in again; in any case, his own set could not receive short wave.

'Well now', Knight revealed, 'Roughly since the invasion of Holland and Belgium that station has been broadcasting material which is ... incitements to revolution'. It was 'panic propaganda' advising people to take all their money out of the banks and into the hills before the oncoming Germans. Donovan agreed that 'no reasonable person' would say that there was a 'word to be said for that sort of thing'.

'Yet', Knight continued, 'A tremendous number of BUF members have advertised that station'. Knight then cited several examples. Donovan agreed and said that the theory was that the broadcasters were using a transmitter on the back of a lorry somewhere. He also agreed that there were some 'fanatical' BUF members but he believed that these were all among 'the lesser fry'.

Knight then turned the spotlight on William Joyce and asked Donovan if he had ever been known as 'The Professor'. Donovan admitted that he had first been introduced to him as Professor Joyce but agreed that it had been 'all tripe'. Knight then revealed that one of the announcers on the New British Broadcasting Station was referred to as 'The Professor'.

Donovan asserted 'You could not mistake Joyce'. Knight disagreed and asked, 'Have you ever heard him mimic a cockney? He used to do a middle class Irishman frightfully well'.

Knight then enquired about where Joyce's first wife was 'the one who married Piercy'[7]. Donovan said that he thought that they were down near Brighton or somewhere near there. Knight then revealed that he had known her before she became Mrs. Joyce when she was a Miss Barr, Hazel Barr. This was perfectly true because Hazel had told the same story to Heather, her eldest daughter. Heather even remembers Knight coming to their house on one occasion when her father was out, probably in 1934.

Knight then enquired about John Angus Macnab, Joyce's close friend and his former partner in a coaching school. 'Do you happen to know whether he was ever interested in codes and ciphers?' Donovan didn't but he said that he was one of the best chess players that he had ever met. Mental gymnastics. He said that 'there would be grounds for thinking that he would be interested at least in the academic side of ciphers and codes'.

Finally, Knight enquired about Captain Ramsay, which Knight regarded as 'dangerous ground'. Donovan said that he would not think much of any conspiracy in which Ramsay was a prime mover. He was just a Jew hater and he hated Donovan because he had once been a Mason.

Knight seemed surprised, 'Because you were a Mason? It's a curious thing about Ramsay. He would just look at somebody's nose, he would condemn you and me right away because our noses are big'. He then enquired how Ramsay and Mosley were getting on now that they were fellow inmates in Brixton Prison.

---

[7] Eric Hamilton Piercy.

Donovan replied, 'They get on quite well', to which Knight responded, 'They used not to at one time'.

That was not what Knight had told Anderson the Home Secretary when he had been 'working up' a case against Mosley on 20 May 1940. On that occasion, Knight asserted that Mosley and Maule Ramsay were 'in constant touch' with one another and that many members of the Right Club were also members of the BUF.

Evidently, Knight had again exaggerated for effect.

# 16: More Spies

Whether or not Tyler Kent was a spy, there was certainly an interesting assortment of authentic spies at loose in Britain in the run up to WWII and beyond.

Isaac Don Levine, a Washington journalist, first made the British Government aware of the activities of Soviet spies in Britain in September 1939. His source was Walter Krivitsky, a former Soviet Intelligence officer for Western Europe. Krivitsky, who had been based in The Hague, had defected in 1937 after receiving an invitation to visit Moscow. He turned down the invitation, after having had the premonition that the visit was to celebrate his having won a place in one of Stalin's purges. He eventually reached Washington, where he became friendly with Levine, a fellow Jewish Russian émigré.

Walter Krivitsky was the cover name of Shmelka or Samuel Ginsberg (1889-1941) and at some stage he had discussed the worsening world situation with Levine. Krivitsky who was normally extremely cagey, unburdened himself by saying that he knew of at least two Soviet agents who were operating 'within the innermost sanctums of the British Government'[1]. He described one as a 'code clerk in the Cabinet' whose name was King. The other was working in the Committee of Imperial Defence but he couldn't remember the man's name.

After Hitler had signed a non-aggression pact with Stalin, Levine decided to act and he obtained an interview with Lord Lothian, the British Ambassador. During the course of the visit, Lothian was briefed on the presence of Soviet espionage in Britain. He learned that King, the spy in the British Foreign Office, had been handing out information to the Soviet authorities 'for a long time'.

This was sufficient for MI5 to get a fix on Captain John Herbert King, a 55-year-old coding expert, but curiously Liddell

---

[1] Gordon Brook-Shepherd, *The Storm Petrels* (1977).

wrote in his diary on 20 September 1939 that 'it is doubtful if we shall prosecute'. Well, of course, the Foreign Office would not have wanted its competence to be thrown into question, particularly not after the recent declaration of war.

On 27 September 1939, Liddell recorded that the King case was developing in 'an interesting way' and the following day King signed a confession admitting that he had been working for the Soviets since 1935. He explained that he had succumbed to temptation because not being a permanent civil servant, he wasn't entitled to a pension and he wanted to put something away for his old age.

There is some doubt on how much King had been earning. The files in the National Archives show that he had been on a salary of £500 p.a., which if true, was very good going in those days and more than enough to set aside something for his old age. However, Gordon Brook-Shepherd[2] observed that the salary scales for Foreign Office cipher clerks in 1939 were in the range £85-£350 p.a. and 'as King was listed thirteenth out of the sixteen clerks his pay cannot have been at the top end of the scale'. The lower levels identified by Brook-Shepherd seem more likely because the Foreign Office would have wanted to avoid any criticism that it might have been under-paying its coding clerks.

Contrary to Liddell's earlier expectation, King was tried *in camera* on 18 October 1939. He pleaded 'Guilty' and was sentenced to ten years. However, the facts were not made public until 7 June 1956 when 'a very brief, factual Foreign Office press communiqué' was released. Obviously, it had not been considered desirable to publicise the 'chinks in the armour' until long after the event. Or was there more to it than that?

As King was employed as a code clerk in the Foreign Office, he would have been a very valuable contact for the Soviets. It has been postulated that if Krivitsky hadn't exposed King, then possibly Stalin may have tipped off Hitler on how woefully ill prepared Britain was in the wake of Dunkirk and things may have turned out very differently.

---

[2] Gordon Brook-Shepherd, *The Storm Petrels* (1977).

This seems highly unlikely because Stalin also had other agents in place and it was reported that Stalin's strategy had been to remain chummy with both sides in the hope that he would then be well placed to pick up the pieces. Obviously, Churchill knew all too well how desperate Britain's position really was and, in this context, his exchanges with Roosevelt through the American Embassy in London take on a new complexion. If both Hitler and Stalin were being kept aware of the developing closeness of Anglo-American relations, it may have given each of them food for thought.

If that had been the grand strategy then it certainly worked because Hitler continually sought a peace deal with Britain from the day that war was declared through every stage of the conflict right to the bitter end. He kept hoping that Britain would agree a negotiated peace but despite all the military and naval setbacks, Britain refused to lie down.

Arising out of Krivitsky's revelations, Liddell noted that another man in the code section of the Foreign Office had been suspended pending interrogation. He was Major Grange. Another man named Raymond Oake was being interrogated although it seemed 'doubtful if he is very closely involved'. In his confession, King had identified Oake as having introduced him to Henry Pieck, his Soviet spymaster, in the International Club in Geneva. At the time, Oake was courting the stepdaughter of Captain Harvey, MI6's spy chief in Geneva, and had since married her.

Krivitsky was then invited to London where travelling as Mr. Thomas he arrived on 19 January 1940. Although initially scheduled for a three-week stay, he was asked to extend his visit. He returned to Canada, from whence he came, on 26 February.

During his stay in London, Jane Archer née Sissmore, MI5's Soviet specialist, questioned him about other leaks from the Foreign Office and the Committee of Imperial Defence. Krivitsky told her that 'a young aristocrat was the source, a young man probably under thirty ... almost certainly educated at Eton and Oxford'.

With the benefit of hindsight, Krivitsky's clue pointed to Donald Maclean (1913-1983) who later achieved notoriety by fleeing to Moscow with Guy Burgess in 1951. He was also one of 'The Cambridge Five'. Maclean had joined the Foreign Office in October 1935 and the investigators may have been thrown off the scent because Maclean had been educated at Greshams and Cambridge. Also, he was then no longer at the Foreign Office, having been posted to the Paris Embassy in September 1938. Having defected in 1937, Krivitsky was rather out of touch but nevertheless he named a lot of names.

Some of these were listed in Jane Archer's report released into the National Archives[3] but evidently this is not a full list and according to Gordon Brook-Shepherd who had been given privileged access, Krivitsky had revealed almost 100 Soviet agents operating throughout the world, sixty-one of whom were located in Britain or working against its interests elsewhere.

Among the names that filtered through into the National Archives was a clerk in the Cipher Department of the Foreign Office, named Oldham. This was Ernest Holloway Oldham who had offered his services to the Soviet Union in 1927. But as Krivitsky had pointed out, he had committed suicide in October 1933.

Krivitsky also fingered a man identified as 'D. Pritt, KC MP'. There could not have been too many candidates around at the time who were both an MP and a King's Counsel to boot. According to Krivitsky, Pritt was 'one of the chief recruiting agents for Soviet underground organisations'. He had spent time in Moscow writing up the trials of Zinoviev-Bucharin in such a way that 'it would be accepted by Western countries'.

MI5 was evidently unable to develop a case against the Soviet's chief recruiting agent, even though there was a Labour MP by name Denis Nowell Pritt, who was also a King's Counsel. Some people might have considered it worthwhile interviewing this man, even if it was only for a brief chat on the terrace at the House of Commons but evidently no one within MI5 did so.

---

[3] KV 2/805.

However, the most interesting name on Krivitsky's list was Kurt Jahnke, the man whom 'Gill of the Foreign Office' would later discuss with Herschel Johnson at the American Embassy in February 1940, as the recipient of the intelligence gleaned from 'The Doctor' at the American Embassy in Berlin.

The MI5 files on Tyler Kent include an extract from an interview with 'Dictionary' dated 10 August 1950[4] and according to this extract, 'Tyler Kent supplied material regularly from the time of his recruitment in 1938 until about September 1940'. Dictionary was unable to give any details for controlling Kent but stated that the photocopies [of the Embassy documents] reached the Jahnke Büro first via the Embassy courier in London and later through Petroff in France. Dictionary said that he couldn't recall the name of Anna Wolkoff.

Dictionary was the code name for Carl Marcus who had been Kurt Jahnke's secretary since 1938. On 13 November 1944, Marcus had crossed over to the Allied lines as Jahnke's emissary with a message for Robert Vansittart, a senior British mandarin who had run his own intelligence service during the thirties. The nub of the message was that with Germany on the verge of defeat, Jahnke had ideas for spreading further disruption and also for managing the peace.

Kurt Jahnke (1882-1945) was a man who played many parts and over the years had many aliases. In the United States, he was known as Kort Border; in Mexico he was Jose Iturber and Steffens; in Britain he travelled under the name of Johnson and elsewhere he was Jensen or Jansen.

Born 17 February 1882 in Gnesen in the Prussian province of Posen, he emigrated to the United States in 1899 at the age of 17. At some stage he became a naturalised American and served with the US Marines in the Philippines. He was discharged due to ill health.

In 1918, he was described as 6ft and 175 lbs. He was broad shouldered, had light brown hair, a small moustache, a thin face

---

[4] KV2/545 - 13

and some gold-filled teeth. He was said to speak good English. In 1941, his dark hair was 'slightly greying at the temples', his social manners were considered 'perfect' and he spoke fluent French. In 1945, his dark hair was going 'very grey' and he sported a small Hitler moustache.

At various unspecified times, he was said to have worked for the US Secret Service and Pinkertons Detective Agency and he often carried a badge for some detective agency or other. He is also said to have joined the US Customs Service and the Border Patrol, which may have been the same thing. He was also involved in smuggling opium and cigars but apparently his most lucrative venture was in arranging for the bodies of dead Chinese to be shipped from the States back to their homeland, by using zinc-lined caskets that satisfied the US authorities. This also earned him the lasting affection of an important Chinese family.

After the outbreak of the 1914-1918 War, he 'put himself at the disposal' of the German Admiralty, at the request of Franz Bopp the German Consul General in San Francisco. In 1915, he joined the Morse Patrol, a night watchman agency, apparently to provide himself with an alibi by having an associate carry out his duties whenever he was getting up to mischief elsewhere.

From his base in San Francisco, Jahnke carried out various sabotage activities against merchant and naval ships as well as organisations that were supplying the British. He also fomented industrial unrest.

Jahnke's own account of his early career in espionage and sabotage has been uncovered in the German Foreign Office records:

> From August 1914 on, I was in California and based in San Francisco, the Central Office for secret military operations of the German government. In March 1916, I took over the western part of the United States as representative of the Admiralty Staff for intelligence and sabotage assignments. In February 1917, I was the representative secret agent

for the United States. My field of activity, however, also extended to England. I functioned as head of the intelligence and sabotage service until the end of the war.

It is claimed that while Jahnke was in San Francisco, he had helped to provoke the famous dockworkers' strike that eventually spread to all western ports in the US. He had also contributed to the sabotage of more than a dozen ships. It is said that he liked to use Americans of Irish descent for his operations, especially members of radical organisations and trade unions because they were willing 'to get at it with utter ruthlessness and blindness'.

Jahnke first came to the attention of British Intelligence in WWI, thanks to the successes achieved by Admiral Hall's Naval Intelligence team who intercepted German diplomatic traffic and also cracked their codes.

After the war, the Lehigh Valley Railroad Company engaged Amos Peaslee, a New York lawyer, to investigate 'The Black Tom Case'. Peaslee found Hall in retirement and ready to help. In *Three Wars with Germany* (1944), Peaslee and Hall recounted their attempts to identify the saboteurs at work in North America and the legal battles to extract damages from various German governments. According to Peaslee, it became 'the most famous international law suit of modern times' but after 17 years, his efforts ended in failure.

The sabotage occurred at 2.08 a.m. on 30 July 1916 at a freight terminal in lower New York Harbour on Black Tom Island[5] opposite the Statue of Liberty. It rocked New York 'as never before in her history' when thirty-seven carloads of high explosives, several large warehouses, a dozen barges and ships, and a complete railway station and yard were 'blown to atoms'. A 'sister case' was tried at the same time. This concerned the destruction of the Kingsland Assembling Plant at Kingsland, New Jersey on 11 January 1917, where supplies for Russia were being prepared for shipment.

---

[5] It took its name from the solitary resident that once lived there.

British Intelligence had intercepted some 10,000 'cables and radios' of which 264 dealt with German sabotage operations in North and South America. According to Hall's biographer, there were also more than forty messages which showed that Germany had systematically distributed anthrax and other germs referred to as 'E and B cultures' in the Argentine and the United States.

Some of the cables contained references to Jahnke. On 3 April 1918, Jahnke had sent a message to the Chief of the Admiralty Staff at Antwerp complaining at having been placed under the orders of Captain Hinsch. It came, he said, 'as a painful surprise' because he was accustomed to working independently ... [and] ... his successes justified the confidence that had been placed in him. An undated response accepted that his 'detailed accounts of successes mentioned appear credible ... [and] ... his co-operation with the Admiral Staff must therefore unquestionably remain'.

According to Peaslee, it appeared that there were two separate groups of German saboteurs who claimed credit for each other's work: Frederick Hinsch had led an 'East Coast group' while Kurt Jahnke had operated principally on the West Coast. After the United States entered the war, both Hinsch and Jahnke moved their operations to Mexico and presumably this had occasioned the instruction for Jahnke to report to Hinsch.

Jahnke and his assistant Lothar Witzke, alias Waberski, would later be described as 'the most deadly sabotage team in history' and Witzke has the distinction of being the only foreign agent sentenced to death in the United States during WWI. He was later reprieved and served a jail sentence instead. In 1929, Peaslee succeeded in tracking him down in Venezuela. Although Witzke declared his loyalty to Germany, he admitted having done some sabotage work [in the United States] during the war but he asserted that 'no one would ever find out what it was'.

A few weeks later, the German Foreign Office rewarded his loyalty by whisking him off to China, where the Hamburg-American Line gave him a cushy job.

Jahnke returned to Germany after the war and was awarded the Iron Cross in 1919. He was back in Mexico in 1920 with a passport in the name of Steffens, posing as secretary to a Professor Hellman who had gone to Mexico to carry out an agricultural study.

In 1923, Jahnke was stirring up trouble against the French who had occupied the Saar, as a response to Germany having failed to make its scheduled reparations payments. He then served as Adviser and Political Chief of the Black Reichswehr, an auxiliary army that was being built up in secret to overcome the constraints on German military strength imposed by the Treaty of Versailles. Terrorist activities and the assassination of those considered traitors were also attributed to the Black Reichswehr.

In 1925, Jahnke worked as an agent for the Fourth Department (Soviet Military Intelligence) while the Locarno Treaty was being hammered out.

In 1927, during the period of close economic cooperation between Russia and Germany, Jahnke advised Walter Krivitsky, the Russian Intelligence Officer who later defected, that Gustav Stresemann had made secret preparations for a visit to Stalin in Moscow[6]. Apparently Stresemann considered that Kristinsky, the Soviet Ambassador in Berlin, did not have sufficient authority. Krivitsky informed Moscow and the visit did not take place.

From 1926 to 1928, Jahnke served as a Deputy of the Prussian Diet and in 1929 he became Chief of 'the Secret Cabinet' for Gustav Stresemann. By this time, he had become a rich man with a house in Berlin and an estate in Mecklenburg.

Following Stresemann's death in October 1929, Jahnke worked principally for Canaris until 1934 when consequent upon Hitler's rise to power, he joined the Abteilung Von Pfeffer that answered to Rudolf Hess, Hitler's deputy.

Franz Von Pfeffer Von Salomon, who had taken part in the Kapp Putsch [March 1920], had become an early Hitler acolyte and had run the SA from 1926 to 1930. The stated aim of Von Pfeffer's department was 'strengthening Anglo-German

[6] MI5 Interrogation of Krivitsky, January-February 1940.

relations' and Von Pfeffer was considered the front man while Jahnke provided the brains. Although Jahnke had an office in the same building as Von Pfeffer, he also maintained an office at his Berlin home. This was the Jahnke Büro, essentially a private intelligence service that worked under the auspices of Rudolf Hess.

Reports and intelligence summaries of the Jahnke Service were distributed to Hitler, Hess, the Reichskriegministerium, Viktor Lutze (Stabschef of the SA), the Gestapo and probably Auswartiges Amt.

Jahnke visited England in 1938. Travelling under the name of 'Johnson', he is said to have met some 'important people' and it can be inferred that Lord Londonderry, Robert Vansittart and Stewart Menzies, who would later become the Head of MI6, could have been amongst his contacts.

In August 1939, Jahnke is reported to have 'mortally offended' Ribbentrop who had hitherto been a good customer, by making a last ditch attempt to prevent the invasion of Poland. Jahnke had apparently encouraged Menzies to send his close friend David Boyle to meet Hitler but when Ribbentrop got wind of the proposed meeting, he persuaded Hitler to call it off.

In February 1940, a British source (presumably Marcus) reported that Jahnke had been receiving a regular supply of top-secret material from the Committee for Imperial Defence, the British Foreign Office and the US Embassy in London.

Sometime during 1940, Jahnke is believed to have visited Lord Londonderry at his home in Mount Stewart in Northern Ireland. If so, then it is likely to have been another peace initiative.

On 26 April 1940, Hitler ordered the dissolution of the Büro 1 (Abteilung Von Pfeffer) but it is not known why. Possibly, this may have reflected Hitler's disappointment at Hess's failure to arrange a negotiated peace.

Then in 1941, the Gestapo seized Jahnke's files and he was ordered to desist from further intelligence activities. The story goes on to say that Heydrich, suspecting that Jahnke was a Soviet spy, had 'requisitioned' his office.

After studying Jahnke's files, Walter Schellenberg decided that his experience and contacts could be useful and he appointed him as his adviser. In 1942, Schellenberg involved Jahnke in negotiations with the Chinese, namely, General Kousi and Chiang Kai Shek. Muller of the Gestapo then accused Jahnke of being a British spy and produced a file of supporting evidence. Jahnke took the accusations coolly and survived the challenge.

According to Marcus, the Gestapo often visited the Jahnke Büro but Jahnke thwarted them by hiding boxes of chocolate in his safe, while any secret papers were scattered casually on his desk. The Gestapo always insisted on inspecting the safe and confiscating the chocolates.

Marcus continued to serve Jahnke through to 1944 when, with Germany on the brink of defeat, Jahnke sent him on his last mission to make contact with the British. He crossed the Allied lines on 13 November 1944. At this stage Marcus became known as 'Dictionary' and he expanded on the American material that had been coming in to the Jahnke Büro up to March 1940 when it stopped.

It may have stopped because Jahnke had been taken out of the loop when Hitler dissolved the Abteilung Von Pfeffer (in April 1940) or the source may have dried up as a consequence of the investigations that had been put in place in February 1940.

Evidently, it was never considered at that time that the source might have dried up as a consequence of Tyler Kent's arrest.


There is a story that says that Jahnke survived WWII and lived happily ever after in Switzerland. This is at odds with a notice that appeared in a Hamburg paper in October 1949. This announced Jahnke's return from Moscow and stated that in future he would reside in Berlin.

More recently, a report[7] from Moscow says that the Russians captured Jahnke and his wife in April 1945. They were handed over to SMERSH, interrogated, tortured and executed in May 1945. By then, the Russians had apparently come to regard Jahnke as a British agent. The Russians may have revised their opinion of Jahnke, as a result of the British Intelligence interrogations of Marcus in March 1945. A copy of at least one of these reports[8] was sent to 'Major Blunt' in MI5. This was, of course, Anthony Blunt who was unmasked as a Soviet spy in 1981.

During his interrogation by the Soviets, Jahnke told them that in 1933, as a consequence of Hitler's rise to power, the Jahnke Büro was placed under the direction of Rudolf Hess. Then, following the outbreak of WWII, Jahnke had been drafted into the army as the commander of intelligence for the 800th battalion of the Brandenburg special designation regiment. The role of the battalion was to penetrate the enemy's front line in small groups, wearing the enemy's uniform and to cause disruptions until their main attacking forces arrived. However, 'for no apparent reason' he was removed from his intelligence assignments in 1940. He speculated that this might have been due to his negative attitude to Hitler's foreign policy and also due to efforts by Hitler and Himmler to rationalise control of intelligence operations within the Gestapo.

Walter Schellenberg, Himmler's Intelligence Chief, tells another story. He claims that Jahnke actually went to work for him and that he ran a spy ring inside Stalin's General Staff at Marshal Rokossovsky's Soviet Military Headquarters. However, at some stage, the SS exposed Jahnke as a British agent but somehow he managed to escape their clutches by fleeing to Switzerland. How he was able to return from Switzerland in time to fall into the hands of the advancing Russians in 1945 is not explained.

---

[7] Russell Van Wyk, a historian at the University of North Carolina.
[8] KV 2/755 (36Z).

Of course, after the war, all the Germans were busily re-inventing themselves to show what good guys they really were and in any event, Jahnke was hardly likely to tell the Russians that he had been a double agent. But if Jahnke really had been a British agent, this was a good enough reason for the Russians to have executed him.

The truth of the matter seems to have been that Jahnke would work for anyone prepared to pay for his services: the Germans, the Russians, the Chinese, the Japanese or the British.

Marcus's claim that Kent had been a Jahnke agent is much more difficult to accept. The line in 1940 was that the espionage material was arriving from the American Embassy in Berlin courtesy of 'The Doctor'. This was not necessarily Marcus's version because when questioned in 1944, Marcus had said that he could not identify the source, claiming that Jahnke was always very secretive about the identity of his agents. However, Marcus did say that he understood that the source was a 'secretary at the American Embassy in London' who had been recruited in Switzerland in 1938.

Marcus completely changed his tune in 1950, when he was not only able to identify Tyler Kent as the source but he also claimed that he had been with Jahnke at the time when Kent had been recruited in Switzerland in 1938. Not surprisingly, Marcus's interrogator formed the opinion that Marcus was telling them what they wanted to hear. In other words, the 'usually reliable' source had now apparently become suspect.

Marcus's tale doesn't hang together because Kent was not a secretary and he was not employed at the London Embassy in 1938. Moreover, there is no record of his ever having been in Switzerland in 1938. However by 1950, Kent had become notorious as 'the spy in the American Embassy', so his name could have slipped easily off Marcus's tongue.

Significantly, Kent was later re-categorised as a Soviet agent. As nothing had turned up to show that he had been a German agent, his alleged connection with Kurt Jahnke may have supported a re-think. Or his re-categorisation may have been more compatible with the times, when Germany was back 'on the side of the angels' and Russia had been restored to its previous position of Public Enemy #1.

In the event, Marcus was later suspected of having been a Soviet agent himself and two other possible Jahnke agents had also been uncovered in Britain. One was a man named Fletcher who, like King and Oldham, had evidently been employed in the Foreign Office and another was a secretary at the American Embassy in London. She has never been named but Maxwell Knight provided some details in a 'Summary of Results' that he compiled in April 1945 when the war was coming to an end.

Knight had got onto Werner Albert Österwald in late November 1938, after Österwald had admitted being a German Intelligence Agent to one of Knight's 'reliable sources'. Knight assigned an undercover agent called 'Frank' to the case. After making contact, Frank soon obtained an admission from Österwald that he was indeed a secret German agent and that he had a contact at the American Embassy.

Österwald had apparently been a member of the Gestapo until the summer of 1938, when he had got himself into trouble over money and had been dismissed. Knight's agent maintained contact and eventually a search warrant was obtained against both Österwald and his woman friend who was working at the American Embassy.

With a lack of sufficient evidence to justify prosecution, a deportation order was obtained and Österwald was deported on 8 March 1939. However, Österwald's woman friend apparently continued to work at the American Embassy.

Could Österwald have been a Jahnke agent? And could his woman friend have been taking documents from the American Embassy? Anything is possible but evidently Maxwell Knight did not consider this to be one of his more important cases.

The possibility that Fletcher of GC&CS might have been a Jahnke agent was also investigated and on 18 February 1940, eleven days after he had written to Herschel Johnson about the leakages from the American Embassy in London, Guy Liddell noted in his diary that the case of Gulla Pfeffer[9] had been brought to his notice. According to MI5's file on Kurt Jahnke[10], Frau Pfeffer was related by marriage to one Pan Pfeffer and Jahnke had sent her money after she had asked Pan Pfeffer for help.

Later, at Jahnke's suggestion, Gulla had obtained a job in the Kolonial Amt and, whenever she visited England, Jahnke asked her to keep her eyes open for any influential people who might be useful to him.

Gulla eventually met Fletcher, 'a youngish man who worked at the Foreign Office (in reality at the GC&CS)' and she had decided that he was exactly what Jahnke was looking for. A proposition was put to him and Fletcher responded by saying that he couldn't do anything without consulting his superiors. This he did and they had agreed that he should meet Jahnke. As a result, Fletcher and his wife visited Berlin in May 1935, where they were the guests of the Nazis although, according to the report, Fletcher only met Jahnke on one occasion.

In Liddell's Diary for the 18 February 1940, the name of Gulla's contact in GC&CS was blanked out but undoubtedly it was Fletcher and he was reportedly suspected of supplying Jahnke with SIS and Imperial Policy reports. Liddell also noted 'He might also be the person giving the contents of Kennedy's telegrams to Roosevelt.'

On 20 February 1940, Liddell recorded that he 'had a long talk with Felix Cowgill[11] on the case of FLETCHER ... [and] ... he has taken full details to report to Menzies[12]'.

On 22 February 1940, Liddell discussed the case of xxxxxxxx with Cowgill and noted that 'he has played his cards fairly well by reporting certain facts as they happen'.

On 23 February 1940, Liddell attended a meeting at SIS in order to discuss the case of xxxxxxxx of the GC&CS. 'It is

---

[9] 'Gulla' according to KV 2/755; 'Gula' according to Liddell.
[10] KV 2/755
[11] An MI6 officer.
[12] The Head of MI6.

obvious that he has a kind of secret service kink … [and] we are going to try to get a look at his banking account.'

On 1 April 1940, Liddell noted that 'Fletcher of GC&CS is going to France for eleven days on a bicycling tour. We discussed the possibility of sending over two girls with him on the boat but the plan fell through as it was found he had already left.'

On 20 April 1940 Liddell reported that FLETCHER had reacted to news of Gulla Pfeffer's arrest by buying several bottles of Chartreuse, which he proceeded to 'consume to excess'. It was then planned to draw up a questionnaire for interviewing FLETCHER.

There is no record of any interview with Fletcher but Liddell returned to the subject on 26 January 1945 when he heard that Carl Marcus had come across to the Allies and he suggested to Menzies that 'there might be an interesting tie-up with the old case of JAHNKE and FLETCHER.

So, if Fletcher had ever been a Jahnke agent then he appears to have got away with it.


The Kent-Wolkoff Affair was more complicated than most because it had been woven around Knight's 'sexed-up' report, the Washington cover story delivered by Kennedy and the much more subtle spin imparted by Jowitt. When combined with a MI5 sting operation, some perjury from MI5's top brass and the mysterious exchanges between Roosevelt and Churchill in the non-confidential Gray Code, it all added up to a Giant Jigsaw, where none of the pieces seems to fit.

Nevertheless, all the pieces do fit together but they produce a totally different picture from any of those projected by the various cover stories.

# 17: Giant Jigsaw

When Maxwell Knight presented his 'sexed-up' report to Herschel Johnson on 18 May 1940 requesting permission to search Tyler Kent's flat, he probably had no idea of the ensuing repercussions because initially it had been intended that Kent should be deported. However, Knight had taken the precaution of having his report approved by Guy Liddell, so if things were to go badly wrong, he had covered his back.[1]

Knight's report had followed Liddell's warning on 7 February 1940 that copies of Embassy correspondence were reaching German Intelligence, via someone known only as 'The Doctor' based in the American Embassy in Berlin. An MI6 man calling himself 'Gill of the Foreign Office' followed this up by visiting Johnson on 14 February 1940, and he gave the story a further twist by referring to Kurt Jahnke, the legendary German spy and saboteur who had led 'the most deadly sabotage team in history'. But the entire story had evidently been made up, because Liddell's diary for 14 February 1940 shows that Felix Cowgill, Gill's boss, had visited him that same day and had told him that Jahnke's informant was 'said to be in the British Foreign Office and to be either a clerk or the wife of a clerk'.

So why the deceit? Liddell's letter and Gill's visit were probably part of a damage limitation exercise. On 7 February 1940, Walter Krivitsky was approaching the end of his visit to London, a visit initiated by the journalist Isaac Don Levine who had taken Krivitsky's story to Adolf Berle, the Assistant Secretary of State. Berle had introduced Levine to Lord Lothian, the British Ambassador, who had then taken matters further. But British Intelligence had to assume that Berle would have been interested in learning the outcome of Krivitsky's visit.

It could be assumed that Berle would have been seriously disturbed by Krivitsky's revelations, so 'The Doctor' may have been invented to suggest that Kurt Jahnke was actually getting his material from an American source. The fact that Carl Marcus

---

[1] KV 2/840 (57C).

failed to mention 'The Doctor' on his later debriefings supports this hypothesis.

It is unlikely that Tyler Kent had been a spy for Kurt Jahnke, despite Carl Marcus's later claim in 1950 when he was telling MI6 what he thought they wanted to hear. Indeed, it is unlikely that Tyler Kent had ever been a spy at all. This was certainly Maxwell Knight's conclusion after having made exhaustive enquiries following his arrest. It is supported by the lack of any corroborating evidence in the German, Italian or Soviet Archives.

Moreover, the presence of 'masses' of Embassy documents in Kent's flat supports his explanation that he was collecting them out of interest. Had he been a spy, then presumably he would have either passed the documents to his 'control' or destroyed them after communicating their contents.

Kent evidently had no access to photocopying facilities, otherwise it would not have been necessary for Wolkoff to visit Smirnoff to arrange for the two documents to be photographed, at Captain Ramsay's request.

Whether Kent was a spy or not, he was certainly extremely naïve. He had wrongly assumed that his diplomatic immunity gave him carte blanche to do pretty much whatever he liked. This was generally true, but he had clearly overstepped the mark by showing copies of Embassy documents to Wolkoff and Ramsay.

But although he was probably not a spy, Kent could certainly have been charged with at least 500 offences under the Yardley Act, and having admitted the offences in writing, he had been let off very lightly with a sentence of only seven years.

Tyler Kent had stirred up a hornet's nest by allowing Anna Wolkoff and Captain Ramsay to view his collection of Embassy documents. Despite the three of them having been incarcerated for most of the war, stories would eventually leak out about the reasons for Ramsay's and Wolkoff's interest which was, of course, the Churchill-Roosevelt correspondence.

James Leutze produced the best appreciation in *The Secret of the Churchill-Roosevelt Correspondence: September 1939 – May*

*1940* published in the *Journal of Contemporary History* (July 1975).

Leutze pointed out that the reluctance of the American Government to open its files even after the usual classification period of twenty years had elapsed 'added to the suspicion of conspiracy'. However, when the files were finally opened, Leutze was unable to detect anything that smacked of a plot to get the United States involved in the war. Nevertheless, he was able to detect clues that the President had been playing 'a distinctly unneutral game' and this might have led to awkward questions, particularly in the run up to the Presidential Election.

Leutze also observed that the Roosevelt Administration had shown no greater relish to open their files after the Election than they had done before, and that the first admission of their secret correspondence had come from Churchill. Churchill had claimed that their exchanges had been confined to 'naval topics' and, indeed, most of the documents published by Kimball in his 'full correspondence', and restated by Bearse and Read, fall into this category. Exceptionally, the telegram sent by Roosevelt on 15 May 1940 also referred to aircraft, anti-aircraft equipment and steel purchases.

Leutze did a penetrating analysis of the various exchanges and pointed out that none of the parties who would have expected being kept in the picture were very impressed with the telegrams routed through Ambassador Kennedy. He referred specifically to the British Ambassador in Washington and the American Section of the British Foreign Office in London; the latter being particularly upset because they had already come to distrust Joseph Kennedy. Welcome to the club! Everyone distrusted Kennedy. Of course, at that stage of the game, and for many years afterwards, it was not generally realised that their messages had been encoded in the non-confidential Gray Code.

Leutze examined Roosevelt's 'distinctly unneutral game' from the time of the Royal Visit in June 1939, which gave King George VI the opportunity to eat hot dogs, 'weather permitting'. The weather so permitted and Roosevelt promised the British monarch 'full support' in the event of a war with Germany, including providing naval patrols in the Western Hemisphere.

According to His Majesty's notes, Roosevelt seemed 'particularly keen' on playing this support role and promised that 'if he saw a U-boat he would sink her at once and wait for the consequences'.

Shortly afterwards, Roosevelt backed up his offer with action, and interestingly in view of the later 'destroyer for bases' deal, agreement was then reached that Britain would hand over its various bases on the Eastern coast of the Americas. But at that stage, Roosevelt was anxious that the transfer should be consummated during peacetime. This was agreed and the details were thrashed out at secret conversations in Washington between Commander T.C. Hampton of the Royal Navy 'travelling incognito' and Admirals Leahy and Ghormley, two bigwigs in the American Navy.

Accordingly, when war broke out America declared a Neutrality Zone and started patrolling the Western Atlantic with naval craft and air patrols. Admiral John Godfrey, Britain's Director of Naval Intelligence, had noted the value of the American contributions as early as 26 February 1940.

Leutze also identified other American initiatives during the phase of its 'Undeclared War' including the destroyers for bases deal, a gradually broadened convoy procedure, replacing British forces in Iceland and the institution of a 'shoot at sight' policy in the Atlantic. Prophetically, Leutze suggested that 'further searching may reveal other instances'.

As far as Tyler Kent was concerned, Leutze suggested that he may have 'seen and sensed' early evidence of a tendency to expand the war-making powers of the executive, contrary to the assertions that Roosevelt had been making during his re-election campaign.

When Maxwell Knight led the search party in the raid on Tyler Kent's flat on 20 May 1940, he made three mistakes; Franklin Gowen, the representative from the American Embassy, spotted two of them and Knight effectively acknowledged the third himself.

Knight's first mistake was to lead the search party directly to Kent's room, without asking the maid who had let them in to tell them where it was. This led Gowen to suspect that Knight had been there before.

Knight's second mistake was not to be seen to apprehend Irene Danischewsky, Kent's mistress, for interrogation. This led Gowen to infer that Irene was one of Knight's agents, which she wasn't. In fact, Detective Inspector Pearson's full report shows that he not only interrogated her but he also went to her home the following day. He found her in a state of great distress lest her husband should learn of her association with Kent. She was 'only too willing to assist the police' and her premises were searched by invitation. Nothing of an incriminating nature was found and Pearson concluded that she had visited Kent at his flat for 'admittedly immoral purposes'.

Knight's third mistake was not to take a comprehensive inventory of the items discovered in Kent's flat. In a report that he wrote on 4 April 1945 about his wartime activities, Knight listed the lessons to be learnt from the Kent-Wolkoff Affair. One of these, possibly written tongue-in-cheek, was that 'the greatest care must be taken to see that these [documents] are properly listed and recorded'.

The most curious aspect of Knight's failure to take an inventory was an inability to determine the actual number of documents in Kent's collection. Joseph Kennedy in his Diplomatic Memoir stated that 'over 1,500 Embassy documents were found in his possession' but at Kent's trial in October 1940 the figure of 500 was bandied around. The State Department Press Release of 2 September 1944 gave the number as 'more than 1,500' and in their book *Conspirator* (1991), Bearse and Read reported the count at precisely 1,929 and they also provided a supporting summary prepared by the CIA.

Of course, if the number had been reduced, then this would have fuelled suspicion that officials had extracted any sensitive documents from Kent's collection but it is decidedly odd that 500 should have been quoted at his trial. It was clever to show a modest escalation as a method of disguising any extractions without arousing suspicion. So, what would have been extracted? Presumably, anything and everything that supported Kent's claim that Roosevelt had been making pre-war commitments to those European countries in dispute with Hitler.

What we now know is that Maxwell Knight had been asked to provide a Commentary on Gerald L.K. Smith's six-page pamphlet *The Story of Tyler Kent* published around September 1944[2]. Knight presented his Commentary on 26 February 1945[3] and in a covering note to Brigadier 'Jasper' Harker, the Deputy Director of MI5, he stated that 'it did not seem desirable that any reference should be made to this':

> I have been careful to point out that the references in the document to the contents of the stolen telegrams in practically every case do not coincide with the contents of the telegrams in connection with which Tyler Kent was charged. This is true but for your own information and for our records, it is necessary to point out that among the mass of telegrams which were seized at Tyler Kent's flat – and many of which I examined myself – there were many telegrams which referred to the projected Lease-Lend Plan. (Author's emphasis.)[4]

The fact that Knight had admitted having 'examined many' of the Embassy documents suggests that he did make an illegal entry, because at Kent's trial he had testified that all the documents had been bundled up and passed over to Franklin Gowen. He had also testified that he had only 'glanced at some of them'. 'Glancing' and 'examining' are at opposite ends of the spectrum, which supports the prior search hypothesis and it may explain why he knew his way to Kent's flat without asking for directions. It also seems unlikely that Liddell and Knight would have sought Ambassador Kennedy's permission to search Kent's

---

[2] The reference to Ramsay having been released (24 September 1944) shows that Smith's booklet was published afterwards.
[3] KV 2/545 piece 128a.
[4] A reproduction of this extract appears in Appendix: Images.

flat without having taken the precaution of a prior search. They would not have wanted to appear stupid.

In Herschel Johnson's report on Knight's visit on 18 May 1940, he said that Knight had 'quoted details from some of the Embassy correspondence that Kent had shown to Anna' but there did not seem to be enough in any of Marjorie Mackie's reports to allow Knight to 'quote details'. This is also indicative of a prior search.

Obviously, Knight could have quoted some of the gossip that was doing the rounds and there was certainly enough to make Kennedy's hair curl. A report from Special Source, dated 16 April 1940, stated that Anna had dined with Kent at the Russian Tea Rooms on Friday 12 April and later that evening, she had told her cronies that Kent had informed her that the North Sea battles then in progress had been greatly exaggerated; that they had only been minor skirmishes and the British propaganda had been merely to cover naval losses sustained at Scapa Flow.

Wolkoff had also disseminated the story that Kennedy had been told by Lord Halifax, the Foreign Secretary, that the reason that the British Navy had been unable to stop the Germans landing in Norway was because of the dense fog. Kennedy was then alleged to have asked Halifax why the fog had failed to impede the Germans. Kent had claimed that on returning to the Embassy, Kennedy had asked, 'How can England hope to win the war with a daft fool like that as Foreign Secretary?'

True or false, the dissemination of such gossip was not conducive to good Anglo-American relations. But retailing gossip is not the same as having been able to quote details from some of the Embassy correspondence that Kent had shown to Anna, as Herschel Johnson had reported.

Whether Knight made a prior search or not, he had clearly seen many telegrams that referred to the projected Lend-Lease Plan and so, after all the stories and speculation, here at last was proof positive that Kent had been telling the truth: Churchill and Roosevelt had been in correspondence about the Lend-Lease (or Lease-Lend) formula months before Roosevelt had supposedly conceived the idea, after his re-election.

Consequently, Kent's knowledge of Roosevelt's pre-war commitments was the only reason for his having been tried in secret and incarcerated during the war; and the assumption that 'the full correspondence' between Churchill and Roosevelt had previously been made public is now proved false.

So, although Kimball and Bartlett had considered it 'an unlikely possibility', the official files can now be seen to have been selective, even though this has taken a vast conspiracy stretching from London to Washington lasting not merely for over thirty-five years but actually for over sixty years.

With Roosevelt scheming with Churchill to bring America into the war, he had to keep a wary eye on Joseph P. Kennedy, his Ambassador in London. Kennedy belonged to the 'Appeasement School of Thought' and he also had designs on offering himself as the Democratic candidate in the Presidential Election in November 1940.

This was not something that Roosevelt would have welcomed and sending Kennedy to London in 1938 as Ambassador was a good way of defusing his plans. Kennedy had actually asked for the job of Ambassador, which had been a stepping-stone for five previous Presidents. Roosevelt had been happy to oblige, but he had also arranged for a close watch to be kept on Kennedy's activities.

Eventually, Kennedy came to realise that he had lost Roosevelt's confidence and that he was no longer 'in the loop'. This was the cue for Roosevelt and Churchill to start a special line of correspondence routed through him, which was designed to give him the comfort that he was privy to everything that was passing between them. It was highly contrived, even to the extent of Churchill inviting Kennedy over, so that he could read Roosevelt's letter that served as a prelude to their exchanges.

Roosevelt wrote to Churchill on 11th of September 1939:

> My dear Churchill
>
> It is because you and I occupied similar positions
> in the World War that I want you to know how
> glad I am that you are back again in the

Admiralty. Your problems are, I realize, complicated by new factors but the essential is not very different. What I want you and the Prime Minister to know is that I shall at all times welcome it if you will keep me in touch personally with anything that you want to know about. You can always send sealed letters through your pouch or my pouch.

I am glad you did the Marlboro volumes before this thing started - and I much enjoyed reading them.

With my sincere regards

Faithfully yours

Franklin D. Roosevelt

Roosevelt's letter, which was sent under seal, had been forwarded in the Diplomatic Pouch to the American Embassy in London, but it did not arrive until either the 3rd or the 4th October 1939[5]. On the Fifth, Kennedy noted in his diary that Churchill had invited him to the Admiralty so that he could read him the letter. Kennedy claimed to have been disgusted, considering it to be 'another instance of Roosevelt's conniving mind'.

Churchill had asked Kennedy to send the response that 'The Naval Person will not fail to avail himself of the invitation and he is honoured by the message'. Kennedy obliged but he also noted his forebodings about Churchill, 'I can't help feeling he's not on the level. He is just an actor and a politician. He always impresses me that he'd blow up the American Embassy and say the Germans did it if it would get the US in. Maybe I do him an injustice but I just don't trust him'.

Later that same day, Churchill sent his first telegram to Roosevelt via Kennedy at the American Embassy and Churchill's message had been marked for transcription in the Gray Code.

Churchill involved Kennedy again on 28 November 1939, when he invited him to the Admiralty to show him a chart on 'the sinkings'. He gave Kennedy a copy to take to Roosevelt on a

---

[5] Warren Kimball says the 3rd; Joseph Kennedy the 4th.

forthcoming visit to Washington. He also asked Kennedy to get Roosevelt's opinion on a plan to lay mines off Norway 'to stop Germans bringing iron ore down'. They worked out a code: 'Eunice would like to come to the party' (if OK) or 'Eunice would not like to go to the party' (if Roosevelt thought it might cause a 'big upset' in America). Roosevelt thought it OK and so Kennedy cabled Churchill accordingly. Again it was highly contrived.

The content of the Churchill-Roosevelt exchanges that went via Kennedy was designed to reassure Kennedy that Roosevelt was observing all the proprieties. Accordingly, when Churchill sent a telegram to Roosevelt via Kennedy on 15 May 1940 begging for 'the loan of forty or fifty of your older destroyers', Roosevelt responded via Kennedy on the 16 May, advising that 'a step of that kind could not be taken except with the specific authorization of the Congress'. But notwithstanding Roosevelt's official response to Churchill, Guy Liddell had noted in his diary on the 17 May:

> Stewart Menzies[6] had some information I gather of a reliable and very confidential kind that Roosevelt was proposing to give us 100 destroyers, somewhat out of date but nevertheless useful. He also proposed to give us a portion of his first-line aircraft provided that we would replace them in due course with Spitfires. There is no doubt that Roosevelt would bring the whole country into the war now if he possibly could.

So it wasn't just destroyers but aircraft as well, both of which were urgently needed, as a consequence of the rapidly deteriorating situation in France. General Ironside, Britain's Chief of Imperial General Staff, had previously noted in his diary on 19 February 1940 that he had wired the US to find out if they had any surplus 74 mm field-guns adding, 'I think that they could be pushed over the frontier to Canada, as the aeroplanes are being handled'.

---

[6] The Head of MI6.

Roosevelt was actively trying to help Britain in its hour of need and, in fact, both Britain and France had already set up Purchasing Commissions in the United States that had agreed to purchase 8,000 engines and 4,700 frames at a cost of $614 million. This major commitment was made on 28 March 1940 and represented 17% of the total amount expended by Britain and France on Defence in 1939[7]. It provides clear evidence that Britain and France had decided that the time for talking was over and that they were determined to take up Hitler's challenge.

Arthur Purvis (1890-1941) represented Britain's interests. Born in Britain, he had been sent to the United States in WWI to buy war supplies. After the war, he moved to Canada where he became Chairman of Canadian Industries Ltd, a chemical company with munitions interests. After the outbreak of WWII, he moved to Washington as the Director-General of the British Purchasing Commission. His importance was such that he was made a Privy Councillor, a rare honour.

On 15 May 1940, Roosevelt telephoned Purvis with some personal suggestions. Would it be possible to 'reserve civil transport planes and private owner planes for transport and light bombing purposes?' Later that same day, Roosevelt pointed out to Purvis 'that it would not be possible for a British aircraft carrier to enter a United States port to load aircraft'. However, he suggested that a carrier could be sent to Botwood, Newfoundland and Purvis 'could then arrange to have the aircraft flown to the Canadian border, pushed across the border and flown to Botwood'[8].

Australia also arranged to have 49 Hudson aircraft that it had on order in the United States to be diverted to Britain[9].

On 17th June 1940 after the collapse of France, M. Bloch-Lainé signed an agreement in Washington under which all the contracts that the French Government had made with American

---

[7] John F. Kennedy, *Why England Slept* (1940) shows Britain had Defence Expenditures of $1,817 million in 1939 and France $1,800 million.
[8] Philip Goodhart, *Fifty Ships That Saved The World* (1965).
[9] H. Duncan Hall, *North American Supply* (1955).

war industry were assigned to Britain, the consideration being a token payment of one dollar.

The way Roosevelt got round his gift of the surplus destroyers was to claim that they were a quid pro quo in exchange for Britain's air and naval bases that stretched from Newfoundland to British Guiana but this was simply a ruse. Before the war, Britain had agreed that America could have the bases *gratis* because it lacked the ships and planes that could have used them. It was also consistent with how the British and American navies had agreed to share responsibilities in the event of war.

On the earlier occasion, Roosevelt had wanted the deal consummated before the war, which it was but after further consideration, he wanted to wrap it up as part of the destroyer deal, so it was re-packaged accordingly.

After Roosevelt had cleared all the legal hurdles to his own satisfaction, he was finally able to advise Churchill on 13 August 1940 that 'it may be possible to furnish to the British Government as immediate assistance at least 50 destroyers ...' This message was routed through Kennedy, who had probably been kept in the dark about many of the other arrangements that Purvis among others had been making directly with Roosevelt.

Joseph Kennedy invited Churchill to dinner on 2 September 1940 and when the party of six was seated, Churchill suggested that they call it the 'Destroyer Dinner' because the deal had been wrapped up and was ready to sign. Six days earlier, Kennedy had complained to Roosevelt at being kept in the dark. 'I do not enjoy being a dummy', he protested, even though Churchill had been feeding him titbits of information. Obviously Kennedy knew enough to realise that he was being sidelined.

At the dinner, Churchill told Kennedy that he had not wanted to link the destroyers to the bases which had been given gratis because he was concerned that if the destroyers turned out to be old and decrepit then it would make the British look silly. However, Roosevelt had insisted because he thought that it would help him to push the deal through, even though the transfer of the bases had already been consummated before the war. In fact, many of the destroyers did turn out to be old and decrepit and, arguably, the British were made to look silly but nevertheless some of the destroyers were put to good use.

Evidently, neither Roosevelt nor Churchill nor anyone else 'in the loop' considered that the spoof messages routed through Joseph Kennedy were 'highly secret'. Indeed, Churchill's code names of 'Naval Person' while he was First Lord of the Admiralty and 'Former Naval Person' when he stepped up as Prime Minister provided the thinnest of disguises. Roosevelt was always identified either by name or as 'the President'. They had not been designed to fool anybody but simply to impress Kennedy or any others who obtained copies. The code names certainly hadn't fooled Kent who told Knight that they referred to Churchill.

However, some of the spoof messages necessarily conflicted with the real exchanges that were being kept away from Kennedy and this led to confusion both in the British Embassy in Washington and in the American Section of the Foreign Office in London, neither of whom had been kept fully in the picture. This confusion was probably the reason that Alexander Cadogan had made the entry in his diary on 27 February 1940 that he 'deprecated the procedure'.

In 1940, Roosevelt's opponents could have made political capital out of the spoof messages, which turned out to have valuable secondary uses, first by providing examples of the supposedly secret messages exchanged between the two war leaders at Kent's trial, and later by being unveiled to the general public as representing the 'full correspondence' of the two war leaders.

In all probability, the spoof messages were also serving as 'cribs' for Britain's codebreakers who were monitoring traffic passing through all the foreign embassies in London. It was reasonable to assume that messages of such apparent importance would be encoded verbatim by any foreign embassies that routed them back to their homelands. The possession of specimens of known 'plain text' could have been a great help to the code breakers.

Interestingly, the spoof messages that supposedly comprised their complete correspondence were not released into the public domain until 1972, three years after Joseph Kennedy's death, possibly because one of the Kennedys might have put the cat among the pigeons by quoting some further examples.

Although Joseph Kennedy knew enough to realise that he was being sidelined, it is impossible to assess the extent that he was being by-passed but it may be relevant that Kent's trial only started after Kennedy had left for the United States to offer his resignation as Ambassador. Conceivably, had Kennedy attended the trial then he might have heard Kent refer to issues that had been previously kept from him.

In the statement that he had made to the Judge before his sentencing, Kent had complained that the Jury had been required to determine his intent from the four documents produced in evidence and that he had been prevented from producing others by the American Embassy.

The transcripts of Kent's trial that are in the public domain were evidently edited, as indicated by the existence of the two Indexes and the disparities between them. 41 pages in the 'Original Copy' referred to Kent's examination and cross-examination compared with 49 pages in 'This Copy', an increase of 19.5%. However, the other 126 pages in the Original compared with 152 pages in the Copy, an increase of 20.6%. Obviously, it would have been easier to produce an exact copy of the original so there must have been a good reason for producing a new copy. The difference was probably due to the deletion of highly sensitive references, such as telltale phrases like 'Lend-Lease'.

If any sensitive references had been edited out, this would have been done for consistency with the general policy of plausible denial with regards to Roosevelt's pre-war commitments.

The use of the non-confidential Gray Code for the Roosevelt and Churchill correspondence routed through the American Embassy in London was entirely consistent with best practice, as laid down in the Diplomatic Service for encoding 'verbatim texts' obtained from 'foreign sources'. The American Foreign Service had long been aware that a verbatim text obtained from 'a foreign source' could provide a valuable crib for any code breakers who obtained possession of both the verbatim text and a coded version. Therefore, the use of the non-confidential Gray Code was perfectly proper for the spoof messages.

There were several other codes and ciphers then in use in the US Diplomatic Service, such as M-138 a military cipher that could have been used to provide higher-grade cryptography. The M-138 was, in fact, used for the transmission of messages between Churchill and Roosevelt after their historic meeting at the Atlantic Conference in a ship moored off Newfoundland on 10 August 1941.

Some other 'highly secret' exchanges between the two wartime leaders were also 'masked' by naval cryptographic systems, rather than State Department ones until 1943[10]. At the Pearl Harbor enquiry after the war, Admiral R.E. Ingersoll had testified that it had been arranged before the war that there should be a 'distribution of codes and ciphers' with the British Admiralty. This was consistent with the cooperative arrangements that had been made for patrolling the high seas in the event of war.

The two wartime leaders were both code conscious and neither would have continually condoned the use of a non-confidential code for the exchange of any truly secret messages.

The most extraordinary feature of the story is why on 13 April 1940 Anna Wolkoff should have arranged for photographs to be taken of the two telegrams that were introduced in evidence at the trials. These were not only the most innocent examples imaginable but they were also stale: one was dated 30 January 1940, the other 29 February 1940.

---

[10] Ralph E. Weber, *United States Diplomatic Codes and Ciphers, 1775-1938*.

Surely, Captain Ramsay could have selected something very much more exciting from Kent's collection to show to Chamberlain than two hoary old telegrams? After all, the shooting war had started on 9 April 1940, there was a wealth of 'top secret' Lend-Lease correspondence, and presumably documents that supported the gossip that had been doing the rounds. Why on earth would Ramsay have wanted to show Chamberlain either of those that were produced in evidence, particularly the one dated 30 January 1940?

### PERSONAL AND SECRET FOR THE PRESIDENT FROM NAVAL PERSON.

I gave orders last night that no American ship should in any circumstances be diverted into the combat zone round the British Isles declared by you. I trust this will be satisfactory.

JOHNSON[11]

The telegrams that had been produced in evidence certainly baffled Kent who did not consider them at all 'interesting'. This gives rise to the possibility that they were not the ones that Ramsay had chosen. Evidently, Kent had taken no interest in which telegrams Anna had taken at the time and although the negatives had been left in his flat, they were unreadable with the naked eye. At Kent's trial, the Prosecution called Detective Inspector James O'Brien from the Photographic Department of New Scotland Yard as a witness and the Prosecuting Counsel had asked, 'As they are in negative form are they too small to read conveniently?' The witness had agreed.

Nicolas Smirnoff the photographer was also called as a witness and he testified that the negatives 'might have been' the ones he had taken because the enlargements made by the police showed documents of the same size. He said that he had never read the documents and as soon as he had photographed them, Anna had put them back in her bag.

[11] Herschel V. Johnson was acting Head of the Embassy in lieu of Joseph Kennedy who was holidaying in the United States.

Substitutions would therefore have been possible and after Captain Stephens, a Deputy Director of Naval Intelligence, had testified that they 'might be useful to the enemy' that would have been good enough. Wolkoff may have realised that they were not the documents that she had arranged to have photographed but making such a claim would not have helped her case because it mattered not whether they were the originals or substitutes.

There is absolutely no proof that any substitutions were made but it would certainly have been feasible and entirely consistent with the other skulduggery that had taken place. Possibly this was the reason why it was considered 'too complicated' to prosecute Ramsay because he would have known for sure which telegrams he had wanted to show to Chamberlain. He might even have let the cat out of the bag on the contents of other telegrams that he had seen. Being an MP with friends in high places, he would not have been so easy to convict on a criminal charge, particularly if he had argued that he was only doing his duty.

For what it's worth, every one of Anna's Right Club friends who had met Kent was interned, as was her father. Nicolas Smirnoff the photographer, who claimed that he had neither met Kent nor read the documents, was also interned.

Britain had bet the bank on winning the war and its commitment escalated dramatically when France fell and Arthur Purvis negotiated the take-over of the outstanding French orders on American suppliers on 17 June 1940. In order to continue the war, which had been optimistically estimated as a three-year project, Britain needed a vast amount of dollar credits. Dollars because its main munitions suppliers were going to be in the United States; credits because its war chest was near empty in terms of liquid assets. It also needed the US Government to turn a blind eye to the legislation, in which it appeared to be straitjacketed.

It would need some conjuring tricks of a high order. During the critical days of 1940, when Roosevelt realised that the Government could not sell any of its own military equipment to a belligerent, he arranged for it to be sold to a local private enterprise, which then sold it on to the British.

However, Roosevelt's trump card was 'Lend-Lease'. If we are now prepared to believe Kent, Roosevelt and Churchill had been discussing the formula for 'at least twelve months', before he revealed the idea at his weekly press conference on 17 December 1940:

> Suppose my neighbour's house catches fire and I have a length of garden hose four or five hundred feet away. If he can take my hose and connect it up with his hydrant, I may help him to put out the fire. Now what do I do? I don't say to him before that operation, 'Neighbour, my garden hose cost me $15, you have to pay me $15 for it'.
>
> What is the transaction that goes on? I don't want $15 – I want my garden hose back after the fire is over ...

The figure would actually turn out to be nearer $50 billion because it was actually a pretty big fire. There was also to be a pretty big debate before the Senate approved it on 11 March 1941 but that was certainly the major turning point of the war and an important stepping-stone was to ensure that Roosevelt was re-elected in November 1940.

Evidently, the US Treasury lawyers had discovered an old statute of 1892 that could be used to suggest a precedent. This provided that the Secretary of State for War could, when in his discretion it was for the public good, lease Army property not required for public use for a period of not longer than five years. Hence, the origin of the term 'Lend-Lease'. It sounded much friendlier than 'War Loan'.

Roosevelt's support was not entirely altruistic because he and his Administration would have been fully aware of the economic benefits that America had enjoyed by becoming 'the arsenal of democracy' in WWI and in providing credit to the Entente in similar circumstances. Conversely, by not supporting Britain in its hour of need, America may have been forced to write off its

WWI War Loans. These had not been fully repaid and most of the borrowers, including Britain, were in default.

In purely economic terms, the Roosevelt strategy was very compelling.

MI5's initial targets were Captain Ramsay and Oswald Mosley but neither had done anything that could be remotely described as subversive, although suspicion centred on Mosley's plans for starting a broadcasting station using German transmission facilities. All the contemporary evidence suggested that they were both fiercely patriotic and that Mosley's broadcasting station would have been essentially a commercial undertaking. Ramsay, for his part, was a staunch supporter of Chamberlain and his pre-war policy of appeasement.

However, Mosley and Ramsay represented a body of opinion that believed that Britain and Germany should arrange a negotiated peace and this became an unacceptable option to those who had a fuller understanding of the potential of the Nazi Menace. For example, it was not generally known at the time that the feasibility of an Atomic Bomb was being actively explored by Soviet Russia, Germany, Japan and, of course, the United States and Britain. If there had to be a war, then better to have an earlier non-nuclear confrontation, rather than risk Hitler getting first use of such a weapon.

In the event, the internment of Ramsay and Mosley and their followers sent an important message to pacifists and it helped to subdue further calls for peace.

But due to the lack of any hard evidence against Ramsay or Mosley, it was necessary for Knight to produce a 'sexed-up' report that exaggerated for effect.

So assuming that there had been a pre-election deal between Churchill and Roosevelt as Kent had alleged, did Churchill keep his side of the bargain by helping to ensure Roosevelt's re-election in November 1940?

He most certainly did, as evidenced by the work of William Stephenson. H. Montgomery Hyde first revealed some details in

*The Quiet Canadian* (1962) and in the North American edition entitled *Room 3603* (1963). At least two Americans, David Bruce and Whitney Shephardson, had evidently requested excisions from the American edition but even the British edition can now be seen as not strictly accurate, following the publication of the more definitive *The Secret History of British Intelligence in the Americas 1940-1945* (1998) and Thomas E. Mahl's *Desperate Deception* (1998). In between times, William Stevenson had produced a fictionalised account in *A Man Called Intrepid* (1976).

British Intelligence agents had evidently used every trick in the book to influence public opinion in America and to discredit both the isolationists and Nazi Germany.

The war had caught Anna Wolkoff at a low ebb. She had recently lost her business, she had been ill, she was very poor and she had gone back to living with her parents. She was probably very vulnerable and would have been easy meat for Knight's group of agents who were undoubtedly encouraging her to do all the wrong things.

The general question of internment had been discussed before the war and once Chamberlain recognised that there was no hope of reaching an acceptable peace deal the Norwegian campaign was given the go-ahead and Knight also swung into action with his sting operation on Wolkoff.

There were real concerns about a Fifth Column, as evidenced by the attention that was being paid to the Nazi black propaganda station 'NBBS' much of which was being scripted by William Joyce. Asking Wolkoff to try to send a letter to Joyce, whom she apparently only knew by reputation, would have certainly appealed to her as an avid listener of what she referred to as the 'Freedom Station' and, accepting that the MI5 undercover agents shared her beliefs, she was understandably responsive to Hélène de Munck's offer to forward the Coded Letter to William Joyce. Maxwell Knight probably compiled the Coded Letter himself because he knew a lot about William Joyce, having known him since 1924, when they were both members of Britain's first

Fascist Party, the British Fascisti.

Knight started off in the Intelligence Department and in 1925 he married Gwladys Poole, later Director of the Women's Units[12]. Knight was described as the Deputy Chief of Staff when in 1927 he had 'to leave London for a considerable time'[13]. In 1928, notwithstanding his having left London, he was described as 'G.H.Q. Council' and was awarded the Order of the Fasces. However, in 1933, Knight was among those deprived of their Orders of the Fasces for 'having failed to live up to their Fascist undertakings'[14].

Joyce joined the British Fascisti in December 1923 and served both as the Officer Commanding Chelsea District and also as a leading light in the organisation's 'X Society', a gang of toughs who 'organised the heckling and breaking up of Communist meetings' and formed the nucleus of the 'Fascisti Police'.[15] He left in 1924, after having been scarred for life when stewarding an Election Meeting held by a Conservative candidate. The British Fascisti had no political ambitions of its own and urged its members to vote Conservative.

Knight may have tipped off Joyce about his prospective internment in August 1939 as an act of friendship or in an effort not to draw unwanted attention to his own Fascist past. Or possibly both, even though MI5 had been fully aware of Knight's work for the British Fascisti when they recruited him in 1931. Indeed, it was because he had already established a valuable network of moles in Communist organisations that he was recruited.

James Hughes aka P.G. Taylor has also been linked with the British Fascisti and Knight immortalised Hughes and Joyce by making cryptic references to them in his first book *Crime Cargo* (1934).

However, when Knight and Hughes invoked Joyce's name in April 1940 to persuade Anna Wolkoff 'to attempt to

---

[12] Announcement in *The Fascist Bulletin*, 23 January 1926.
[13] Announcement in *The British Lion,* December 1927.
[14] *British Fascism*, Summer 1933.
[15] KV 3/57.

communicate' with the enemy, they signed Joyce's death warrant because if Joyce should survive the war, which he did, then he would have been able to embarrass the authorities, first by revealing his knowledge of the backgrounds of Knight and Hughes and also by confirming that he had never received Anna's letter.

The obvious solution was to send Joyce to the scaffold for his Nazi propaganda activities, even though he was an American by birth and he had taken out German nationality before America entered the war.

Similarly, Tyler Kent could not have been allowed to throw a spanner in the works in May 1940 and Maxwell Knight rose to the occasion admirably with his 'sexed-up' report, which had been designed primarily to ensure that the Labour Party would support the National cause. Maybe, if Knight had failed to deliver then some other plan would have evolved, but critically he did perform when it mattered; and so he deserves credit for the small but important part that he played, which is possibly why he was promoted to the Honorary Rank of Major on 1 October 1940 and awarded the OBE in 1943.

It was unfortunate that so many members of the BUF had to be interned when in all probability, they would have served their country valiantly in its hour of need but it was all for a good cause. Sadly, many former Mosleyites were also given a hard time after the war as well.

Nevertheless, the 750 or so internees served several important purposes: they ensured that Labour supported Churchill when the chips were down; they sent warnings to many others who were anti-Churchill or anti-war; and they sent signals to Hitler, Mussolini, Stalin and Roosevelt that Britain was determinedly anti-Fascist.

As for Anna Wolkoff, her friend Christabel Nicholson told the Advisory Committee that Anna 'was always full of wild statements and one did not really believe more than 25% of anything she said. I think she likes to Edgar Wallace[16] herself and make out she really knows something'[17]. Nicholson also revealed that Anna was 'very poor', which is probably why Marjorie Mackie was able to get close to her. Presumably, Mackie would have been given a generous entertaining allowance to support her investigations, which she mainly pursued by indulging herself at the Russian Tea Rooms.

Dorothy 'Dolly' Newenham, another associate of Anna's had also been an avid listener to the New British Broadcasting Station and on 29 June 1940 she had been at Admiral Wolkoff's home when they heard that 'the Germans would come simultaneously at 25 British ports. They will come over in their wonderful new invention, extraordinary tanks that go on water and land; 5,000 planes will bomb England and 55 divisions will take the country'. She finished by saying, 'I am so impatient and wish Hitler were already here. I can hardly wait.' She was detained on 2 July 1940[18].

An MI5 informant with the initials 'N.M.R.' reported a conversation with Dolly on 4 February 1942. On that occasion, Dolly claimed that Tyler Kent had discovered 'something so terrible between England and America that if it came out it would have stopped the war'. However, she also said that 'all Anna's friends felt that she had only herself to blame for her imprisonment but that she was not a spy nor had she transmitted any information to Germany'.

Dolly claimed that the authorities knew this and Anna had told her that the jury had refused to convict her and that the Judge had to 'rant and roar' at them for two hours before they would return a verdict of 'guilty'. When Anna re-told her story to an Immigration Officer in 1954, the time taken by the jury to reach its verdict had escalated to three and a half hours and in this later version 'even the judge was surprised at the verdict of guilty'. But Anna wasn't because 'there was a Jew on the jury'.

---

[16] A popular British writer who scripted *King Kong*.
[17] KV 2/902 piece 32a.
[18] KV 2/677 piece 55y.

Gabriel Wolkoff, her father's brother, had given vent to his own feelings by placing an announcement in the Personal Columns of *The Times* on 14 November 1940, a week after the sentences were announced:

> I, GABRIEL WOLKOFF, wish to place on record
> my severe condemnation and complete disavowal
> of the activities of my niece, Anna Wolkoff,
> resulting in her sentence.

The *Daily Herald* had asked her sister Kyra for a comment and she was quoted as saying, 'My sister, Anna, has done a very wrong thing but she is still my sister'.

The views expressed by Uncle Gabriel, sister Kyra and friend Dolly Newenham give our story a happy ending because if Anna's family and friends considered that she had done a very wrong thing and had only herself to blame for her imprisonment then 'justice was seen to have been done'.

# What Happened To ...?

## Winston S. Churchill (1874-1965)

In WWII, Churchill almost single-handedly willed Britain to victory against all the odds by forging a critically important alliance with Roosevelt. It was his finest hour and he is now rightly regarded as the Greatest Briton Ever. He was kicked out of office on 26 July 1945 when Labour came to power at the first General Election after the war. A Conservative Government was returned on 26 October 1951 when he again became Prime Minister, the second oldest after Gladstone. He handed over the reigns to Anthony Eden on 5 April 1955.

## Irene Danischewsky (1910-?)

Irene Danischewsky was born in Moscow and her parents brought her to Britain in 1915. Whilst her husband was in the Army, she worked as a Welfare Officer employed by London County Council. She corresponded with Kent and visited him in prison on several occasions. After MI5 had her telephone tapped and her letters examined, it was concluded that there was nothing to connect her with Kent other than a love affair.

## James McGuirk Hughes alias P.G. Taylor, etc. (1897-1983)

Prior to the big round up of May 1940, Hughes had been very active gathering Intelligence on various Right Wing organisations. Later, it is believed that he may have gone to South America on some Intelligence assignment.

## William Joyce aka Lord Haw-Haw (1906-1946)

Joyce was captured after the war and, controversially, he was found guilty of High Treason and executed. Had he lived, he could have exposed the MI5 sting operation against Anna Wolkoff. His case was even discussed by the Cabinet during his trial, which was heard by Mr. Justice Tucker, the same judge who had heard the Kent and Wolkoff trials.

## Joseph P. Kennedy (1888-1969)

Kennedy won a lot of friends during the early part of his spell in Britain as Ambassador and then proceeded to lose them with his defeatist talk and his belief that America should not get dragged into the war. Had Kennedy been elected President in 1940, which was a possibility until Roosevelt sidelined him in Britain, the war could have had a very different outcome. After returning to America, he attracted criticism for his 'machinations' with Charles Lindberg and his claim that he 'would prefer the Germany with Hitler to the England of Churchill and Bevin'. He had also used all his influence in the film world, which was considerable, to prevent exhibitors from showing pro-British and anti-Nazi films.

## Tyler Gatewood Kent (1911-1988)

Kent had been let off lightly because had he been sent to the US for trial under the Yardley Act, he could have been jailed for the rest of his life. Instead, he lived in some style off his wife's income, until a series of poor investments brought him down to earth. He had no children.

## Maxwell Knight (1900-1968)

Knight enjoyed a second career after the war as a broadcaster and he had numerous naturalist books to his credit. He evidently found fulfilment in his third marriage to Susan. He had no children.

## Guy Maynard Liddell (1892-1958)

Liddell later came under suspicion as a possible Soviet agent because of his close friendships with Anthony Blunt and Guy Burgess. The suspicion appears to have been unjustified.

## Marjorie Norah Mackie née Amor aka Agent M/Y (1898-1975)

After having worked as an MI5 undercover agent and then as a stool pigeon in Holloway, Mackie appeared as a prosecution witness at several trials, including those of Kent and Wolkoff. MI5 used her again in 1941 as an *agent provocateur* to try to incriminate a Bristol rector. She finished up as a Domestic Manciple and died in Cambridge with obesity and overeating listed among the causes. She left a son, James.

## Joan Priscilla Miller (1918-1984)

Miller changed her name to Jones at some stage prior to her marriage to Lt. Commander Thomas Kinloch Jones on 29 December 1945. They had one daughter, Jonquil. Latterly, Joan was in a relationship with Julian Phipps, an artist and cartoonist, and she became known as Joanna Phipps. In February 1980, Julian wrote to his previous employers advising them of his plan to retire in Malta in October. He made no mention of Joanna being either his wife or partner.

## Sir Oswald Ernald Mosley (1896-1980)

Although hero-worshipped by many of his pre-war followers, Mosley soon retired to Paris where he became chummy with the Duke and Duchess of Windsor.

## Captain Archibald Henry Maule Ramsay (1895-1955)

Ramsay wrote a book *The Nameless War* (1952) in which he bemoaned 'the deliberate ruin of the landed class' and proved to his own satisfaction that *The Protocols of the Learned Elders of Zion* was genuine despite being a cruel hoax. He also still considered Hitler a splendid fellow despite or perhaps because of the Nazi invasion of Soviet Russia in contravention of their Non-Aggression Treaty.

### Enid Riddell (1903-1973?)

Enid stayed in touch with Anna Wolkoff and it is believed that they were both killed in a car crash.

### Franklin D. Roosevelt (1882-1945)

A charismatic leader, he died soon after being re-elected for a fourth term and shortly before the cessation of hostilities in Europe. Roosevelt was Britain's saviour in its hour of greatest need. Of course, his motives were not entirely altruistic because he and his advisers realised the value of becoming 'the arsenal of democracy'. It took America into new technologies and levered it out of the depression in which it had been bogged down in the Thirties.

### Anna Wolkoff (1902-1973?)

Wolkoff was a model prisoner and took an interest in gardening. Her British nationality was revoked while she was in prison and upon release she became a stateless person, and had to request Home Office permission whenever she wished to travel overseas. A request to have her name changed was refused. She continued dressmaking and painting, signing her pictures as 'Roussoff', the name that her grandfather had used on his paintings. She never renewed her friendship with 'Cotty', the 6th Earl of Cottenham, who died in 1943 at the age of 40. She never married.

# Appendix: Images

## Reproduced by permission of the National Archives, Kew

# SECRET

The JOYCE Cipher

Instructions for Enciphering.

1.      The system is VIGENERE with straight alphabets.

2.      The keyword is HACKENSCHMIDT.

3.      To encipher, take the Vigenere slide (model en-
closed) and proceed as follows:-

Find each letter of the keyword HACKENSCHMIDT in
succession on the moving alphabet and place it above the
letter "A" on the fixed alphabet.   Find each letter in
succession of the clear text on the fixed slide, and use the
letter immediately above it (i.e. on the moving alphabet) as
its cipher-equivalent.   When each letter of the keyword has
been thus employed, thirteen letters of the clear text will
have been enciphered; repeat the same process for the next
thirteen letters of the clear text, then again for each
successive thirteen letters of the clear text until the end
of the message.

4.      Example:-

To encipher the clear text "TALKS EFFECT SPLENDID BUT ..."

Place first letter of Keyword (H) on moving alpha
bet over A on fixed alphabet: find first letter of clear
text (T) on fixed alphabet, and read the letter above it
(=A) as cipher-equivalent.

Place second letter of Keyword (A) on moving alphabet above A on fixed alphabet; find second letter of clear
text (A) on fixed alphabet, and read letter above it (=A) as
cipher.

## The 'Joyce Cipher' provided instructions for Enciphering the Coded Letter. (KV 2/345)

263

## Anna Wolkoff's Letter to Vernon Kell, the Director General of MI5

### Page 1 (KV 2/840)

18ᵃ Roland Gardens,
S.W.7.

22. 2. 40.

Dear Sir Vernon,

The one and only time I had the pleasure of meeting you was, if you remember, at a dinner given by Mark Ottenhausen last winter at which a certain subject came under a very lively discussion.

In view of the fact that you confessed to having been a student of this particular subject for the last forty years — I enclose herewith a copy of "Truth" of the 19.ᵗʰ 40, which I am sure will amuse you as much as it amused me. It has only just come into my hands and I hasten to post it on to you.

Since I saw you, many waters have

## Anna Wolkoff's Letter to Vernon Kell,
## the Director General of MI5

Page 2

flown under London Bridge. I have
lost my business, gone into another as employee
and thence then discharged as "not wanted" on
the outbreak of war! Alas! one has scruples
God knows why, and I deemed it beneath
my dignity to sue, although a two-year
contract was treated like a scrap of paper.

I then joined the A.F.S. as I had to
live, but the conditions of billeting were such
at the substation to which I was appointed
that I fell ill and was obliged to resign.

So here I am, a P.C. in my parent's
home and back again where I was 18 years
ago: the dressmaker round the corner!"

Plus ça change, plus c'est la même chose...

Yours sincerely,

Anna de Wolkoff :

## Maxwell Knight's Report
## to Brigadier O.A. Harker,
## the Deputy Director General of MI5
## dated 31 January 1945

### Extracted from KV 2/545

You will, I am sure, appreciate that in the commentary
I send you now, I have directed my remarks towards potential
American readers:    I have, for instance, been careful to point
out that the references in the document to the contents of the
stolen telegrams in practically every case do not coincide with
the contents of the telegrams in connection with which Tyler KENT
was charged.        This is true;    but for your own information,
and for our records, it is necessary to point out that among the
mass of telegrams which were seized at Tyler KENT's flat    -and
many of which I examined myself-  there were many telegrams which
referred to the projected Lease-Lend Plan.        In writing my
commentary, it did not seem desirable that any reference should
be made to this

In this report Knight advised Harker that he had
examined many of the documents seized from
Kent's flat on 20 May 1940 and that there were
many telegrams that referred to the projected
Lease-Lend Plan, thus confirming Kent's
allegations.

# APPENDIX: IMAGES

## Maxwell Knight's Report
## on Tyler Kent
## after visiting him in prison
## on 11 May 1945

### Extracted from KV 2/545

After a somewhat long discussion regarding the Duke del MONTE,
I succeeded in getting an admission out of KENT that, when he met this man
with Anna WOLKOFF, he did know perfectly well that he was an Official from
the Italian Embassy, and he also knew that the pseudonym "Mr. Macaroni" was
indeed an alias, and a rather silly one at that. He maintained that he had
no idea that Anna WOLKOFF was going to transmit information which she had
obtained from him out of this country, via del MONTE or anyone else. I feel
forced to record that I am now prepared to believe KENT. I consider that
KENT's weakness is his incredible ingenuousness. He is even more naieve than
most Americans regarding diplomatic matters and Intelligence work. I think
that, although KENT was bereft of all sense of honour with regard to his
actions while employed by the United States Government, the Espionage angle
simply never occurred to him. I have no doubt that his inexperience was
cleverly exploited by flattery, both by del MONTE and WOLKOFF.

Knight was prepared to believe that Kent had no
idea that Anna Wolkoff was going to transmit the
information that she had obtained from him 'out
of the country'.

## Colonel Francisco Marigliano, Duke del Monte

The Assistant Military Attaché at the Italian Embassy in London.

After dining and clubbing with Tyler Kent, Anna Wolkoff and Enid Riddell on 9 May 1940, he was assumed to be Anna's conduit to the Germans.

After the war, this was 'strenuously denied' by the Italians. (KV 2/1698)

# Glossary

| | |
|---|---|
| BBC | British Broadcasting Corporation |
| BUF | British Union of Fascists (Later known by other names) |
| GC&CS | Government Code & Cipher School (British codebreakers) |
| GCHQ | Government Communications Headquarters (Successor to GC&CS) |
| KC | King's Counsel (A Top Barrister) |
| MI5 | British Security Service |
| MI6 | British Secret Intelligence Service (SIS) |
| MP | British Member of Parliament |
| NBBS | New British Broadcasting Station (Nazi black propaganda radio station) |
| NKVD | A Soviet State Security Service 1922-3 & 1934-43 |
| OBE | Order of the British Empire – an 'honour' bestowed on deserving civil servants, among others |
| OGPU | A Soviet State Security Service 1923-44 |
| Okhrana | Tsarist Secret Police |
| PJ | Perish Judah (Slogan of several anti-Jewish groups) |
| SA | Sturmabteilung (Nazi 'Assault Detachment' or Stormtroopers) |
| SIS | Secret Intelligence Service (MI6) |
| SMERSH | Death to Spies! (Soviet Military Counter-Intelligence) |
| SS | Schutzstaffel (Nazi 'Protection Detachment') |

# Bibliography

## Books

Alvarez, David & Graham, Robert *Nothing Sacred - Nazi Espionage Against the Vatican 1939-1945* Frank Cass Publishers, London, 1997

Barnes, Harry Elmer (Editor) *Perpetual War for Perpetual Peace* Caxton Printers, New York, 1953

Beard, Charles A. *President Roosevelt and the Coming of the War 1941* Yale University Press, New Haven, 1948

Bearse, Ray & Read, Anthony *Conspirator - The Untold Story of Churchill Roosevelt and Tyler Kent* Macmillan, London, 1991

Bechhofer Roberts, C.E. *The Trial of William Joyce* Jarrolds, London, 1946

Brook-Shepherd, Gordon *The Storm Petrels* William Collins, London, 1977

Charnley, John *Blackshirts & Roses* Brockinday Publications, London, 1990

Cole, J.A. *Lord Haw-Haw and William Joyce: The Full Story* Faber and Faber, London, 1964

Cookridge, E.H. *Secrets of the British Secret Service* Sampson Low Marston, London, 1948

Costello, John *Ten Days to Destiny (alt: Ten Days That Saved The West)* William Morrow, New York, 1991

Crowson, N.J. (Editor) *The Journals of Collin Brooks 1932-1940* The Press Syndicate, Cambridge 1998

Dilks, David (Editor) *The Diaries of Sir Alexander Cadogan 1938-1945* Cassell, London, 1971

Farago, Ladislas *The Game of the Foxes* Hodder & Stoughton, London, 1971

Firmin, Stanley *They Came to Spy* Hutchinson & Co, London, 1950

Fuller, Capt J.F.C. *The Star in the West* Gordon Press, New York, 1974

Gillman, Peter & Leni *Collar The Lot!* Quartet Books, London, 1980

Goodhart, Philip *Fifty Ships That Saved The World* Doubleday & Co, New York, 1965

Griffiths, Richard *Patriotism Perverted* Constable, London, 1998

Hall, H. Duncan *North American Supply* HM Stationery Office, London, 1955

Hall, W. Reginald & Peaslee, Amos J. *Three Wars With Germany* G.P. Putnam's Sons, New York, 1944

Hyde, H. Montgomery *The Quiet Canadian* Hamish Hamilton, London 1962

James, William *The Eyes of the Navy* Methuen & Co Ltd, London, 1955

Jowitt, The Earl *Some Were Spies* Hodder & Stoughton, London, 1954

Joyce, William *Twilight Over England* Imperial War Museum, London, 1996

Kahn, David *The Codebreakers* Weidenfeld and Nicolson, London, 1966

Kennedy, John F. *Why England Slept* Sidgwick & Jackson, London, 1940

Kern, Gary *A Death in Washington* Enigma Books, New York, 2003

Kessler, Ronald *The Sins of the Father - Joseph Kennedy and the Dynasty He Founded* Hodder & Stoughton, London, 1996

Kimball, Warren F. *The Most Unsordid Act - Lend-Lease 1939-1941* The John Hopkins Press, Baltimore, 1969

Kimball, Warren F. *Churchill & Roosevelt - The Complete Correspondence* Princeton University Press, Princeton, New Jersey, 1984

# BIBLIOGRAPHY

Knight, Maxwell *Crime Cargo* Garden City Press Ltd, London, 1934

Landau, Captain Henry *The Enemy Within* Van Rees Press, New York, 1937

Lash, Joseph P. *Roosevelt and Churchill 1939-1941* W.W. Norton, New York, 1976

Lownie, Andrew *Tyler Kent - Isolationist or Spy? Essay in North American Spies* University Press of Kansas, Lawrence, Kansas, 1991

MacDonogh, Steve *Open Book - One Publisher's War* Brandon/Mount Eagle Publications Ltd, Dingle, County Kerry, Ireland, 1999

Macleod, Colonel Roderick (Editor) *The Ironside Diaries 1937-1940* Constable, London, 1962

Mahl, Thomas E. *Desperate Deception* Brassey's, Dulles, Virginia, 1998

Masters, Anthony *The Man Who Was M - The Life of Maxwell Knight* Basil Blackwell, Oxford, 1984

Miller, Joan *One Girl's War* Brandon, Dingle, County Kerry, Ireland, 1986

Muggeridge, Malcolm *Chronicles of Wasted Time - Part 2 The Infernal Grove* Collins, London, 1973

Pratt, Fletcher *Secret and Urgent* Blue Ribbon Books, New York, 1942

Schellenberg, Walter *Invasion 1940* St Ermin's Press, London, 2000

Simpson, A.W. Brian *In the Highest Degree Odious* Clarendon Press, New York, 1992

Singer, Kurt *Spies and Traitors of World War II* Prentice-Hall, New York, 1945

Singer, Kurt *The World's Greatest Women Spies* W.H. Allen & Co Ltd, London, 1951

Smith, Amanda (Editor) *Hostage to Fortune - The Letters of Joseph P. Kennedy* Viking, New York, 2001

Snow, John Howland *The Case of Tyler Kent* Domestic and Foreign Affairs/Citizens - New York/Chicago, 1946

Stettinus, E.R. *Lend-Lease: Weapon for Victory* Macmillan, New York, 1944

Stewart, Graham *Burying Caesar* Weidenfeld & Nicolson, London, 1999

Trythal, Anthony John *'Boney' Fuller* Rutgers University Press, New Brunswick, 1977

Weber, Ralph E. *United States Diplomatic Codes and Ciphers 1775-1938* Precedent Publishing, Chicago, 1979

West, Nigel *MI5 British Security Service Operations 1909-1945* The Bodley Head, London, 1981

West, Nigel & Tsarev, Oleg *The Crown Jewels* HarperCollins, London, 1998

West, W.J. *Truth Betrayed* Duckworth, London, 1987

Whalen, Richard *The Founding Father - The Story of Joseph P. Kennedy* New American Library, New York, 1964

Wheatley, Dennis *The Time Has Come...The Memoirs of Dennis Wheatley* Hutchinson & Co, London, 1978

Wolkoff-Mouromtzoff, Alexander (A.N. Roussoff) *Memoirs* John Murray, London, 1928

Young, Kenneth (Editor) *The Diaries of Sir Robert Bruce Lockhart 1939-1965* Macmillan, London, 1980

## Other Material

Harris, Robert *The American Tearoom Spy* The Times, London, 4 December 1982

Hope, John *Fascism, the Security Service and the Curious Careers of Maxwell Knight and James McGuirk Hughes* Lobster No 22, December 1991

Kent, Tyler *Speech at Fourth International Revisionists Convention, Chicago*, September 1982

# BIBLIOGRAPHY

Kimball, Warren F. & Bartlett, Bruce *Roosevelt and Prewar Commitments to Churchill: The Tyler Kent Affair* Diplomatic History, 7 September, 1981

Leutze, James *The Secret of the Churchill-Roosevelt Correspondence: Sep 1939 - May 1940* Journal of Contemporary History, Vol 10 No 3, 1975

Penrose, Barrie *MI5's Mistress of Espionage* Sunday Times Magazine, London, 18 October, 1981

Smith, Gerald L.K. *The Story of Tyler Kent* Gerald L.K. Smith, Detroit, September 1944

US State Department *Press Statement* Washington, 2 September 1944

Whalen, Richard *The Strange Case of Tyler Kent* Diplomat, November 1965

Yale University Library *Tyler Kent Collection* Sterling Memorial Library, New Haven, Conn, 1970

# Index

Smirnoff, Nicolas Eugenovitch:
81-82, 85, 88-89, 101-102,
167, 191, 205, 236, 250-251

Smith, Gerald L.K.: 67-72, 74,
83, 96, 240

Snow, John Howland: 49n, 73

Somervell, Sir Donald: 209

Special Branch: 17, 82, 97, 115-
116, 118, 120-123, 135, 167,
174, 181-182, 207

Special Source (MI5 Informant):
32, 148, 188, 190, 214, 241

Spiro, Edward: *see E.H.
Cookridge*

Stanford, Mary ('Molly'): 183-
184

State Department (US): 47, 51-
59, 63-65, 71, 80-82, 87,
150, 153, 159, 195, 239, 249

Stephens, William Derek: 100,
251

Stephenson, William: 253

Stevenson, William: 254

Sting Operation: 6, 30, 36, 105,
145, 149, 157, 187, 234,
254, 259

Stokes, Richard R.: 11

Straker, Mrs. Betty: 29n

Strangeways Prison: 115, 208

Stresemann, Gustav: 227

Stumfegger, Ludwig: 90

*Sunday Dispatch*: 79

*Sunday Telegraph Magazine*: 76

*Sunday Times Colour Magazine*:
27n, 188

Swinton Committee: 125, 134

Taylor, Elizabeth: 185

Taylor, Henry J.: 59, 62

Taylor, P.G.: *see James Hughes*

Taylour, Fay: 43n, 201, 207,
210, 212, 214

Tavistock, Marquess of: 178,
201

*The Times*: 37, 41, 257

Thompson, Detective-Inspector:
130

*Time*: 45

*Toronto Daily News*: 47

Treachery Act: 92

Tregear, Joyce: 123

Trenchard, Lord: 17

*Truth*: 133-134, 142

Tucker, Mr. Justice: 9, 39, 131,
259

Ustinov, Klop 110

Van den Kieboom, Charles: 91-
92, 102

Van Lennep, Anne: *see Anne de
Lennep*

Vansittart, Sir Robert: 154, 202,
204, 223, 228

Van Wyk, Russell: 230n

Printed in the United States
65345LVS00005B/151